GLASGOW CRIMEFIGHTER

Also by Robert Jeffrey:

Glasgow's Godfather

Glasgow's Hard Men

Gangland Glasgow

Blood on the Streets

The Wee Book of the Clyde

The Wee Book of Glasgow

*

The Herald Book of the Clyde

Doon the Watter

Clydeside, People and Places

Images of Glasgow

Scotland's Sporting Heroes

(all with Ian Watson)

GLASGOW CRIMEFIGHTER

THE LES BROWN STORY

LES BROWN
&
ROBERT JEFFREY

BLACK & WHITE PUBLISHING

First published 2005
by Black & White Publishing Ltd
99 Giles Street, Edinburgh

Reprinted 2006

ISBN 1 84502 060 X

A CIP catalogue record for this book
is available from The British Library.

Printed and bound by Creative Print and Design

CONTENTS

ACKNOWLEDGEMENTS

Les Brown and Robert Jeffrey would like to thank colleagues in the police and the press, Sheila Brown and Marie Jeffrey and the staff of the *Daily Record* and Newsquest (publishers of *The Herald, Sunday Herald* and *Evening Times*) for their assistance in the production of this book.

LB & RJ

This book is dedicated to police officers everywhere.

1

The Inside Story of the Meehan Stitch-up and his Seven Years in Solitary

A success for 'good old-fashioned policing' – it's a phrase that has become something of a cliché to be mouthed by top cops at the conclusion of a big murder trial. But it contains an element of truth, as I well know. Many a case is solved by sheer relentless detective work during which every door in the neighbourhood of the crime scene is knocked on by tireless plain-clothes and uniformed officers at all hours and in all weathers. Every dank tenement staircase climbed. Every lead, however unlikely, followed up. The usual suspects are rounded up. Every possible connection interviewed. Neighbours, workmates, folk in the local shops, pubs, golf club, bowling club, cinemas – all are quizzed. 'Wanted' bills are printed by the helpful local press.

This is the Glasgow detective's equivalent of saturation bombing and it can work. Often what is called 'a result' is achieved and, at the end of a long slog, the investigating force can enjoy the feeling of satisfaction that comes when the gates of Barlinnie or Peterhead slam behind a villain. The celebration cup of tea – on occasion laced with a drop of something stronger – back at the station tastes sweet. It is one face of policing and it is a familiar one to the tabloid readers who follow, daily, the war between the boys in blue and the criminal fraternity in this city, a place some observers have dubbed the Chicago of north-west Europe. But it is only one of several faces – some of which are benign, others disgraceful.

There is a pleasing face of successful policing, the intuitive leap of deduction brought on by years of experience and the ability to see into the criminal mind in a way that comes from a life spent rubbing against the villains. In this, my tale of more than twenty years as a detective, there are many examples of just that – occasions when my colleagues and I instinctively headed in the right direction when faced with a puzzling case. You can't beat experience. I found it interesting, for example, that, when the CID are called in, those in the uniformed branch, who are often the first on the scene, just don't know where to start and are sometimes slow to grasp the significance of simple little matters – the tiny clues that point in the direction of a solution. The same happens when the sleuths from the big city are taken out of the tenements and schemes into the countryside to investigate a rare crime in farmland areas or a market town. And it is no wonder this is so – the rural cops might only see a murder once every few years but, here in Glasgow, you could have a couple of bloody killings on your hands before breakfast. I remember one New Year when we solved four killings – albeit fairly simple cases mostly arising out of drunken rammies – in the space of a day and still had time to enjoy a bite of turkey and a glass or two before heading home.

The student of detective fiction knows, from the days of Sherlock Holmes to TV's Colombo onwards, that it is often the sum of little things that points to the big truth. Incidentally, most real-life detectives enjoy a thriller on the TV as much as the next man. And, when I look at my scrapbook pictures of Glasgow CID's finest in action in the fifties and sixties, I reflect that Peter Falk didn't have the copyright on shabby gabardine raincoats and turned-up collars! Or the trademark battered felt hats.

But it is a sad fact that dogged detection and brilliant leaps of intuition are not the complete face of police work in this part of the world. There are also stitch-ups and cover-ups and, inevitably, outrageous miscarriages of justice. Glasgow has had more than its share. The convictions of Oscar Slater, Paddy Meehan and Joe Steele and his co-accused, big TC Campbell, are the most obvious. These were men incarcerated – and, in one case, nearly hanged by the neck till he was dead – for long years on what the TV detectives would call 'bum raps'. Serious bum raps! I have had my own share of controversy – the Albany drugs trial for a start (there is more, much more, of that later in this book). But I was never a fit-up merchant, though I have met some in more than twenty years as a crimefighter in Glasgow. It is my view that the bent cop deserves to be exposed. Cover-ups are an insult to the brave majority of officers who risk their lives and sometimes that of family members working long hard hours to try to contain the villains and let the citizens sleep peacefully of a night. When they succeed, they deserve the praise of the public and the media. When they step out of line, they should be hammered – hard and without pity.

Now, despite what any of my ex-colleagues might tell you, I was not personally involved in the Slater case – it began in 1908 after all! This particular fit-up is often said to be the worst of all these miscarriages and I suppose that is so since it came so close to ending on the gallows. Interestingly, it has connections with some of the modern miscarriages. Slater was a German Jew who just happened to be in the wrong place at the wrong time and he suffered the bigotry of his era as well as becoming the victim of incompetent, malicious policing. The cover-up by the authorities lasted for years – shades of what was to happen to Steele and Campbell in the Ice-Cream Wars.

The victim in the Slater case was a rich eighty-three-year-old spinster who had cash and jewellery, about three thousand pounds' worth, an enormous sum for those days, stashed in her west-end flat. Not wise! Even today, it is not a clever move to have large sums of readies and attractive pickings like precious stones lying around your Glasgow home. It is even more reckless to let people know that it is there. Right now, I could name you

3

half a dozen or so badfellas who would be up the tenement stairs two at a time after such a haul and to hell with the fact that someone might die.

The crime that led to the Slater stitch-up was never solved and, to this day, no one knows who killed Marion Gilchrist. The age of the victim, the scene of the crime – the douce gas-lit streets of the wealthy west end – all combined to put the police of the day under enormous pressure to make an arrest. This need to assuage the public hunger for action in such cases is still the major motive of a cop who goes wrong and takes up 'planting' – the dropping of evidence on a suspect or in his home.

I remember one famous city detective who did not normally believe in such doings but who in extremis once asked me to lock a particular villain up. 'What's the charge?' I asked. 'Possession of "jelly" (gelignite),' I was told. 'Where is it?' I asked. 'In his loft,' I was told. I asked, 'How do we know that?' and was told, 'Because you will put it there.' This request was an uncharacteristic lapse by a top operator and I refused to do it but other cops were, on occasion, not as scrupulous as I was.

The pressure on the cops to 'do something' in the Slater case was no less strong at the turn of the twentieth century than it can be today when the public is wound up and poked into a state of outrage by the media over some particularly horrific unsolved crime – no one likes to look a blank wall. As the police thrashed around hopelessly trying to find someone to put into the frame for the murder of old Marion, the sleazy figure of Slater came along. A womaniser and gambler, he was suspected of trying to pawn a brooch that had been stolen from the scene. But this was not the case – indeed, as well as not having stolen the brooch, he had a cast-iron alibi for the murder. There is no need to go into the details of the murder here – it has entertained true-crime readers in dozens of books and dramatisations – other than to identify a link with crimes I have investigated and one particular link with modern detection – the discredited identity parade.

4

The public has little faith in ID parades and everyone knows a tale or two about detectives holding out four or five fingers behind their back to indicate a number in the line-up to help a victim identify an attacker or robber, to help separate the bad guy from the volunteers grouped around him. Some tales are true. Most are disgraceful though there can be humour in some of the identity parade stories. Legendary Glasgow defence lawyer Laurence Dowdall used to raise a laugh with his story of an ID parade where a man with a limp was the accused. When the person who had been attacked admitted he could not recognise the man, the line-up was asked to walk in a circle. The guilty man had told the others about his predicament and, when they were asked to walk, everyone in the line-up had a limp! The ingenuity of a Glasgow villain should never be underestimated.

Even the infamous bank robber Samuel 'Dandy' McKay, who was active in the 1960s and 1970s and is still remembered in the city today, suffered at the hands of an identity parade. But this was a parade with a difference. With his record and infamy, McKay was often the subject of police surveillance and, on one occasion, he was seen walking a dog in the Linn Park near his luxurious south-side bungalow home. The cop noted the dog was a black Staffordshire bull terrier – something of a fashion accessory for today's drug dealers, Dandy was ahead of his time. Shortly after this, there was a burglary in the area and a dog was left behind. In an identity parade at Cardonald Cat and Dog home, the dog was picked out as Dandy's and the game was up. I often think it is just as well that Dandy never knew that the other dogs in the parade were two greyhounds, an Alsatian, a border collie, a lab and a cross-breed!

In the Slater case, the fact was that the cops were determined to get an arrest and they did. An identity parade was rigged to ensure that he was picked out as a man who was seen fleeing the scene of the old lady's murder. It was garbage, of course, and that parade is now often used to show trainee cops how not to do it. Slater, however, was convicted but mysteriously reprieved just before he was due to hang and it took almost twenty years before he was freed from prison for a crime he did not commit.

On his release, he lived a life of quiet respectability in Ayrshire, coincidentally the scene of the crime that would result in the unjust conviction of one Paddy Meehan in a case in which I had some first-hand involvement. This was also a case where another flawed – but not fixed – identity parade played a major role.

Detectives working the streets of Glasgow soon build up a bulging mental notebook on known criminals and, just because someone is in the category of the 'usual suspects', it doesn't mean that they were involved. Owing to a lifetime of crime, mostly fairly minor, Paddy Meehan was often in that category as he was a man with a talent for breaking into well-defended premises and blowing a safe or two. He was not a violent man and, in my mind, certainly no killer. Nor would I have believed that he was the sort of man who would leave an old and frail woman and her injured husband tied up in their burgled home, over a weekend – a cruel act that would result in the death of the woman. Yet this is what Meehan was supposed to have done. I knew him well enough to have alarm bells in my mind about his involvement and other aspects of the case also puzzled me.

It's probably best to begin at the beginning in this saga that has become a fascinating part of Scotland's criminal history. What was to be the concluding and definitive episode in Meehan's career in crime began on the night of Saturday, 6 July 1969. He and an associate, Jim Griffiths, headed out of Glasgow for Stranraer by car. In the south-west port there was a motor taxation office which attracted the attention of this dubious duo. Their idea was to do a recce of the office with a view to, at some time, breaking in to steal vehicle registration forms which would be an invaluable aid in getting rid of stolen cars that came their way. Griffiths and Meehan were men whose work often took them out in the dark of night on missions of no good. There was

seemingly nothing special about this excursion that the two set
out on that night – but it was about to start an epic tale of crime
that ended with a bloody shoot-out, the death of one of them
and the unjust incarceration in solitary for seven years for the
other. It was also to leave an innocent man, a sixty-five-year-old
newsvendor called William Hughes, dead on the streets of
Glasgow and others injured and terrorised in a mad rampage in
which shots were even fired into a children's playground.

Griffiths, Meehan's companion on the fateful night of the Ayr
murder, was a Lancastrian, not too well known to the Glasgow
police, but a man with a prolific record for car theft. On the night
that Meehan and Griffiths left to case the taxation building in
Stranraer, two other villains, of whom we will hear later, were
on the roads south-west of the city. Their target was the bungalow
home of Abraham and Rachel Ross in Blackburn Place, Ayr. Mr
Ross owned a bingo hall in a converted cinema in Paisley where
he worked on Mondays, Tuesdays, Thursdays and Fridays. He
often kept some of the proceeds in a safe at home. The robbery
at his house took place in the early hours of the Saturday. Mr
Ross and his wife were asleep when two men broke in through
a window and woke them up. Mr Ross was hit several times to
subdue him and the couple were tied up and frequently struck.
After nasty blows to the head, Mr Ross was forced into revealing
where their safe was located.

Despite his age, old Mr Ross struggled hard against the
intruders and, in a remark that was to assume great significance
at the trial of Meehan, one of them was heard to remark to the
other, 'Get this c**** off me Pat.' Both the intruders had strong
Glasgow accents and, in conversation, one referred to the other
as Jim. Seemingly the two burglars and tie-up merchants in this
case were called 'Pat' and 'Jim' and Pat Meehan and Jim Griffiths
were on the prowl that night. But an experienced detective would
not put too much force to this. I have noticed down the years
that it is not uncommon for two robbers to decide beforehand to

call themselves by assumed names during the crime. They figure, often rightly, that the phoney names will be reported to the police. Another version of this ploy, which I ran into from time to time, was the deliberate use of Irish accents and names to give the impression the IRA or UVF were involved. Mind you, hindsight is a fine thing, as they say, and account must be taken of the pressure the police were under as the tabloids banged on about at the callous and barbarous horror of the Ayr bungalow attack and the lack of arrests.

The phoney Pat and Jim made off with about a grand in cash and other items from the house. At around 5.30 a.m., one of them went away to get the car. However, he was delayed and it was turning daylight when he returned. The Rosses were left tied up, in pain from their injuries and in fear of their lives. Their screams to attract attention were unheard and it was only at 9 a.m. on the Monday, when their cleaning lady turned up for work, that they were discovered. When Mrs Ross died in hospital at Ayr on 8 July, a particularly dastardly and horrific robbery turned into a murder.

At this time, early in that hot July, I was pounding the streets far from the cooling breezes of the Ayrshire coast on the hunt for villains who attracted less media attention. But, in a twist of fate, I was soon to be part of the drama. As is often the case, the investigators had a look at the usual suspects. Meehan had a track record of break-ins, if not murder, and he soon had a knock on the door from men determined to find out what he had been up to on the fateful night. Pencils scribbled fast on notepads as the wily old safe breaker admitted that he and his pal Griffiths had travelled through Ayr that night en route to Stranraer. The excuse was that they were looking at a car they planned to buy. For obvious reasons, the real story that it was a journey to case a break-in at the motor taxation offices was not mentioned.

Meehan also brought up an interesting tale that was to feature in his eventual trial. He told of an encounter with a teenage girl he and Griffiths had assisted. The girl and her friend had been in a white car with a couple of guys and, in the way that sometimes happens late at night on country roads, there had been some sort of dispute or whatever and she was put out of the car. Meehan and Griffiths, the men who stopped when they saw she was in distress, were hardly knights in shining armour but they did the right thing and took her in to their car. They drove at high speed after the white car, overtook it and the foursome was reunited. To this day, it strikes me as odd that the prosecution would believe that the killers of old Mrs Ross would pick up a hitch-hiker.

Back at home, Meehan mentioned the incident to his wife in the context of a discussion about the bungalow killing which had upset Mrs Meehan who was outraged, like most people, about the way the old lady had been left so callously. Paddy phoned the cops, realising that, if the girls had told of the incident, he and Griffiths might be suspects. That way, he would get in first and he told his version of the incident with the girls and the white car without giving the Ayr police his name. But a hare had been started and Meehan was arrested at his home on 14 July.

Almost inevitably, an identity parade was swiftly held at the Central in Glasgow with Meehan in the line-up. What happened is in some doubt and it has become one of the most controversial parades in the history of crime. At the trial that was to follow, the prosecution claimed that Mr Ross, the survivor of the attack, viewed the line-up as the first witness but Meehan's defence claimed he was the last. The other witnesses were the two girls from the white car.

Meehan's solicitor at the parade was Peter McCann. I have seen the identity parade form completed by Detective Sergeant John Ingles and it clearly shows that Meehan chose to stand at position number one. It was his choice. There were six other males of similar age and appearance in the line-up. Mr Ross collapsed after hearing the person in number one position say,

'Shut up! I will get you an ambulance, all right?' and was assisted from the room.

The running of the parade took the normal form with the witnesses and those in the line-up being kept apart. The witnesses were all in a side room – in this case, the Detective Sergeant's room. The actual parade took place in the detective constables' room and, as each witness passed through, having viewed the line-up, they were taken to a separate room, making sure they did not mingle with witnesses still to have a look at the line-up. The officer running the parade, Detective Sergeant Ingles, would complete a form detailing the running of the parade. As a witness entered the parade room, he would be addressed by the officer in charge and his particulars noted and then he would be asked to look at the line-up of men and, if he recognised the person referred to in the witness statement, he should point at the person and state the number at his feet.

Unless there was some specific reason otherwise, Mr Ross, as the main witness, should have been called first. Regardless of his order on the witness list, there is no doubt in this case about one thing that happened. Old Mr Ross asked if the men in the line-up would say the words, 'Shut up! I will get you an ambulance, all right?' Meehan did so and the result was electrifying. Mr Ross, obviously distressed, said, 'That's the voice. I know it. I don't have to go any further.' During the attack one of assailants used a hood and as Mr Ross was struck he was cowering under a blanket so the voice identification was vital since he had had no real sight of the burglars.

Mr Ross's statement on the voice and the fact that it was so positive was to play badly for Meehan at the trial. When he heard Mr Ross speak, Paddy replied, 'Oh, sir, you have the wrong man, honest.' Meehan also denied to the police right from the start any involvement. Incidentally Meehan was right to fear the danger of the girls identifying him: one did and also told of the driver referring to his passenger as 'Pat', important evidence that he and

Griffiths had been in the area on the night of the killing.

But I had a big personal surprise in store. A couple of days after Meehan had been picked up, on 15 July 1969, I was in the High Court in Glasgow as a witness in a trial. It was a case that was attracting a lot of media attention, so much so that there were as many as ten reporters, big guns from the crime desks, waiting for the trial to start. I was quite well known to the readers of the crime pages in those days and, as we waited, a colleague jokingly said to me, 'You know how you get involved in these high-profile cases? Well, I'm about hit the front pages – I'll show you what real publicity is like.'

He had a disappointment coming. About an hour after our chat, he strode into court to take centre stage in a criminal drama, as he thought, and he was just about to take the oath when the entire media pack jumped up as of one and literally ran from the court. I grabbed one of the scribes as he headed for the door and asked what was up. The reply was a real shaker: 'A man with a number of guns has run amok in Lansdowne Crescent and a number of people have been shot.' My witness pal's big case was going to be small beer now!

Tom Goodall, the legendary head of the CID who was on the court precincts, asked me if I had a car. I didn't but said I did. 'Get it!' said the boss. It took only a minute or so to get a CID car from an officer waiting to give evidence and, with Goodall in the passenger seat, we headed for Lansdowne Crescent. We used the police radio to let HQ know that Goodall was on the way to the scene. The radio barked back the info that the suspect, Paddy Meehan's pal Jim Griffiths, had appropriated a car, having shot the driver, and was heading north. We immediately changed direction in an attempt to head off the mad dog gunman. The radio continued to give a commentary on a truly sensational scene. Griffiths was driving towards Springburn, tyres screaming and tailed by a convoy of police cars. Somewhere along the route, he had slugged a bottle of brandy.

11

Next he dumped the car. He got into a stolen lorry and drove off in that. As we joined the chase, he turned into Kay Street, a cul-de-sac. He was a cornered rat. We blocked the street with police cars and he leapt from the lorry, ran into the last close on the right and disappeared from view. His whereabouts didn't remain a mystery for long – he started to fire a rifle from the top floor of the tenement building. He fired alternately from windows at front and rear of the flat, causing havoc in both directions. Uniformed officers responded by sealing off the entire area and stopping all traffic on the busy thoroughfare that is Springburn Road. The corporation swimming baths at the end of Kay Street were thronged with children. The building was sealed off and the kids were secured behind the doors.

Glasgow police are not routinely armed. The use of firearms is taken with extreme seriousness and they are only issued in extremis. If ever Tom Goodall and the rest of us needed them, we needed them now. The boss sent to HQ for the guns and they arrived in a squad car. Many innocent people were at risk of death in this mad affray. Weapons against Griffiths were vital. Apart from the newsvendor who had been killed, nine men, two women, a child and a police officer were shot as Griffiths fled to his final gory hiding hole after being questioned by police at his lodgings miles away.

Tom Goodall immediately handed a revolver to Chief Super Callum Finlayson, commander of the Maryhill Division, and Detective Sergeant Ian Smith. They legged it into the close and up the stairs toward the gunman. For a further five minutes, the firing from the windows of the flat continued. Then the shots stopped. The sudden silence in the midst of this mayhem was so painful you could almost feel it. What had happened in that dark canyon of a close? A few minutes later the two officers reappeared dragging the bleeding body of Griffiths.

Goodall and I listened as Finlayson told of getting to the door of the top flat and looking through the letterbox to see the crazed gunman stamping around the hallway. The door was damaged and, through a gap in it, Griffiths could see the officers. He raised his gun that he had already used to kill and wound during his rampage and the officers knew they were in mortal danger. As Griffiths took aim, Finlayson fired off a shot – perhaps to wing him in the shoulder, perhaps to make even surer the siege was over. The bullet bounced off the Englishman's collarbone and into his heart. It was over.

But some formalities remained. Tom Goodall turned to me and said, 'Mr Brown, you are in charge of the body. Do you know what that entails?' I did and so I arranged for the body to be taken to the city mortuary. There I searched the body and removed a small amount of money and other personal items – an Omega wristwatch, an AA membership card, a driving licence (in the name of C R J McCartney), a passport office pamphlet and four bank notes, including a Bank of England £10 note. There was nothing of real significance on the body. He was wearing a suit and I noticed a bullet hole in the jacket just under the left shoulder. I asked the mortuary attendant to leave the clothing on to assist the medical team in determining the path of the bullet. It turned out it had entered the body and struck the collarbone and ricocheted down through the heart, causing instant death. Someone unkindly remarked that it was 'a bloody good shot'.

A loser to the end, Griffiths had only the gravediggers for company as, on the first of August 1969, he was lowered into a pauper's grave in the Linn Park cemetery. His family refused to come north. The undertaker said a short prayer. The men who had ended his reign of terror were given honours for their brave actions on that fateful day – Callum Finlayson received the MBE and Ian Smith the BEM.

What happened in Kay Street had another effect on the saga. Remarkably, the Crown Office issued a statement saying that 'with the death of James Griffiths and the apprehension of Patrick

Connolly Meehan, the police are no longer looking for any other person suspected of the incident concerning Mr and Mrs Ross at Ayr'. This was in 1969. Many years later in 1981, Lord Hunter produced his report – ordered by the then Secretary of State for Scotland, Bruce Millan, in 1977 – into the case. It is fascinating that, in it, Hunter wrote that 'the terms of the Crown Office Statement were such as to indicate that, in effect, the case was closed' – so much for Paddy Meehan's chance of a fair trial. In the same lengthy report, Lord Hunter also wrote, 'It was a failure not to interview and question officers who had been on duty on the night of 5 and 6 July (1969).' More on that later.

When Griffiths had panicked at the police knock on his door – he was known to be terrified of being jailed – and gone on his bloody rampage, he unwittingly made sure that many would prejudge the accusation against Meehan. When Griffiths had phoned Goodall prior to the shoot-out, he was told he should surrender to the police and Goodall even gave him his home phone number. Had the Englishman taken this advice, Paddy Meehan would not have undergone the ordeal he did.

The Kay Street siege had one amusing sidebar. The morning after the shooting, Tom Goodall sent for me. Before I had time to wonder what was going on, I noticed a fine spread of national newspapers on the desk. He was direct and asked, 'Mr Brown, how do you explain the fact that your photograph is on the front page of all these papers?'

Without a smile I remarked, 'Sir, I stood beside you!' Then it was back to the daily grind of a Glasgow detective.

The question remained. Who were the real 'Pat' and 'Jim'? The true story took years to emerge from the slime of the Glasgow underworld. And, for a long time after the famous trial, there was speculation among lawyers, the police and criminals about the real culprits.

The trial itself was a remarkable affair. Joe Beltrami was involved in the defence, as was Nicholas Fairbairn and the late

John Smith, the former Labour leader. The trial has been well documented in books by Beltrami and Ludovic Kennedy who both campaigned to overturn the wrongful conviction. I look at the trial in a different light. As a detective familiar with the working of the CID – particularly in murder inquiries – I consider I have an advantage here. I also know most of the officers concerned in the case.

Setting aside the ill-advised Crown statement, Meehan was on trial because of the coincidence of the names Pat and Jim and the fact that he had been in the vicinity on the night of the murder. Then there is the identification parade. Knowing the detectives involved in conducting the line-up, I do not believe that it was fixed. However, it was disastrously flawed. In my opinion, Meehan's defence blundered when he was allowed to stand in position number one. They should have ensured he had a middle position so that Mr Ross would have heard several versions of the words spoken at the time of the crime. This would have helped clarify the recognition or otherwise of the voice.

The trial also heard of the finding of scraps of paper from the Ross safe in the pocket of clothing Griffiths wore on the night of the crime. This takes some swallowing. Later events confirm that Griffiths and Meehan were not the perpetrators. Therefore, it follows that the only explanation for the scraps of paper has to be that a police officer removed paper from the safe and put it in the pocket to be found by another detective. There is no doubt in my mind, knowing the officers involved, that the Identification Bureau Officers, Detective Inspector Cook and Detective Constable Beaton, examined the pieces of paper, believing them to have been found in the place that had been indicated to them – in other words, Griffiths' coat. Their evidence proved that the pieces of paper found in the pocket were identical to pieces in the Ross safe. But that's all it did. Because we now know beyond doubt that Griffiths and Meehan were not 'Pat' and 'Jim', it is clear that someone fabricated evidence against Meehan by planting the paper. And, at the trial, there was reference to fragments of stones from mineral felt on the Ayr bungalow roof said to have found their way on to Meehan's shoes. Clearly Meehan was to take the blame for this horrific crime.

The fit-up worked. Meehan was found guilty by a majority on the murder charge with nine of the fifteen-strong jury believing that the evidence was sound enough to prove beyond reasonable doubt that the safe blower, with no previous record of violence, had committed the crime. He was given life.

Who actually did it? For years after the trial, the name of an infamous Glasgow criminal called William 'Tank' McGuinness was whispered on the streets as being implicated. But, sensationally, McGuinness could have come into the frame right at the start of the investigation if the cops in the seaside town had done their duty.

You will remember that it was earlier shown that, after 'Pat' and 'Jim' were said to have finished with Mr and Mrs Ross, one of the pair went out to get the getaway car but he failed to come straight back and was away for some time. The explanation for this almost beggars belief. On the night of the break-in at the bungalow, two policemen were called to a rowdy party that was taking place nearby. When they arrived in their van, they met McGuinness in the road and asked his name and what he was about. He said he was looking for the bus station. The cops gave him a lift there and, after he had been dropped off, he walked back to the getaway car and picked up his accomplice.

But it was five years after the trial – with Meehan in solitary pleading his innocence – before further evidence emerged about what had really happened in Ayr that night. As we now know, while Meehan and Griffiths made their way to Ayrshire, another duo was also heading south-west from the city that night – McGuinness and, as it subsequently emerged, another well-known Glasgow criminal, Ian Waddell. In 1974, two city reporters were investigating information that Waddell and another man, only known at that time as Mr X, were responsible for the killing. Waddell was interviewed in the presence of his solicitor and admitted being in Rosses' house on the night of the murder. He was able to give details of what was in the house, what was stolen, including a watch which had been torn from the wrist of Mr Ross. This fact had never before been made public. Clearly Waddell was involved. But who was his partner?

In September 1976, I was on an inspectors' course in Ayr. During a weekend leave at home in the city, my phone rang. The caller asked, 'What colour is your dog?' This was a pre-arranged coded signal that, if I went to a secret corner of Linn Park, my informant 'Sam' (aka the bank robber Dandy McKay) would tell me something of interest. 'You know the Paddy Meehan case? The two men really involved were Ian Waddell and Tank McGuinness. McGuinness left the house to pick up their car and was stopped by two cops in a police car. McGuinness pretended he was drunk and looking for the bus station,' he said.

I gave Sam a hard look – this was dynamite. 'How do you know all this?' I asked.

'McGuinness told me.'

'How well do you know him?'

'I've done turns with him – he's a tie-up merchant and a nutcase.'

This was all true – Tank had serious form, as they say. Known to be dangerous, he was suspected of several bank robberies and night visits to businessmen's houses and pubs where the victims were tied up and battered to reveal the location of money, jewels and the like, so he fitted the profile of the man in the Ross house that fateful night. Even among the Glasgow neds, there were few who would have left the old couple injured and tied up to await their fate. Many a Glasgow criminal would have phoned the police after the robbery to make sure their victims survived. Not McGuinness.

What was I to do with the information? On the Monday, I

returned to the police training college, adjacent to the police office, where, during the following week, I made discreet enquiries. Having the advantage of knowing the time and the date McGuinness had been picked up by the officers, it didn't take me too long to come up with the name of an Inspector William Hepburn. Curiously, the man in charge of the inspectors' course in Ayr I was on at the time was called Hepburn. He was the sort of guy the cops call 'genuine' and very popular. If he was the same Hepburn who had picked up McGuinness, I had no doubt that he would confirm it.

I waited till the right moment and spoke in private to him. Without hesitation he told me that he had been on patrol with a Sergeant McNeill that night and they came across a man walking not too far from the bungalow in Blackburn Place. The man was apparently the worse for drink and said he was lost and looking for the bus station. Hepburn told me they took him to the bus station and dropped him off. On learning of the murder, he put two and two together and he told me that he had submitted a detailed report of the encounter. I pointed out to Hepburn that he had briefly had one of the most dangerous men in Glasgow in his hands and, had he investigated further, he could have saved Mrs Ross's life. Hindsight comes into play again but the fact is that he didn't do anything other than file a report. And, according to him, that report was 'shelved'. Someone, somewhere, had added 'cover-up' to the 'fit-up' in the saga of the wrongful incarceration of Patrick Connolly Meehan.

Had the two officers searched McGuinness, they would have found the keys of the Ross bungalow. However, the action book at Ayr Police Office did not contain a note on Hepburn's contact with McGuinness. Hepburn told me that he reported the interception of McGuinness (or he may have given his name as McGuigan) to the CID the day of the discovery. The collator for the inquiry later reported that he had no knowledge of such a report. The first he knew of this was when he was interviewed by a Crown agent in October 1969. No statement by Hepburn was included in the case papers.

Joe Beltrami later wrote to the Crown Office with the information that the police had given a lift to a man. The reply he got expressly stated that 'no such event had occurred'. On 8 October 1969, a detective superintendent was sent to interview all back-shift and night-shift officers in the area of the murder on the fateful night and that is when Hepburn's version was officially recorded.

I had a clear duty to file a report so I did. In it, I claimed that, in my opinion, Tank McGuinness was almost certainly one of the two men responsible for the murder of Mrs Ross and I outlined the circumstances that had led me to this belief. My report, like that of Hepburn, was ignored. Any information that went against the belief that 'with the death of James Griffiths and the apprehension of Patrick Connolly Meehan, the police are no longer looking for any other person suspected of the incident concerning Mr and Mrs Ross at Ayr' was unwelcome – even years after the trial and with a man in jail for a crime he did not commit. The whole case was a disaster from beginning to end.

Could it be that the ill-advised statement after the violent death of Griffiths was what drove years of establishment cover-up? Scrutiny of the documents of the time indicates there was real ferocity in the refusal of the Edinburgh legal establishment to accept the fact that Meehan was innocent. Even after Lord Hunter's report into the case was published, the establishment was reluctant to properly clear Paddy. In petty and grudging comments, it was even suggested that Meehan and Griffiths could have moved on to the Ross house after McGuinness and Waddell had broken in. There was no evidence whatsoever for such comments which gouged into Meehan's psyche. Could clinging on to the belief that Meehan had done it make that statement back in 1969 – and the cover-ups and fit-ups – less damaging to authorities? It looks that way to me.

The only people to take any credit out of the Meehan saga were the campaigners, principally Joe Beltrami and Ludovic Kennedy, who fought for justice on his behalf and ultimately secured a Royal Pardon for him on 19 May 1976.

But my involvement with the cast of bad guys who people the Meehan story wasn't quite over. In March of that year, I had been involved in a murder inquiry in which I arrested one of the sleaziest denizens of Glasgow gangland at that time – John 'Gypsy' Winning. Tank McGuinness had been battered to death and Winning was suspected of murdering him so we picked him up in a pub in the Gallowgate. Once said to be close friends, McGuinness and Winning had fallen out big time as a result of Winning's suspicions that McGuinness was 'messing about' with his daughter. The resulting trail was the worst prepared criminal trial I have been involved in. Winning was found not guilty and the judge in the High Court was moved to remark, 'If I didn't know better, I would form the opinion that the police could have prepared a better case.' He got that bit right. However, Winning had rid Glasgow of a very dangerous criminal.

Meehan may have died a free man in August 1994 in Swansea but he had spent almost seven years in solitary and, even on his release, he was treated abominably by the authorities. Embittered, he ended up a sad figure, trudging the streets of Glasgow trying to sell a controversial book on his astonishing life. Like McGuinness, Waddell also died in bloody circumstances when he was murdered by a 'friend'. Andrew Gentle was given two life sentences for killing Waddell after the two of them had stabbed a girl to death in a flat in Easterhouse. John 'Gypsy' Winning was also murdered. In his case, the location was a house in Fife so his life ended far away from the city streets where he had built such a reputation as a dangerous 'head banger'.

When I reflect on the Meehan case, I find it ironic that, from among the huge cast of infamous underworld men of violence, Meehan, a minnow without a record of blood-letting, was the one who was involved in an establishment cover-up and was fitted up and then banged up for the sort of cruel crime that was never part of his criminal CV. Seldom has bad luck, coincidences and circumstance had such an effect on a minor criminal figure.

2

DOWN ON THE FARM AND ADVENTURES IN THE GORBALS

The cop on the beat in a tough scheme, the detective with his ear to the ground and even the police administrators driving a desk thick with paperwork tend not to pay too much attention to the ragbag of opinions and theories that spout from the mouths of psychiatrists, psychologists and academic criminologists, filling newspapers and magazines. The cops just get on with the job of nailing the bad guys.

But even the most brief acquaintance with what goes on in the underworld in a city like Glasgow or any of the many of other similar places round the world gives the hardened cop some food for thought. It is impossible to miss the fact that violence and evil-doing does seem to run in some families. In Glasgow, in the modern era, those who fit this trend include: Hugh Collins and his father; the various members of the Ferris clan; Jimmy Boyle and his associates; and, above all, the Thompsons – Arthur Snr and Arthur Jnr. Could it be that crime really is in the genes as some of the shrinks think?

Who knows? Whatever is in my genes that caused me to end up as a crimefighter and on the right side of the law seems to have been in the family. My father Harry was a prison officer at Barlinnie from the start of the Second World War. Born in 1931, I was the right age to be able to take in some of what was going on as Herr Hitler marched through Europe. My early years were spent in

Bedlay Street in Springburn and I attended the local Hydepark Street Primary School. But, as happened to hundreds of other youngsters in Glasgow, the war and the threat of Nazi bombing raids on the factories and shipyards on the banks of the Clyde, which winds its way through the centre of the city and heavily populated areas down river, meant I became an evacuee. Moved out of the Luftwaffe target area, along with my brother Harry, then ten, and my wee brother Arthur, aged five, we were sent to Cuminestown in Aberdeenshire. Young Arthur was moved into a family in the village and Harry and I went to a farm, Thornhill, where the Smiths and their seventeen-year-old son Patrick looked after us well enough but soon introduced us to the daily hard work that was farming in those days. Up in the cold at seven, we assisted Mr Smith and Patrick with the feeding of cattle, horses and hens before going to school – it was a day's work before the school work! It was hard going for city youngsters aged eight.

I did well at school, finishing top of the class for several years, but I could have made more of it if it hadn't been for the tiring work on the farm which made homework difficult. But, as they say, there was a war on!

At home in Glasgow cycling was a youthful passion and Harry and I pedalled our way round the Campsies on summer days. Nights were often spent at the pictures, as we called it. My favourite was *King Kong* at the old Kinema (we had five or six cinemas within walking distance). It was a toughie and I enjoyed it but I also remember standing in a massive queue, round the block, waiting to see *Gone with the Wind*, something of a weepie. Dad used to take us to Hampden to see the big football games – Scotland and England and the like. After Springburn we moved to Aikenhead Road in the south side and then to Pollok. After I married, we spent some time in Croftfoot before moving to Old Castle Road, Simshill, where neighbours included Glasgow politician Bashir Mann, TV star Carol Smillie and Celtic legend Billy McNeill.

In our time in Aikenhead Road, I had my first brush with what you might call the underworld. Aged around fifteen, I became pally with the Crosby family who stayed not far away in Govanhill. George Crosby was the same age and we were solid friends and I was always welcome in the family home, dropping in for meals and so on. I must have been a touch naïve in those days for it took some time for the penny to drop that they were gangsters. George and I would swan around the local billiard halls and cinemas and we never had to pay a penny. Eventually I twigged that the Crosby reputation as hard men was the reason we had such a free ride! My illusions about the family were completely shattered one night when I was in the house as the older members 'tooled up' with bayonets and left in a taxi to meet and do battle with a rival gang. I heard later that in one fight an opponent died.

My friendship with the Crosbys had a remarkable postscript years later. In my early days as a cop in the Gorbals, I accompanied some officers to help arrest a man wanted on warrant. It turned out to be my old pal George who not only recognised me but told my colleagues he was proud that I was doing so well.

But there were other adventures ahead before I first pulled on the blue serge and the chequered cap of a Glasgow cop. I left school at fourteen with no academic qualifications and started work at a bookstall in Buchanan Street station. This lasted a year and I earned some badly needed cash. The job was also very enjoyable as I was the only guy in a staff of five – those girls spoiled me! But this little idyll was to end after a year as my grandfather wisely insisted I learned a trade. He took me to Weirs, the world-famous engineering firm based in the south side at Cathcart. I served my time as a fitter there and thoroughly enjoyed it.

I had also loved my jaunts with my father to Hampden. After a revamp in the nineties, Hampden became Scotland's National Stadium and it features later in my life as a policeman. But, at

Weirs, I was to get more of an insider's view of football. One of my mates there was Archie Robertson who played for Clyde at Shawfield. Archie died tragically young but is still well remembered in Scottish football circles as an elegant straight-backed player with tremendous ability to distribute a ball effectively. Had he played these days he would have been a millionaire. As it was, he shared his love of Clyde with Weirs.

At eighteen, National Service beckoned. There was some fun in this too and I well remember our first day at Padgate, an RAF induction centre. A flight sergeant ushered us into a hangar and seemed desperate to find good sportsmen among us. 'Any champions?' he asked. One lad, an Englishman as it turned out, was a table-tennis champ. A Scot had raised his hand as well and, when he was asked where he came from, he replied, 'Wishaw.' 'Where the hell is that?' said Mr Officer. But his putdown didn't last long as he went on to say he was looking for footballers but didn't expect another Stanley Mathews. 'Who the hell is Stanley Matthews?' I asked. That got a laugh.

No one who did National Service forgets it and mine did produce some memorable moments. Maybe I was always destined for the police but, at any rate, in the services, I volunteered for the RAF Regiment. I spent two years at Fassberg in West Germany, a few miles from Belsen. Being part of a crack mortar squad, we had a high old time entertaining the dignitaries and plane lovers at the Farnborough Air Show. Another highlight has a modern resonance. We took part in a massive operation called Heavyside. We played the part of a terrorist unit being hunted by the British and American armies. This was dammed near the real thing – the simulation was so realistic that soldiers could lose their lives, some as a result of so-called friendly fire. My lads almost copped it when an American fighter accidentally dropped a napalm bomb on us. For some reason, it did not ignite and I was spared to return to Weirs in 1951 to continue with my apprenticeship.

A couple of years later, I was qualified and ready to indulge my itchy feet with a spell as a marine engineer. My first ship was an old coal burner called *City of Worcester*, an Ellerman Line vessel. Travelling from Chalna in India to Dundee with jute was not the most romantic of occupations, but a life at sea looking after the engines did bring the occasional reward – and I had an early experience of crime. We stopped at Aden for coal and one of my duties was to check the bunkers. On one occasion, I was convinced that we had been short changed by 100 tons. I reported the matter to the chief engineer but he attempted to persuade me I was mistaken. I soon realised there was a scam going on between the chief and the coal suppliers. I protested again and, when I returned to my cabin, I found a pound note pinned to my pillow. For the first and last time, I had been got at.

A transfer to the *City of Perth* brought a string of exotic destinations including Baltimore where I watched the premiere of *Oklahoma!* – a long way from the Kinema in Springburn. Long Beach was another destination and there we had a look at the *Spruce Goose*, the gigantic wooden flying boat built by Howard Hughes. At San Francisco, we had lunch at Fisherman's Wharf and met Ann Sheridan in the flesh. Until then, she had only been an alluring flickering figure on the Springburn screens.

It was an interesting few years, not least the experience of being strafed in the Straits of Formosa by three aircraft returning from a bombing raid over China. We radioed the Royal Navy for help and got the less than reassuring message from the nearest vessel, HMS *Newcastle*, saying, 'Don't panic – we will be with you the day after tomorrow.'

But, after three happy years on the *Perth*, I decided to call it a day for several reasons – one of them being that I had fallen in love. My youngest brother, Leonard, was a professional ice skater and I went down to Crossmyloof Ice Rink in Shawlands, not far from my old stamping ground at Weirs, to see him train. Although Leonard went on to be third in the British championships, I soon lost interest in watching him because my eyes were on a certain young woman. She happened to be the Scottish champion and she was also doing a spot of practising. That day in 1955, it was love at first sight when Sheila Fotheringham came into my life. Along with Jeanette Altwegg, Sheila had been selected to represent Britain in the 1952 Olympics and, indeed, Jeanette won the Gold Medal for figure skating. Leonard always used to thank me for supporting him as he trained but, by now, he knows I had an ulterior motive in all those trips to the ice rink at Crossmyloof, which, sadly, is now a supermarket.

The wisdom of Harry, Arthur and me being evacuated was underlined by a tale Sheila could tell of the Clydebank Blitz and a remarkable escape from death. One night, a bomb shelter they had used in Beattie Street was hit by a land mine. Minutes before it struck, Sheila and her mother had gone back to the house to collect something. They returned to a scene of devastation – the brick wall had blown out and the concrete roof fallen in, killing several relatives who were later buried in a mass grave in Clydebank Cemetery.

During our courtship, Sheila was one of the stars of the show *Holiday on Ice* down at the Glaswegians' favourite resort, Blackpool. It was a great thrill for me to travel down and see the beautiful redhead who was my girlfriend electrify the arena. Happy days! We were married in Croftfoot Parish Church on the south side on 20 August 1959. By then, I was a humble police constable and the press had a field day with the story, contrasting me with Sheila, the gorgeous skating star.

There was a Weirs connection even in me joining the police. When there, I had worked in the power house along with a maintenance fitter called Dougie Black who was the most genuine guy you could want to work with. His cousin, uncle and brother were all cops and it was Dougie who first suggested I joined the police. I took the big step in November 1956 and, after attending police colleges at national and local level, I was ready for the final interviews and a posting in the City of Glasgow.

I enjoyed my training, particularly the days at the police college in the Gorbals' Oxford Street where I first met one of the officers I admired most in my career, Chief Inspector Fred Casely who was in charge there. In Oxford Street, we sat at old-fashioned school desks – for the big guys, it was a case of knees up at our chins – and Fred and other experienced cops lectured us. Well, lectured is the wrong word – we were introduced to a world where accuracy and procedure were vital and where an interest in and understanding of your fellow man were essential. There were tales of days in the Gorbals station when cops were rolling on the floor trying to subdue a violent prisoner while upstairs the police choir rehearsed 'Abide with Me'!

The choir and the pipe band were world famous and formed an important part of the social fabric of the police. They toured abroad a lot and I remember one tour to Denmark in 1963 when, in a concert in Copenhagen, the choir of fifty serving officers under Fred entertained with a wonderful rendition of 'Loch Lomond' and other traditional airs while the pipe band belted out 'Scotland the Brave' and even managed a version of '76 Trombones'.

But Fred was superb at the 'day job' and the ranks of the police are thronged with cops who were made into top-class men by him and his colleagues and his legacy.

After all the slog of training, the day arrived when we were to be 'posted'. The list was to go on a notice board and, as I approached it to see my fate, I heard a colleague say, 'Les Brown has got the Gorbals.' Sure enough, I saw that I had been given the number D69 and was to report to Gorbals Police Office, in Nicholson Street, about 250 yards from Gorbals Cross, the following Monday – on the night shift. The great day came and it was bitterly cold and threatening to snow. I looked at my watch, confirmed I was in good time, took a deep breath, opened the swing doors and stepped into what was to be my world for the next twenty years or so.

I walked through the outer public part of the office and into the muster hall. Most of the shift were already seated and I was introduced to them. I got a friendly welcome and some interesting news about my number. The last bearer of D69 had been a police officer who was hanged in Barlinnie for the murder of a prostitute. This was James Robertson and his was a remarkable case. He had run over and killed his girlfriend with his car. Initially thought to be a hit-and-run incident, good policing spotted what had happened – the victim had been deliberately run over several times. But Robertson's death has a controversial note to it and he could have saved himself from the gallows. In a convoluted piece of thinking at his trial, he maintained his victim was an acquaintance, not someone with whom he had a strong ongoing relationship. In his view, this protected his wife from the truth but, in reality, it made the killing more horrific as it removed any crime of passion defence. His lawyer, the legendary Laurence Dowdall, was convinced he could have escaped the death sentence if he had told the truth about the relationship and its complexity. But he stuck to the story that he had killed an acquaintance rather than a lover and took the short walk to the drop in the infamous Barlinnie hanging shed.

A new world was opening up to me – the life of a cop on the beat. Gorbals section in those days had beats numbered from seven to sixteen and, on good nights, each beat had a patrolling officer. In addition, we covered the Kingston Docks. As a newcomer, I was given the docks as my first assignment. We left the office and walked to our various beats. When I arrived at the docks, I was pleasantly surprised to see that my 'office' was the dock's accident box. Located just inside the main gate of the docks area, the shed was fairly spacious and was equipped with a cooker, running water, a fire and a telephone linked directly to the Gorbals Police Office.

However, it was not long before I was to sample the lively life of a police officer out on the streets of the Gorbals. A few days later, I was given a beat that included the Cross area itself. On a Friday and Saturday night, this place was something else. Trouble generally came as the pubs emptied. By this time, their customers, who were mostly of Irish descent, would be drunk and, with no attractive homes to go to, they would stand around on the pavements. Inevitably, heated discussions were held and they often ended in violence. On my first Saturday, a woman ran into the outer room of the police office, where we were waiting to go to our beats, screaming that a cop was being attacked by a mob. We ran from the outer office and I heard on the radio my first 'Code 21 Red'. (If a police officer requires assistance that is not urgent, a radio message is transmitted, to a specific police unit, to attend a Code 21. If it is urgent, the message is Code 21 Red and, in Glasgow, such assistance will arrive within two minutes.)

Being the youngest and fastest, I arrived at the Cross at the head of the pack and saw a cop curled up on the ground being kicked by a uniformed soldier. I was still in full flight when I punched him full on the face, knocking him to the ground. He was quickly frogmarched to the office. On the way, he threatened me with violence and added that he intended charging me with assault. On hearing this, my partner reached over and tore the lapel clean off my jacket. As he did so, he said, 'Charge him with assault now, you bastard.' The officer at the end of the kicking was black and blue but recovered.

It was a night of violence in the Gorbals and it was to be the first of many for me.

3

Scarface Russo, Johnny Ramensky and on my Bike in Castlemilk

Police work in the old days in the Gorbals required a good pair of boots – stout and well shined, for all the walking involved – and the ability to think on your feet. The inhabitants of this much-maligned area might not have had much in the way of formal education, and they were often unemployed and short of cash, but they were certainly quick on the uptake. It also helped to have a good pair of fists. This was a lesson quickly drilled into me by my colleagues.

The Gorbals area needed policing virtually 24/7 as they say these days. The coppers on the beat worked three shifts – nights for six weeks (starting at 11 p.m.), then six weeks of day shift (7 a.m. till 2 p.m.) and then there was a back shift (2 p.m. till 11 p.m.). However, on Friday and Saturday nights, the back shift stayed on till midnight and the night shift started at ten. This meant that, between ten and midnight, we had the maximum head count on the streets when the pubs came out – the time it tended to be most needed. There were plenty of drunks and troublemakers and it could be a hard task to keep the peace.

The Bonnington Bar was one place where the atmosphere or the drink made the customers reluctant to leave swiftly at closing time – I suspect it was largely the drink! I remember we entered it one night to be greeted by a customer who had overindulged and fancied himself as a bit of Glasgow wise guy. He was a cocky individual and, as this would-be comedian approached Arthur Waugh, the constable I was with, he looked at Arthur in his blue uniform and declaimed, 'Christ, it's a lamplighter!' Arthur handed me his cap and, with an almighty punch, felled the guy, saying as he did so, 'That's put your gas at a peep.'

The pub emptied briskly after that and I immediately got another lesson about life on the beat. The pub owner, pleased to get some peace at last, placed two glasses of whisky on the counter. Arthur carefully poured one glass into the other and drank it, turning to me to say, 'You can't drink – you're a probationer.' Arthur Waugh was a legend in the Gorbals and I learned a lot from him. Any time we saw a battered woman on the street, Arthur would establish where the husband was and, while I stood guard, he would pay him a visit. Summary justice was administered and many an evil husband would think twice the next time he thought of raising his hands to his wife.

These were exciting times for a young cop. It is true that the majority of the folk in the area were honest and hardworking and the many books available detailing reminiscences of life in the Gorbals tenements are right in that there certainly were true friendships, humour and harmony up many a close. The locals did tend to look out for each other but it was far from the cosy, 'we are all in it together' sort of a place that is described through rose-coloured spectacles by folk who have been away from the reality of urine-smelling closes and squalid backcourts for too long.

Houses and pubs in the area were frequently broken into and it is undeniable that there was a lot of drink-fuelled fighting on the streets – even in daylight. Crowds tended to gather around the Cross, where well-known Gorbals hard men would flex their muscles. There was a lot of minor battling but serious assaults were also commonplace and they were dealt with by the CID. When I first saw the detectives in action, I thought that this was the direction I wanted my police career to go in.

One particular night, I was on Beat 8 and I was 'neighboured up' with a copper called Albert White on Beat 9. It was a sticky night and the crowd at the Cross were restless. Before we had completed our late shift, we had arrested eleven people on separate charges. Most were run-of-the-mill offences except for the arrest of one guy who had scars criss-crossing his face and who proudly identified himself as Victor 'Scarface' Russo. On this occasion, he was locked up and charged with breach of the peace and challenging the police to a fight. In later years, Russo was to become an infamous underworld figure and our paths were to cross again.

The most active local gang in the area at this time was the Cumbie, who took their name from Cumberland Street; this was in our section, but, strangely, we didn't have too much trouble with them. This was because they did most of their fighting with gangs in Bridgeton and Govan and tended to travel to 'away' battles in those areas, causing endless trouble for the officers there. They could be a fierce mob and, on one occasion, as I was walking along Cumberland Street on my own, I turned a corner to find at least thirty of them heading menacingly towards me. It was scary but I was determined not to lose face on my own turf so I kept on walking towards them. They split into groups of four or five and went on past me. It could have been nasty.

The Cumbie and their doings sparked my lifelong interest Glasgow's gangs, which some crime historians number well into the hundreds over the years. At this time, I reckon there were around forty gangs active in the city, the largest being the Maryhill Fleet.

However, there were more mundane duties than gang-busting to be attended to in my early days on the beat. On night shift, the idea was that the copper would check vulnerable local properties – front doors, front windows and the rear of the properties – twice during each shift. If the cop stuck, as most did, to a rigid routing, it was easy for criminals to time their appearances at

various places on the beat and act when the coast was clear.
Right from the start, I did things rather differently, moving
about the beat and stopping in shop doorways and close mouths
for a minute or two just to see what was happening. It seemed
to work as I was catching more criminals than my mates. Of
course, by gambling that the premises were secure, I was taking
something of a chance but I was seldom caught out.

There are incidents that you just can't forget and one I wonder
about to this day occurred when I was patrolling in Abbotsford
Place. I had heard the sound of police whistles – the humble
whistle actually played a major role in crime-fighting before
radios and mobile phones were common – and, in the distance,
I saw a young man running towards me and he was pursued by
two policemen. I dived into a close mouth, waited and, as the
fugitive ran past, I sprang out and seized him. The cops who had
been chasing him soon arrived and told me he had stabbed a
policeman with a screw driver in Allison Street, not too far
away. Apparently he had been disturbed breaking into the rear
door of a shop. We escorted him to the Gorbals station where a
police van was detailed to take us to divisional headquarters. As
I made to enter the van with the other officers, I was surprised
when they indicated that I was not required.

Later that morning, out of natural curiosity, I enquired about
the charges brought against the prisoner I had helped arrest and
the answers I got certainly made me think. The prisoner never
made it to HQ. Apparently, he had 'jumped', handcuffed, from
the van when it was travelling at 40mph and was in intensive
care in the Victoria Infirmary. At first, I thought, 'The Lord
works in mysterious ways.' But the beat cop who had been
stabbed died a couple of weeks later and his attacker lives on.

One of the most remembered names in Scottish crime history
is that of Gentle Johnny Ramensky whose story is currently
being turned into a film. Johnny was an extraordinarily skilled
safe blower who was much in demand to open 'cans' for his

fellow burglars. His skill was such that, during the Second World War, he was parachuted in behind enemy lines to crack Nazi safes in search of secret plans. He did tremendous work in the service of his country but, after the war, he could not control a passion for the adrenalin brought by creeping across darkened rooftops and breaking open the toughest of safes.

He had something of a Robin Hood reputation, usually breaking into business premises rather than stealing from the private householders. His nickname came, by the way, from his acceptance of his fate whenever he was caught – he always went quietly, never resisting arrest. On one occasion, he even took the trouble to tip off the authorities about a couple of safes he had been working on unknown to them. He didn't want anyone to be hurt by explosives going off unexpectedly.

I never ran into Johnny on the beat although he did have a house in our section, a tenement flat in Eglinton Street where he used the name Ramsay. Johnny was away a lot spending time inside but he often used his skills to make an escape from prison. Several times, word reached our patch that he was on the loose and that we were to keep an eye on his home in case he returned. What the bosses back at the station did not know was that most of the local cops were on first name terms with the legendary safebreaker's wife. Whenever he escaped, we didn't hang about backcourts spying, we just joined Mrs Ramsay for a nice wee cup of tea and, of course, Johnny was too smart to head back to Glasgow from Peterhead or Perth or wherever he was serving his latest sentence.

The tenement used by the 'Ramsays' featured in another incident when I was on the beat – a more tragic happening, this time. A resident had reported to the police that a chimney appeared to be in a dangerous condition. I was on the early shift and detailed to go and have a look. I am no builder but it only took a glance to see that the danger was real and anyone passing below would be hurt if it fell. I set about erecting barriers and diverting pedestrians. At 1.55 p.m., the back-shift cop arrived to take over. I pointed at the chimney and said, 'When that comes down, make sure neither you nor anyone else is underneath it.' A year later, I was to repeat those very words at the Court of Session as what had happened was probed. An hour after I had gone off duty, the chimney head did crash to the ground and the poor cop who took over from me was so engrossed in ensuring the pedestrians were safe he had lost track of his own position on the pavement. He received terrible injuries and eventually a large compensation payment.

As the months went by, I was learning my trade and enjoying some success in the lock-up department. But, as is often the case, any notions of great success I had were disguising the fact that I was heading for a fall. These were the days before betting shops were legalised and the backcourts and tenements of the city were thronged with illegal bookmakers, their armies of runners and the punters after a quick buck, a way of life now almost forgotten with centrally heated, carpeted bookmakers' shops on every second city street.

I was on a late shift in the Tradeston area when I noticed considerable numbers of men entering a close in Weir Street. I nipped up the next street, climbed the stairs and, from a top landing, could see a major illegal betting operation in full swing. Racing papers were hung on boards on the back wall, two men were sitting at a table and punters were scanning their racing papers and placing bets. I decided to act. I contacted a cop on a neighbouring beat and together we took observations for about twenty minutes. We then got further assistance and raided the set-up. We arrested the man in charge and about ten of his customers. We seized the boards, table and newspapers and hauled the lot off to the Gorbals office.

To say the reception I got from the duty sergeant was a surprise is more than an understatement. I found out that the bookie had forcibly complained that, not only had he not received his usual warning from the police, it wasn't even his turn to be raided. I was absolutely gobsmacked. However, they were all booked and a case was prepared against them. If I thought that this was the end of the matter, I had another shock coming.

I was, it seems, too naïve or too conscientious for the area so it was decided I needed a move. Off I went to report to my new base: Cathcart Police Office on Merrylee Road, a douce residential area far removed from the tenement life of the Gorbals. But, as a seeker after real policing – and real excitement – I was at least lucky in that the section included the huge Castlemilk housing scheme. In a well-meaning move after the war, the city councillors attempted to alleviate the overcrowding and bad housing around the city centre and built new greenfield housing estates. As well as Castlemilk – which alone had a population the size of Perth – new schemes were constructed in Easterhouse, Drumchapel and Pollok. The snag with such places was that, although the houses themselves were a million times better than the old tenements, the councillors in their wisdom omitted to provide shops, libraries, pubs, swimming pools and so on – all the diversions that helped keep a large population stable.

And they didn't really consider that, when they decanted thousands from the Gorbals to Castlemilk, there were significant gang members among them. The gangsters found themselves away from their normal haunts and without their normal diversions. Many members of the Cumbie found themselves in pastures new. It was a recipe for a crime wave and it happened.

The move of thousands out of the slums to the schemes was a well-meaning disaster in many ways that was eventually corrected, to some extent, by belatedly building the libraries and pools that should have been there in the first place. Permission for pubs and, ironically, betting shops was also eventually given. But, as well, as a lack of amenities on the new schemes, the residents had to contend with policing that was nothing short of a joke. Castlemilk was built between Croftfoot and Cathkin Braes and, to cover this vast place, there was never more than one officer on duty. When required, he could be backed up by officers on mobile patrol. And this was in the days before personal radios! The officer delegated to patrol the huge scheme did so on a bike.

Soon after my transfer, I found myself doing just that. It was depressing and demoralising for an ambitious young cop. The scheme was home to plenty of villains and most of my time was spent delivering citations for court and an assortment of legal and other messages. There was always a hint of violence in the air and it soon turned to reality for me. I was on a back shift in Ardencraig Road when I heard a woman screaming. I pedalled as fast as I could round the corner and saw a woman on her knees beside the figure of an obviously distressed teenager. It seemed that the lad had been attacked by a gang of about ten local youths and stabbed. The woman indicated that some of the gang were in a house nearby. I told her to go to a neighbour's, phone the police and say, 'Code 21 Red at Ardencraig Road, Castlemilk.'

I then summoned up my courage and knocked on the door of the house where the gang members were suspected to be. There were seven youths inside, along with the mother of one of them. I told the woman what had happened in the street and said I was arresting all seven. With her assistance, I marched the suspects to a nearby police box where her son handed me a surgeon's scalpel, saying, as he did so, 'It was me who did the stabbing.' I noted everything that had happened carefully in my notebook and got the mother to sign her name under it. This was a procedure I was to follow faithfully throughout my police service and I found it invaluable. The mother of the young thug would make a good prosecution witness for the High Court where this affair would undoubtedly end. I had barely closed my notebook when the wailing of police sirens on squad cars was heard and out leapt two detective officers. A van was summoned and all seven were whipped off to the cells at Craigie Street Police Office, just off Victoria Road.

Needless to say, my actions were the talk of the division and had been noted by senior officers. The good news was that I was on my way back to the Gorbals. The bad news was that the cops there didn't welcome me back with open arms – that bookie incident was too recent in their collective memory. Instead, the section inspector and sergeant made life as difficult as possible for me. It was a troublesome time for me but it did nothing to dampen down my ambitions and a bit of controversy has never bothered me. But I sought the advice of the senior inspector, John Little, who later went on to become Chief Constable of Tayside. He listened with sympathy and suggested yet another change. He thought I might be good material for the traffic department and he said he would sponsor me in a bid to get the transfer. It sounded good. So I applied to join the traffic department without telling John I had never sat a driving test because I obtained my licence during a time of petrol shortage.

I realised I would have to sit an advanced driving test to gain entry to the department. Right away, I was hell-bent on gaining experience of driving all sorts of vehicles and I even took a two-day course on driving a single-decker bus. My application was processed and I was sent to the police garage at Helen Street, in Govan, where I was interviewed at length and then taken out in an assortment of vehicles ranging from a rather racy Sunbeam Talbot to the sort of huge prison van used for transporting prisoners between offices and jails and courts. It was quite a day but after all the formalities I was accepted for the first vacancy.

The endless hours of plodding the dark streets of the Gorbals were over and so, too, were the days on my bike in Castlemilk. The world of four wheels beckoned . . .

4

RACING JAGUARS, MURDER HUNTS
AND BENT COPPERS

In recent years, there have been many tragic incidents involving police cars in what is known as 'high-speed pursuit'. Since I left 'the traffic', cars have got faster, roads busier and even the most minor law-breaker often drives a top-of-the-range model capable of outrunning even a cop car. The potential for accidents is much increased. Mind you, we had our own incidents and one was particularly memorable. It was serious but there was also an amusing tinge to it that gave it the potential to be interesting from the point of view of a Hollywood filmmaker. Indeed, it involved the sort of comedy car-chase scene that is often portrayed in the movies but this happened in real life and in the world-famous thoroughfare of Argyle Street.

One of our top drivers, Roy Harvey, picked up a stolen car heading eastwards towards Glasgow Cross and chased it at high speed. Just as they got to the area of the Cross, a vehicle suddenly appeared in front of him – out of nowhere, as they say. He had no choice but to take rapid evasive action. In those days, the area was famous for furniture stores and the police car crashed through the front entrance of one, careered along the full length of the store, disappeared down a flight of stairs and, still travelling at considerable speed, ran into a stack of rolled up carpets!

Roy was knocked out by the impact and had to be shipped up the road to the Royal Infirmary. It took him three days to regain consciousness and, when he did, the first thing he saw was Inspector Bob Moyes sitting at his bedside. Noticing the first flickers of life in the driver, Bob said, 'Constable Harvey, it is my duty to caution you . . .' The long arm of the law!

My transfer from the Gorbals took a couple of weeks to come through but finally the three-year slog on the tough streets was over and I reported to the police garage in Helen Street and this time it was as a member of staff. Helen Street was the base for five shifts of officers who would drive daily from there to their respective divisions. At the start, very much the new boy, I was allocated to cars whose usual crews were off ill, attending court or on holiday.

They say things run in threes and I was to be in 'the traffic' for the next three years of my career. The crew of each car was usually headed by a senior officer with around fifteen years' experience. The steadying influence of such men was very evident and it resulted in very few accidents – although Roy, the driver who went shopping in his car, was an exception.

Our job was to help ensure a free flow of traffic, to attend and assist at serious road accidents and arrest drunk drivers (to be nit-picking, they should actually be described as 'drink drivers' since you did not have to be blind drunk to be over the limit) and pick up the speedsters who ignored posted limits as much in those days as they do now. If you liked cars, it was a good job and the posts generally attracted guys who took their work and responsibilities seriously.

However, even in the traffic department, you could find a really bad apple. Before I was in the department long enough to be allocated a regular mate, I worked with an assortment of officers. Right away, I sensed one of them was in the wrong job and, from the start, there were bad vibes between us. That I was right to be uneasy was soon confirmed. We were driving back after attending a pub break-in when this cove told me that he had taken the opportunity to nick a couple of bottles of whisky while we were at the pub investigating the break-in and one bottle was under my seat. I was driving at the time and we turned round straightaway and headed back to the pub. The two bottles of whisky were handed over to a cop who was stationed back at the pub door while the inquiry went on. I reported the incident to the shift inspector Bob Moyes and I knew I would have to be on my guard as I had clearly run into a dishonest cop.

Sure enough, the rota threw us together again and, the following Sunday, I found myself again on duty with this guy as we sped to a burglar alarm call at the famous old Goldberg store in the Candleriggs. The key holder had been called out and he stayed in the street as we entered the shop. Normally, the procedure was to search the ground floor first and work our way upwards but this was not what happened in this case. My partner had a look at the direction board for the various departments at the front door and stated that he would start on the third floor. That, surprise, surprise, was where the jewellery department was. He was the senior man so we went there first. He perused the cases of valuable jewellery and was not in the least amused when I refused to leave his side.

Back at the station, I again told the gaffer what had gone on and that I believed this officer was heading for the Bar-L. It didn't take long to prove me right. A few weeks later, he was arrested for soliciting money from the manager of the Dennistoun Palais who had been pulled up for speeding. Six months was the sentence and good riddance.

Not long after this, I was given a new partner, Willie Smith, and we worked well together. Things were looking up and we were chuffed to be allocated a new car. Code-named Tango 18, it was a top-of-the-range 2.8 litre Jaguar in a nice shade of green. In those days, cars had to be carefully run in and we were urged not to get into high-speed chases after stolen cars till the engine had bedded in. We were even instructed to take it on long gentle runs – which explains why on some sunny day in the fifties tourists at Stirling Castle were treated to the sight of a couple of Glasgow traffic cops enjoying an ice cream. All round it was a nice car but it was fitted with heavy-duty police radio batteries which were located in the boot and this made the vehicle a little unstable at high speed.

We had a sort of routine and it often brought us face to face with celebrities. On the early shift, we would patrol major incoming roads to the city in the hope of catching speeders and we usually bagged a few each day. On one occasion, the victim was the famous golf professional Eric Brown who was often all over the sports pages and even wrote a column for the old *Evening Citizen*. Although he was a Bathgate boy, he was a very well-known face in the city. He didn't enjoy being stopped and seemed agitated when it looked as if we didn't recognise him. He went into the old 'Do you know who I am?' routine and was on the verge of blowing a fuse when I asked him if he was a footballer. It was time to end the wind-up so I told him, 'As you only came second last week in the Los Angles Open and as we only clocked you at 40mph, I will simply give you a verbal warning.' I can still remember that huge grin that spread over his face. Mind you, it was not his golfing prowess that had earned him special treatment – it was our policy to give a 'verbal' to those not too far over the speed limit.

In those days, there were no radar guns or remote cameras to clock the errant driver straying over the limit. The cops had to show in evidence that we had followed fifty yards behind an offending vehicle, for three tenths of a mile. One day, while waiting to give evidence against a guy I had picked up, the Procurator Fiscal asked me if I would measure the distance from his court to the wall of the building opposite. I promptly did so and gave the court officer a note that read '56 feet 6 inches'. After lunch, I was called into court to give evidence for the prosecution. The defence solicitor took me through my evidence and averred I had not been the correct distance behind his client's car. He asked me if I could estimate the distance between the courtroom window and the wall of the building opposite. I indicated I would give it a go. I asked the sheriff for permission to leave the witness box and made my way to the window where I took a good look. I returned to the box and the question was repeated. I replied, '56 feet 6 inches.' The game was a bogey for that defence!

You often got a laugh out of such days off the road and it was satisfying to see a case through to completion at court. For example, not long after the measurement case, Willie and I were back giving evidence against a wealthy builder accused of drink driving. Willie was called first. Normally, our evidence would go along the lines of 'We saw the vehicle being driven erratically and, when the driver was spoken to, we could see his eyes were glazed and, when he got out of the vehicle, he had to support himself on the car door.' This time, it seemed to me that Willie was in the box longer than usual. As I was led into court by the court officer, he said in a whispered aside to me that the accused had a glass eye. As I stepped into the box, I looked at Willie who was sweating profusely and, when I looked at the defence solicitor and saw that he was wearing a wig indicating that he was a QC, I had the feeling that this wasn't going to be quite as easy as I thought – especially when I also realised the defence brief was J Irvine Smith, a man who was to go on to become a legendary sheriff.

The Procurator Fiscal took me through my evidence and then came the feared cross-examination. 'Constable Brown, you have told the court that my client's eyes were glazed. What did you mean?' I looked at the accused and could see the ceiling light reflected in his glass eye. I hesitated and the sheriff asked if the question was giving me a problem. I replied that I was being careful not to insult the accused. 'Answer the question,' said the sheriff. I answered by saying, 'You could not tell his bad eye from his good one.' The accused was found guilty and, some months later when Irvine Smith, by that time a Sheriff, spotted me, he signalled me to follow him into his chambers. I did and, over a coffee, he asked if I remembered the drink driver with the glass eye. I confirmed that I did and he asked me, 'When did you first realise he had a glass eye?' I told him the truth that the first I knew of it was when the court officer warned me. Later in my career, I was in Sheriff Irvine Smith's court many a time and I am sure that, when administering the oath, one of his eyes always narrowed slightly!

Mind you, long before that I got a wee fright and wondered if my career in the traffic was about to end suddenly. Another celebrity was involved and, this time, it was the film actor Richard Todd. My regular partner Willie had gone on holiday and I was teamed up with PC Tom Mitchell for two weeks. One day, the radio buzzed and we were to go to an address at Park Circus. Sure enough, two men were there, one of whom was the film star. The other guy told us that Richard Todd was due on the *Bill Tennant* programme, STV's early evening news flagship which at that time was very popular viewing. Bill had a huge and faithful following for his show which was broadcast from the old STV studios at the top of Hope Street – a fair distance from Park Circus. The show started at 6 p.m. and, by now, it was 5.55 p.m. – hence the call for assistance. With the famous passenger in the back and the horn howling, we set off at what I must admit was a fair rate of knots down Sauchiehall Street and arrived at the studio at 5.59. The star thanked us and said to get in front of a telly when the programme was on and he would give us a mention. We went into a nearby television shop and heard Bill say to Richard Todd, 'I believe you just made it here in time?' Todd replied on air and for the benefit of millions of listeners, including our gaffers, 'Yes, a police car brought me along Sauchiehall Street at about 90mph. So thanks to Tom and Les.' It could have been the end of what I saw as a promising career but we survived.

Driving at high speed was something we did regularly. When chasing a stolen car, our Jag was capable of speeds of anything between 20mph to 108mph in third gear, which was a tremendous advantage because it allowed us to keep both hands on the wheel most of the time. Incidentally, the fastest speeder we caught was on the Edinburgh Road. We were following a car doing 80mph when a sports car whipped past as if we were standing still. We fell in behind this new speedster and accelerated to a point where we could accurately estimate his speed at 108mph. It took about two miles to pull him over and the driver was, to say the least, most surprised to see us. 'Where did you guys come from?' he asked. We told him he had passed us and he couldn't believe it. Maybe it was because our car was unmarked and we had our hats on the back seat.

The speed game was a bit cat and mouse in those pre-technology days. We once had our eyes on a regular speeder who travelled home every evening, keeping a good eye in his rear view mirror. He was proving very hard to catch. Once, when he whizzed past us, we got close to him and dropped back to our 50 yards and stayed there. The distance between us did not decrease so we pulled him over, charging him with driving at more than 50mph in a 30mph area. He turned out to be a well-known criminal lawyer but clearly he was not above making a bad mistake. In reply to the charge, he said, 'You weren't 50 yards behind me when I was doing more than 50.' When he realised what he had said, he begged us not to log the remark. No chance.

Those Jags made speed a temptation and I have to admit that, at one time, many of the drivers on the shift would meet at the west end of the dual carriageway on the Edinburgh Road and race to the Baillieston lights. This 'sport' soon came to an end when a woman who had witnessed our bit of fun put pen to paper in a letter to the Chief Constable, complimenting our driving skills.

Not all the 'celebrities' we met were film stars or sportsmen. I remember getting mixed up with one of the most infamous names in the history of Glasgow crime when I was in 'the traffic' in the fifties – one Walter Scott Ellis. The name of this one-time bank robber is forever linked with changes in the way the Scottish press reported criminal matters. He was cleared of murdering a taxi driver and, after the case was over, there was an almighty scrum of newsmen trying to whisk him away to get his story. The scene led to a judgement by Lord Clyde placing strictures on reporting that are still in place to this day.

However, our involvement was a tad more mundane. During the trial, the advocate depute, who would be handling the prosecution case, travelled through from Edinburgh to Glasgow where we were detailed to take him for a look at the scene of the crime. The murder had taken place in Castlemilk but, as we were driving out there, we got a shock when the legal luminary looked at the rain beginning to splatter on to the windscreen and asked us to turn round and take him back to the station. We ignored the request and took him to the scene at Tormusk Road where he did get out of the car and have a good look around. We then took him back to Queen Street and the comfort of his first-class carriage for his journey home to the capital.

We, of course, followed the case closely and it was interesting to note that the sort of good old-fashioned policing mentioned earlier in this book came into play – at that time in the city there were 650 taxi drivers and every one was interviewed. In spite of this, Scott Ellis was cleared.

Our paths crossed again when he was arrested for being in possession of a sawn-off shotgun. His defence claimed he used this to shoot rabbits. He was convicted on a majority verdict which meant that some of the jury at least believed that this sort of weapon was used to control rodents! Any one with even the most passing acquaintance of juries in the city can testify there is no telling which way they will jump.

I had now served more than four years in the force and, by that time, I was eligible to sit more police exams. I was beginning to think of a different sort of life in the police as the challenge of driving high-speed cars and catching speeders and drunks was losing its appeal. I had no worries about the police sections of the exams – I knew procedure inside out and I was experienced – but there was a big section on general knowledge that might not be so easy. I got a hold of the exam papers for the previous few years – legally, I should add! – and, in an early nod in the direction of becoming a detective, I noticed that, in the geography section, every continent had been covered except Australia. So I turned swot on the cities, mountains, national products and the economy down under and it paid off. The exams were held in the precincts of Glasgow University, that ancient and impressive pile in the west end. As I figured, the police questions did not trouble me. The first words of the general paper were, 'What do you know about Australia?' Three hundred cops sat that exam. Twenty-one passed. I was one of them.

Now the proud possessor of sergeant's and inspector's certificates, I took stock of my position and my future. Being one of only two officers in the traffic department with those qualifications, my next logical move would be to the traffic inquiry department which investigated road accidents and prepared prosecutions. This I did not fancy and my thoughts turned to a career in the CID.

Sometimes fate can take a hand. Bob Kerr, the then boss of the CID, had a driver from the traffic department who was about to go on holiday. I was well in with the garage sergeant and I suggested that I might take over the duties of whisking Mr Kerr around for a couple of weeks. It happened. I was told I would not be in uniform and that I would arrive at Bob Kerr's house at exactly 8 a.m. on the Monday morning, armed with a copy of that day's *Glasgow Herald*. At the appointed time the big man arrived, stepped into the car and told me to take him to his office which, at that time, was in Turnbull Street. As he left the car, I held out my hand and said, 'Sir, you owe me three pence for the paper.' He dryly remarked, 'I usually get my paper for nothing.' But he handed me the money!

I was to wait in the CID office across the street, ready to take him wherever he needed to be. After a week of ferrying Bob Kerr about, he went on holiday for a week. His place was taken by Detective Superintendent Tom Goodall so suddenly I had the privilege of driving the famous detective around.

Once, he came over and found me helping out in a case of a stolen car inquiry and he asked why I was assisting the CID staff. In truth, I couldn't wait to get involved in detective work but I replied, casually, that they were busy and all I was doing was helping out. But I was about to get a lucky break. I drove the great man to a suspicious death in a backcourt in Polmadie on the south side. We entered the close and saw a group of officers including senior detectives standing around a man with a gaping wound in his head – he was obviously dead. There was a discussion taking place and the conclusion seemed to be that it was murder with robbery as a motive. As Goodall's mere driver, I took deep breath and said, 'Sir, I think it is a suicide.' Looking back on it now, I suppose it was a bit of a cheek but there was a stunned silence and I heard one voice say, 'Who the hell is that?' Tom Goodall asked me to explain.

I had seen a similar death during my time on the streets in the Gorbals when I watched as a man jumped from a top-floor stair-head window with his hands in his pockets, taking them out on the way down. He had landed on his head and his injuries were similar to those of the body before us. When I finished, everyone turned to look at the stair-head window. It was shut. Someone sarcastically said, 'He must have shut the window before he jumped.'

I replied that maybe someone had noticed the window was open and had shut it. Goodall sent some one up the stairs to check and found that this is what had happened. Soon we were joined by a detective who had been sent to inform the dead man's relatives of what had happened. It seems, the previous week, the dead man had thrown himself off the Suspension Bridge over the Clyde at Carlton Place – a favourite spot for suicides – and had been rescued by a policeman. This time it turned out that the dead man had told people, when he last left his home, that he wouldn't be back. The inquiry was handed over to the uniformed inspector.

On the way back, Goodall thanked me for my input and said, 'Bob Kerr tells me you want to be a detective . . . Be outside my office at 10 a.m. on Monday. Do you know why?' 'I'm either in trouble or I'm about to become a detective.' Goodall smiled. 'Yes, it is one of the two,' he said. On the Monday morning, he told me I was now an acting detective constable and I should report to Partick Police Office in the Marine division the following week. Exciting and controversial times lay ahead.

5

GANGS, SLASHINGS AND THE FIERY DEATH OF A LANDMARK

The old Locarno dance hall in Sauchiehall Street was famous in many parts of the world – in some ways, it was as well known as the Gorbals. I was told the story of a Glaswegian seafarer who was standing in queue for a cinema in the Bronx when he was approached by four very tough-looking New York black guys. He needn't have worried – they had recognised his accent and all they wanted to know was if the Locarno was still going strong as they had been regular dancers there when they were stationed with the US Navy at the Holy Loch nuclear submarine base. On nights out, they visited the Locarno in the hope that they might meet up with some attractive Glasgow girls.

During my career in the CID, this dance hall has featured several times. It was, on occasion, a focus for the gangs. You still get folk who tell you that Glasgow's reputation for gangs has been exaggerated over the years. Even the well-remembered Chief Constable James Robertson once averred that there were no gangs in the city – talk about false memories and rose-coloured spectacles. The cops on the street knew far better. At any given time, there could be up to fifty gangs in action and, over the years, the numbers ran into hundreds. Likewise, the whitewash merchants try to tell us that the razor-slashing tales are exaggerated. I had not been in the detective business long when I saw for myself what the true story was. The Maryhill Fleet and the

Shamrock from Royston were two gangs that seemed to think the streets around the Locarno were there to serve as their battlefields. On Friday and Saturday nights, they were regularly involved in bloody clashes and, as members of the Northern Division, my colleagues and I would frequently be required to intervene in such events.

Sometimes, in the early sixties, the fighting actually took place inside the dance hall itself. I called on the Lorarno's manager who was concerned with the well-being of his regulars. These were the good Glasgow folk who just enjoyed the glamour of a night at the jigging and the young bucks who saw it as a chance to pull the birds. I told the manager that, next time fighting started, he should lock the doors and tell the cop in the street outside what was happening and reinforcements would arrive.

We had only to wait till the following weekend for a Code 21 Red to hit the airwaves. When we arrived at the front door, the biggest cop I have ever met, Alex Adair, greeted us. A youth from Roystonhill had been slashed and an ambulance was on its way. I told Alex to tell the ambulance guys to hang on outside till we had made our enquiries. It was a dreadful sight – blood was flowing from a huge wound in the victim's neck in frightening fashion. Nonetheless, we got him to sit in a chair just inside the front door, with a red blood-soaked dishtowel, the stain spreading by the second, round his neck. The staff helped out and we got everyone in the hall, male and female, to file past him. Just as he was passing out, I had a quick word and learned that his attacker had been red haired. This information cut the number of suspects down to about half a dozen and the assailant was soon identified and locked up. Those who don't accept the reality of the razor-slashing days should have been around that night and the next weekend which happened to be Easter.

We had been expecting trouble and we got it. There were running battles all along Sauchiehall Street right down to Parliamentary Road. Nineteen slashings were reported and we spent the entire night interviewing gang members and neds who were, to say the least, uncooperative. This was what it was like on the front line in the days of slashings. One of the tasks was to collect the victims' bloodstained clothing and there was a shocking sight the next day in the corridors of the Northern Division office with the area piled high with sacks of clothing soaked in blood.

After a street dust-up of such proportions, more trouble was expected the following night. Officers were drafted in from other divisions and there were a further fifteen arrests for serious assault, making thirty-four arrests over two nights in a relatively small part of the city centre. The young men arrested were mostly members of the Shamrock or Fleet. However, the Chief took it upon himself to issue a press release along the lines that there were no gangs in the city – wishful thinking that was echoed by many local politicians.

My original transfer to the CID had got me out of uniform and into the Partick Police Office. The senior detective constable at that time there was one David McNee, the man who was to be nicknamed the Hammer. He went to the top in Glasgow before he left for London where he ran the Met and he eventually became one of the most respected figures in Scottish police history. On arrival in Partick, I was introduced to my new partner, Detective Inspector Alex Hume. Alex wasn't keen on too much detective work and was more of an administrator. This suited me fine because any mundane inquiry handed to him tended to end up in my hands and it was a great way to get experience.

Working in Partick underlined my growing belief that you should conduct each inquiry according to how you felt about it and not get too bogged down in the 'we usually do it this way' sort of thinking. A good example of this happened on my very first serious crime investigation. A man had been assaulted and robbed as he left a pub near Anderston Cross. On talking to the victim, I got a description of a valuable watch which had been taken in the robbery. I went to the pub to try to find a witness

– no joy – so I popped into a nearby pawnbroker's to leave details of the missing watch. Back at the station, I told Hume and the others how I was doing and they collapsed in laughter at the thought of me imagining that a criminal would be daft enough to pawn the watch. They were still laughing when the phone rang and the pawnbroker said he was dealing with a man trying to pledge the watch! There was a mad dash to the door and we nailed the attacker who got five years. I had made my mark.

But not all of the detective work was the sort of thing that taxed a budding Sherlock Holmes. We had a bogus coalman reported to us – a guy with a typically blackened face who roamed the streets hollering 'coal for sale'. He collected the cash but neglected to deliver the coal. This idiot followed a set route and was there for the catching. A few days after the first complaint, a call came in that he was in the area. We lifted him and I was feeling that I was a pretty good sleuth until I was given sixty-odd crime reports to write up and was still typing at 11 p.m. That knocked some of the cockiness out of me – some of it.

There is quite a difference between a fraudulent coalman and a murderer but I made the leap a few weeks later. The killer was just ten years old. It happened on the night when the famous West of Scotland world champion boxer Walter McGowan was fighting in the Kelvin Hall. It was a sporting occasion graced by the presence of the top men in the CID – as if there wasn't enough fighting on the streets. A call came into Partick that a cop required assistance near Byres Road, where there are trendy shops and restaurants and the many pubs are full of students.

The officer told us that a six-week-old baby had been reported missing from a pram that had been left unattended for a few moments in the common close outside the mother's front door. As we stood discussing the matter, a ten-year-old girl – I will call her Susan – appeared and started coming down the stairs. On spotting me, she turned around and disappeared. I knew that this particular little girl stayed at this address because, not long before, I had interviewed her about a watch that had been stolen at her school.

A massive police search took place by uniformed officers with the help of the dog branch but there was no trace of the missing baby. I nipped round to the Kelvin Hall to keep the big boss Tom Goodall informed and then returned to the scene to be joined by Detective Sergeant Fred Tiplady, a good detective who got results. We agreed to conduct a door-to-door search of the building. We were told that the little ten-year-old lassie, Susan, was on her own but soon located her mother who had no objection to her house being searched. Wee Susan was in a bed recess in the kitchen. Turning to the bed area, Fred looked under the bed and the mother told Susan to get out of bed and she did.

I will take what happened next to my grave. Fred took hold of the mattress and as he did so the wee girl blurted out, 'Don't faint, Mummy.' The mattress was lifted to reveal the body of the missing baby. No words can describe the scene and Fred and I just stood there, shell-shocked and numb. At this point, Tom Goodall arrived to take charge of the inquiry. Tom said Fred and I would be the arresting officers and we should charge the girl at the bar in the police office, which we did.

The murder was then discussed and I put forward the theory that wee Susan had taken the baby to nurse it and was about to return it when she saw me. The sight of the police had caused her to panic and she headed back up the stairs with the baby. When the infant had started to cry, she silenced it. Tom Goodall agreed that this must have been the scenario. Months later, the High Court was a tearful place when Susan stood in the dock, her head barely showing, and a plea of guilty was accepted on her behalf.

Policing is a diverse business – one minute there's a horrific child murder to deal with, the next it's fighting gangs or investigating a fire. The old St Andrew's Halls, near Charing Cross, was a source of joy for thousands in the city. The home of the

Scottish National Orchestra, it hosted concerts by visiting tenors or touring jazz bands. It is a place that touched the lives of most of the city's inhabitants so it was a shock when, one morning in 1962, the citizens woke up to the news that it had been almost destroyed in a massive blaze. The night before the disaster, it had hosted an international boxing match.

This was one of the biggest stories for years in the city and the papers were full of pictures of the burnt-out shell. There were many column inches dedicated to the memories of magical nights in the magnificent old place. The file to investigate the fire was handed to Hume who immediately handed it to me, the junior, with the remark, 'I'll give you a hand with it.' When we arrived at the still-smouldering remains of the building, the first man we met was Mr John Evans. A real gentleman, he said he would be the investigating fire officer and would liaise with us on a regular basis.

It turned out that the loss of the landmark building, now rebuilt albeit in different form, was down to a fairly mundane happening – as is often the case with accidents and disasters. It could have been avoided if heat detectors had expanded as they were designed to do and sent a message to the fire service. In the ruins, we found the units, some of which Evans handed over to us so that the police lab could take a look them. The fire department experts would do the same with some of the others. Anyone who remembers a visit to the old Halls will recall that they were always spotless. The gold leaf would be shining and the red plush would be immaculate and everything would be polished and well cared for. But it was this desire to keep the Halls looking good that, ironically, contributed to their loss. Both the police and the fire department came to the same conclusion. Each of the metallic strips within the fire detectors had sixteen coats of paint on them, insulating them from the heat they were supposed to detect. A joint report was signed by Evans and ourselves and, although we felt we had done good job on tracing the cause, there was real sadness that a great Glasgow institution was no more.

I loved my new career as a detective and I must have been doing something right because, after a year as acting detective constable in Partick, I was promoted to detective constable and posted to the Northern Division and based in Maitland Street. Here, at last, I was to mingle with some of the most famous names in Glasgow's crime story – such as Joe Beattie, who it was said could 'smell out a criminal', and Joe Jackson, with whom I would investigate many a crime in the years ahead and who was an ideal man to work with when things got sticky. David Frew was another Northern man who worked hard and got results. The area we covered was huge – from Sauchiehall Street to the Baillieston lights and it took in Springburn, Ruchazie, Gartham-lock and the huge housing scheme of Easterhouse. Villains galore infested this massive patch and there was never a shortage of work.

As I mentioned earlier, Sauchiehall Street alone could give us a few headaches with gangs and slashings. The whole city centre in those days had its share of lowlife and I was soon involved in a murder inquiry that was to become a part of Glasgow criminal history – a killing that was to lead to plays, books and even some controversial sculpture. My partner was Andy Stewart, a great guy to work with, and one night the inevitable Code 21 Red took us to a location given as West Nile Street at Bath Street and the Lunar Seven, a busy pub. A body lay in the street and it was clearly beyond help. A sergeant told us that the dead man, a fellow called Mooney, had been involved in a fight in the pub with the Shamrock gang. A woman then approached us and asked if I was a cop. She told me that three men were involved, pointed to a youth standing in the crowd that had gathered and said, 'That's one of them.' Andy recognised the guy concerned and got round the back of the crowd and arrested him. We were also told that some of the Shamrock were still in the pub – it can take quite a lot to get a Glasgow ned to leave a pint unfinished. We then took arbitrary action – we instructed the sergeant to hijack a cream-and-green Corporation bus that had just appeared in Bath Street. We dumped the passengers, had the bus brought to the door of the Lunar Seven and got everyone who had been inside the pub on board the bus and down to the Central Police Office. I doubt if such decisive action would go down well in today's force.

It took most of the night to complete the interviews but, as a result of the information gleaned from the questioning, the name of the killer became clear – Hugh Collins. After he had done his time, Collins went on to become an author and sculptor and something of an international celebrity. Because of this, he was touted as one of the success stories of the Barlinnie Special Unit. I didn't know him but Andy did and, at the time of the murder, we searched several houses in Roystonhill looking for him but without success. (Later Collins was to write in his book, *Autobiography of a Murderer*, that he knew we were hunting him down and that he had armed himself with a shotgun – something that made me relieved we hadn't found him!) In the event, Collins, a remarkably intelligent and complex individual who often was contrite in print over having taken a man's life, turned up at the Central with a solicitor and gave himself up. He was given life.

Religion is a stranger to many who pass through the hands of the Glasgow Police and it is seldom a factor in solving a crime but there are always exceptions. The time we were unleashed and went in search of the person who had slashed a member of the Fleet at a showground in Saracen Street was just such an occasion. For the benefit of those without much knowledge of the facts of razor slashing and those, including politicians, who claim the stories of it are exaggerated, I would point out that this poor individual required to be patched up with no fewer than sixty stitches and was left marked for life. The victim was in

Stobhill Hospital and, in Mafia style, was refusing to name his attacker. Incidentally, this is reminiscent of the tale from Chicago in the days of Alphonse Capone when one gangster was carried into hospital with five or six gunshots wounds and, when the cops asked him who did it, he said, 'Has someone been shot?' Anything a Chicago gangster can do, a Glasgow hood can do too.

My buddy and I visited the victim at 3 a.m. and, when I asked the duty nurse if much was happening, she told me that a priest had been called to the next ward to administer the last rites to a dying patient. As we stood by our victim, his head swathed in bandages, I asked if he would be prepared to name his assailant or assailants. He replied in two words the second of which was 'off'. I turned to the nurse and asked, 'Is the priest here yet?' She replied that he was on his way. I put my hand out to the victim and said, 'You won't be seeing me again. Do you want me to bring your relatives here?' He declined the handshake and seemingly taking the point he said, 'Are you not going to ask me who did this to me?' 'That's up to you,' I said. He named three members of a gang called the Barnes Road Mob.

We left the hospital and picked up big Alex Adair, of Locarno fame, on the way. On arrival at the suspects' address, I asked Alex to get out and stand beside the car. All three named were inside the house and, for some reason, they were stripped to the waist. The leader let me in and, taking up a confrontational pose, he asked, 'When did you ever see a body like that?' I replied, 'We have a cop with a body just like yours – except he is six foot six inches tall.' The three of them looked out the window and quietly got dressed.

Months later, in the High Court, the victim claimed he had been conned into naming the attackers because of the reference to the priest but, nevertheless, the three were convicted of serious assault to permanent disfigurement. The guy with the body got eight years to do his bodybuilding behind prison bars and the other two got seven. In this case, a touch of religion did the business!

The fear of God is one thing but, on the streets, there is another fear – meeting someone tougher than yourself. And there was a cop in the sixties who instilled fear in the neds on the infamous Blackhill scheme – so much so that, at one time, there was a petition going the rounds to get him moved. There's nothing new in a tough Glasgow cop. In the late thirties, Sir Percy Sillitoe's 'untouchables' met force with force in their war against the gangs. Retaliate first was often the motto and it worked. There was also another cop, nicknamed PC Hitler, who kept peace on his patch in Maryhill with his fists. The Blackhill cop was Neil Fisher and the villains were genuinely terrified of him. Neil didn't have much truck with the CID but I seemed to be an exception and we got on well.

One incident sheds some light on what life was like in a place such as Blackhill. It occurred one night when I was on the back shift and I received a report that two young boys had been seriously assaulted in Royston Road. They had been shipped to the Royal Infirmary Casualty Department, a place much used to stitching up slashed faces. A colleague and I went to the hospital and even I have to say that I had never seen such horrific slashing injuries. The emergency surgeons put more than 100 stitches into each boy. The boys said that they were attacked by four men who had been talking about a party they were going to in Blackhill.

We decided to head for the party. On the way there, I was delighted to hear Neil was on duty and we picked him up. Although Neil was fearsome, we also picked up some beat cops before going to the house. We arranged that some of the cops would conceal themselves halfway up the close stair while I knocked at the door. When it opened, I was confronted by three neds and, behind them, I could see and hear the party in full swing. I identified myself and asked to enter the house and, in response, I was told that, rather than be invited to step inside, I was about to be thrown down the stairs. At this point, I shouted, 'Neil!' and the cavalry thundered up the stairs as the neds attempted to shut the door.

Our little posse smashed the door in and separated males from females. There were about thirty of each so it was a major party even for that area! The scarred and bandaged victims had been brought from the Royal and we proceeded to hold an identification parade in the living room. Three men were identified and a fourth, who had a beard, was making a nuisance of himself by interfering in everything so we decided he would have to accompany his pals to the station to ensure, as we put it, fair play. The three that the victims had identified were locked up and Beardy was charged with breach of the peace. The following morning, I was still on duty writing up reports when the phone rang and it was a parent of one of the victims to say the man who had actually done the slashing was the guy with the beard. The boys had been too scared to identify him in the house. We immediately raced to the district court but the bird had flown. We went round to his home where he was arrested and locked up with the other three. I was curious to ask why he had inflicted such terrible injuries on two young boys. The answer was a familiar one. He said that, because he was known as 'Mad Mac of the Pak', he had a reputation to keep up. He got five years and, in my opinion, ten would not have been enough. The other three were dealt with less severely

Neil had played a major role in the resolution of the crime. Neil was involved in a lot of action in Blackhill and it was not always bloody battling. One night, he had been sent to a house where a rowdy party – there were always plenty of these – had been reported. He warned the householder that, if he received any more complaints, he would take action. An hour later, Neil was posted as missing and it was decided the right place to start the inquiry was at his last port of call. The duty inspector did so and found the party in full swing with Neil entertaining all and sundry on the piano accordion. He was soon transferred to Central Division where he quickly made his mark. A gents' toilet in Clyde Street was a known haunt of homosexuals. Neil arrested ten men who were hanging about the toilets and marched them into the charge bar area and informed the staff, 'Watch these guys, I'm going back for more.' The last time I saw Neil, he was playing mine host in a pub in Ayr. What a guy!

It is often surprising how many citizens are brave enough to pick up the phone and call the cops when they suspect something out of order. By 1965, I was a detective constable and, one night in September of that year, I was on the night shift with Constable Tom Joyce when he answered the phone and found himself talking to a woman who refused to be identified but said that a man who was wanted by the police was in a house in Northpark Street. Within the half hour, we were in the ground-floor flat after being admitted by a young woman who was obviously the one who had phoned.

I got a shock for who did I see in the kitchen but Victor 'Scarface' Russo? I had last bumped into him in my early days in the Gorbals. I also saw the sleeping figure of a man in the bed and, without speaking, Russo made the sign of locking a door. The guy in the bed was our target. As I approached, Russo whispered, 'Watch yourself.' The man woke up and asked who we were. We told him and he gave us a name and address backed up with a driving licence and other documents.

Russo's warning had put me on edge and I told the suspect to wash up at the sink and get dressed. As he ran the water, I reached over and took a carving knife that had been lying by the side of the sink. He smiled and, at that moment, I knew we had made an important arrest. I told Tom to handcuff him and back at the office we searched him carefully. Amongst other items, we found a postcard filled in and addressed to a prisoner in Blundeston Prison, north of Lowestoft. The message read, 'Wish you were here.' and was signed 'D'. His explanation was that a friend had asked him to post it. It was 3 a.m. but I phoned the prison and spoke to the senior officer on duty who became excited and asked for a description of the suspect. It appeared that our man was almost certainly a David Whittaker who, along with a couple of other prisoners, had escaped from Blundeston. We checked photographs in the current edition of the *Police Gazette* and the identification was easy. One of the other two was a notorious criminal called Archibald Hall, alias Fontaine. The tabloids followed Hall's exploits and dubbed him 'The Mad Butler'.

Whittaker admitted who he was and told us that, when he was working in the prison kitchens at 5 a.m., he had dug through the kitchen wall and climbed the outer wall. He became a fugitive and he boasted he was wanted in many parts of Britain for all sorts of crimes, including armed assault in Perth. He then said that, when we had arrested him, he had had a loaded revolver under his pillow and, given the chance, he would have used it. The CID in Perth were contacted and they sent an escort for him.

We called back at Northpark Street where the woman who had called us confirmed that there had been a gun but that Victor Russo had thrown it in the Clyde. As we waited for the escort from Perth to arrive, we talked to Whittaker over a cup of tea and bacon sandwiches and what he told us was quite an education. He said that this was only the latest in a series of escapes he had made and, at the time, he had been serving fourteen years' preventative detention – prisoners under this sentence are not allowed out for any reason. He would say nothing about where Hall and the other guy were but he had a piece of paper with the words 'Charing Cross 2 p.m. fountain' on it. This looked like a meet with the other two and it was to take place the next day.

Word had spread about this big fish and, when the day shift came on, they had a peek at him chained to a wall radiator. Not long after that, a couple of detectives from Perth arrived to join in the bacon rolls and take the prisoner back north with them. I told them to watch him like hawks and they both laughed, one making a sarcastic remark. We flooded the Charing Cross area with detectives – I actually spent two hours sweeping the streets of the area with a road cleaner's brush – but there was no sign of the escapees. In a book he wrote later, Hall said that there was indeed an intention to meet at that time but, when they had arrived in their hired car, they had found the area 'crawling with cops' – so much for our disguises!

Two days later, I was on a bus on the south side of Glasgow when the passenger in front of me opened up his *Daily Record*. The headline read 'Three escape from Perth Prison' – Whittaker was back on the run. Roadblocks were thrown up round Perth and, in an incident not connected with the escape, a police sergeant was knocked down and killed when, in the darkness, a driver had not seen a police signal to stop. Two of the prisoners, including Whittaker, were recaptured but the third died of exposure on the highland hills. Several months later, when Whittaker appeared in the High Court in Glasgow, he told me that, as he went over the wall, he thought of my warning to the Perth cops and laughed it off. He also said that, if he was given a sentence of more than eight years, he would kill himself. He got seven and they were added to the fourteen he was already serving. He was convinced I was responsible for keeping it under the figure he said would lead to his suicide.

Around the time of the Whittaker business, I got information from a man in custody that a prisoner in the untried section of Barlinnie, John 'Mad Dog' Duggan, was going to escape with outside assistance from an Andy Steele. I telephoned the governor, Mr McKenzie, and passed on the info, which was noted. But the governor was not too concerned – he seemed to have more faith in the security in his prison than Duggan had. At about 3 a.m., I got a message to contact the prison. Duggan had removed the bars from his cell window, climbed out on to the roof and then, moving hand over hand, had used telephone wires to climb on to the gatehouse roof. On jumping to the ground, he found his getaway car had gone without him so he just legged it.

Mr McKenzie wanted him back. About a week later, I got a call from Duggan's wife who said he wanted to give himself up to me. I went with a detective sergeant, Jim Montgomery, to the Duggan house in Stronend Street, Possilpark, and, when Mrs Duggan ascertained we had not had breakfast, we all sat down at the kitchen table for the bacon and eggs. Duggan was then handcuffed and taken back to prison. He was later convicted and this time he was sent to Peterhead. He next came to my notice during one of the many riots in that trouble-torn prison when he was seen on the roof, holding a placard which read, 'Fuck Nelson Mandela – free me.'

There is an amusing tale about how Duggan had got into the Bar-L in the first place. Attempting to blow a safe in the Scottish Gas Office in Sauchiehall Street, he had used a touch too much 'jelly' and, when he dropped the switch, the safe landed outside the building in middle of the street. When we arrived, we were told that the safe blower had been seen climbing on the roof of the adjacent Apollo Theatre. We surrounded the building and a squad entered the theatre. The hall had been booked by an Asian community organisation to show an Asian film and the audience were all wearing turbans. We got the lights switched on and there for all to see was the bold Duggan. He had removed his tee shirt and had attempted to make a turban out of it but his pale face shone out like a beacon. When he was collared, he asked, 'How did you recognise me?'

Amidst this sort of criminal high jinks, there was, from time to time, the inevitable involvement in nasty sex crimes, rapes and attacks on young boys and girls. Among the nastiest cases I ran into as a detective was the story of 'The Box Man'. Reports had been flooding in to the police about a man who approached young boys and asked them to help him hide a box and, when they agreed, he would take them to an unoccupied house where they were assaulted. The frequency of attacks increased and they took place in a wider area – they had originally started in Partick but spread to Cowcaddens. And the victims seemed to be getting older. Getting good descriptions out of people who have been traumatised in an attack is difficult. In this case, we had claims that the suspect was anything from five feet to six feet in height and that he was variously blond and dark haired.

The Box Man was at large for five years and all the trademark attacks occurred in Glasgow except one – it had happened in Southampton. A police officer was suspected but eliminated and another man made a false confession. But, as the rate at which the attacks were occurring over the years was building, a better picture of the suspect was emerging. He was around fifty, with a thin face and brown hair and, on most occasions, he had worn a blazer with a lion rampant or similar device on the breast pocket. He also wore a red and black striped tie. Being ex-Merchant Navy, I should have twigged that the clothing was a useful clue.

In 1969, we broke this troublesome case. A sixteen-year-old boy was approached in Maryhill Road and asked by a man driving a Jaguar car if he would help him lift a heavy box. The teenager agreed and was taken to a caravan on Loch Lomondside and assaulted. He reported this to the police but he hadn't taken the number of the car. He was, however, able to show them the caravan and they discovered it was owned by a man who lived in Minerva Street. When the police got there, the Jag was parked outside. It transpired the suspect was a steward on the *Queen Mary*, hence the Southampton connection. When told he would have to take part in an ID parade, the man laughed and told us to go ahead. As the time of the identity parade approached, an officer went to his cell to tell him his solicitor was on the way.

He found him on the floor with deep cuts in his wrists that were pouring with blood. He had made the wounds with a razor blade he had hidden in his shoe. He was taken to the Western, where he was stitched up, and then returned to his cell. He bit the stitches out with his teeth and the whole rigmarole had to be repeated. The ID parade verified his identity and a trial confirmed his guilt. He faced forty-five charges of sexual assaults and five of breach of the peace. The exact number of his victims will never be known but some put the figure in excess of 100. He was sent to the State Hospital for the Criminally Insane but, after ten years, he was released on conditional discharge with his movements closely monitored.

The case of The Box Man was to mark another turning point in my career. Not long afterwards, I was told that I had been nominated for secondment to the Flying Squad. I left the office floating on air!

6

BIBLE JOHN, DANDY INFORMANTS AND WOULD-BE SPIES

Life in the Flying Squad provided a lot of laughs and some serious insight into police methods that, effective as they were, would often not be tolerated in today's politically correct climate. Giving the odd suspect a bit of a belting to assist his memory is, in these days, more likely to feature in a Hollywood cop flick than happen in reality. Incidentally, some of the biggest names in crime in this city like nothing better than a night in with a bottle of wine and a gangster DVD, the bloodier the better. How much art influences life in such cases or the other way round I leave to the shrinks and there are plenty of them making a good living out of analysing the criminal classes. My experience was on the streets and I tell it like it was. Sometimes we bent the rules to get a result and sometimes we used ingenuity that was worthy of the most cunning and devious lawbreaker.

When I joined the Flying Squad, which was innovative for its time and the forerunner of the Serious Crime Squad, it was a remarkably small unit given the area we had to cover and the fact that Glasgow was a major industrial city with a thriving dockland. It was a place where only a few of its citizens would pass up the chance to turn an illicit pound or two – where the shedding of blood to avenge some supposed slight was the norm and where honest businessmen were squeezed into sharing their wealth with parasites who could offer protection.

I was immediately put to work with Detective Inspector George Walker and a couple of detective sergeants – one was John Watson and the other was Jack Beattie. There was, of course another Beattie in the force at this time – a man who was to feature prominently in the hunt for Bible John, the still-to-be-found killer who haunted the Barrowland Ballroom in 1968 and 1969 and is suspected of killing three young women who were enjoying a bit of big band dance music under the glittering lights of that famous east-end hall. That other Beattie was Joe, who, in his own way, was just as remarkable a character as his namesake, Jack. A former RAF pilot with superb night vision – handy in a cop – Jack's off-duty passions were tweeds and the country life. He was also, to use the old cliché, a master of disguise – something that he used to great effect in a controversial police career. Later in my own career, I was to be part of that controversy, as you can read in the chapter on the Albany drugs raid, which led to the downfall of Jack Beattie whose nickname in the force and the newspapers was 'The Flea' because of his ability to disguise himself and pop up everywhere. It was an apt nickname – a flea can be a real, almost invisible, irritant.

There were also some real characters in the other squads and one who sticks in my memory and who is something of a legend, when the boys in blue gather for a chinwag on the old days, is Roddy Anderson. The stories of Roddy are many and memorable. I assisted him once on a visit to the home of a dangerous criminal. This guy lived up a close and our info was that he was 'two up, right'. In view of his reputation we were going to go straight in with no niceties like a knock on the door. We piled up the stairs and crashed the solid door wide open with splintering and banging loud enough to wake the neighbourhood. The shocked occupants lay peacefully in bed wondering what the hell was going on. Clearly we were in the wrong house. Roddy simply apologised and attempted to replace the door without much success; moments later we were up the right close and the villain was arrested on a warrant.

Roddy had some style, too, when giving evidence. In the High Court one day, he referred to five four-pound notes. The astonished judge asked, 'Don't you mean four five-pound notes?' Nonplussed Roddy replied, 'Well, Your Honour, it was £20 anyway.' On another occasion, some officers and I were with Roddy. We were armed and had arrived at the house of a suspect. One cop was reluctant to stand at the door of the house and instead stood at the bend of the stairs. 'What are you up to?' asked Roddy. The officer replied that he was afraid of being shot. Roddy calmly told him that the only danger he was in was from a ricochet of a police bullet.

I learned a lot in my couple of years in the squad with Beattie often demonstrating the effectiveness of disguise. On the other hand, another colleague, John Watson, was a brilliant user of information and a man who knew every criminal of note on the south side. On the back shift, I would regularly drive John to the Gorbals area where he would meet an informant, usually an active criminal. John would get out of the car for a surreptitious chat and, not long after, we would team up with another couple of guys in the squad and raid a house that John had directed us to, where we would inevitably recover stolen property. Often, if there had been a serious crime in the Gorbals, Polmadie or Govan area, one of his team of informants would call him and the crime would quickly be solved. I learned a lot about how to handle informants from him and I also got a wee lesson on surveillance.

One day, when the four of us were sitting in an unmarked car in Battlefield Road, near Victoria Infirmary, waiting for a contact, suddenly a man of about fifty, approached. He knocked on the window of the car and, when we opened it, he asked what we were up to. He claimed he was a special constable and that he was arresting us for acting suspiciously. Without a word, we all got out of the car. We were six footers plus and pretty hard detectives, even if I say so myself, and he was about five foot six on a clear day. Nonetheless, he bravely marched us to a police box where he rather spoiled this act of playing the tough cop by fumbling in all his pockets and failing to find the key. Our detective inspector handed over his and asked, 'Is this what you are looking for?' The expression on the face of the Special when he realised what he had done was wonderful!

But life in the squad wasn't all laughs and one particular little bit of ingenuity could have landed us in serious bother. We got a radio call directing us to an address in Govan. There, we were met by a young cop who told us there had been a break-in at a nearby shoe shop and that the stolen goods were in a house at the top flat, on the right. It was 3 a.m. and the chances of getting a search warrant were zilch so we did what we were good at – we got the householder's permission to search his flat. It was easy. An experienced criminal, he refused us entry when we knocked on his door in the dead of night. He wanted to see the warrant. The detective inspector in charge told me to go back downstairs to the car and get the warrant. I told our driver what was wanted and he handed me a sheet of paper on which was written 'search warrant'. Back upstairs, I gave the sheet to the boss who read out details of the suspect and his address. The criminal asked to see the warrant but was told that wasn't possible!

The arrest was made and the stolen goods were recovered. The suspect was locked up and, three months later, the case went to trial, sheriff and jury. We all gave our evidence and we were each examined regarding the warrant. The last police witness was the young cop who had met us at the door. He marched confidently into the witness box with his cap under his arm. He had around six months' service. He gave his evidence confidently. When cross-examined and asked if the detectives were in possession of a search warrant he replied, 'Yes, sir.' The defence solicitor then asked what kind of search warrant it was and he replied in a firm voice, 'It was a kid-on warrant.' There was stunned silence in the court. 'What is a kid-on warrant?' asked the sheriff. He got a truthful, if surprising, reply from the young cop. 'It's where you don't have a warrant and so you just write the words "search warrant" on a piece of paper and read out the nonexistent contents!'

Not surprisingly the defendant's lawyer leapt to his feet demanding that his client be freed immediately. The judge had a different idea and said, 'Recall Detective Inspector Walker.' George had to squeeze past me to return to the witness box and, as he did, he whispered, 'What will I do?' I whispered back, 'Faint in the box!' and that is what he promptly did. The trial was then adjourned till the afternoon when George told the court we had a Justice of the Peace warrant and had kidded the young cop into believing we didn't have one. It was quite a 'kid-on' all round but justice was dispensed – even if what led to it was not what the rulebook dictates. However, it was a minor bending of the rules when compared with what sometimes went on but it was still certainly no example to set for the cops of today. And it left us with a few sleepless nights as the case papers were submitted to the Crown Office and there was an anxious wait for the four detectives involved until we were ultimately told that no proceedings would be taken against us.

In any city, there is always a crew of what are known as 'the usual suspects' and, in the Flying Squad, much time was spent dealing with guys known to be criminals – guys with form who were often proud of their wrongdoing and the misguided respect it earned them in some quarters. Ironically of course, when we nailed them and they ended up in court, their previous records, often page after page, were not known to the jury.

In a lot of cases, a quick visit to the likely villains could pay off. Many of them had little trademarks and give-aways when doing a job and detectives were adept at spotting the telltale signs. And, when you looked at the usual suspects, it was also clear that many had specialities, certain types of break-in or certain weapons they always used. We got to know most of them the hard way.

At this time, in the sixties, one of the best-known villains in the city was a character called Samuel 'Dandy' McKay, a man who got his nickname because he was better dressed than his contemporaries. In the twenty-first century, many of the biggest fish in the underworld wear snappy suits, silk ties and well-laundered shirts, giving them the appearance of the businessman rather than the sleazy drug dealer or extortionist, but, in McKay's day, the well-dressed villain was the exception. Although I had heard a lot about him, I had never actually met him when I was in the Flying Squad but this was about to change. McKay's infamy lay largely in his association with the tabloids for whom he provided a series of criminal adventures that grabbed a lot of headlines.

He and a man named Alex Gray had committed one of the biggest and best-reported bank robberies at a bank in Shettleston. They hadn't crept in over the roof or, in the manner of TV bank robbers, dug a secret tunnel into the vaults, pretending to be sewage workers or whatever. Oh, no – McKay did it the easy way. He had recruited one of the workers in the bank, who had given him the necessary key, and he simply turned the key in the lock and made off with a large sum of readies. They had been smart enough in getting into the bank but McKay, Gray and the bank employee were not so good at covering their tracks. They were soon arrested and Dandy got ten years behind bars for his trouble. Incidentally, villains were always on the lookout for key holders who had money problems or woman trouble that they could exploit in order to coax them into helping them with 'inside' jobs.

'Dandy' was a devious fellow and it was no surprise when the tabloids told of his escape from prison and that he managed to make his way to Canada. But he was rearrested and returned to Scotland although he again managed to break out! It was some saga for the followers of crime in the Glasgow papers who had McKay down as a cross between Robin Hood and the Scarlet Pimpernel. The Robin Hood bit came when he helped the police trap mass murderer Peter Manuel. McKay, like many a professional criminal, had his own code and it didn't include murdering innocent teenagers or shooting down families in their homes.

Dandy was to become an important informant to me – his involvement in the Meehan case has been discussed earlier – but my first real encounter with him in the flesh was an odd one. Even when he was enjoying a spell of freedom, he still attracted police attention because, whenever he was around, you could never be quite sure what he was up to. On this occasion, he had aroused some suspicion. We were keeping an eye on him and I was detailed to follow him on foot when he was in the city centre. Other cops would follow me, also on foot, and even more would be in a squad car further behind. Sure enough, one morning at about 10 a.m., he parked his black Mini on the south side of the Suspension Bridge and walked smartly over the Clyde into St Enoch Square. He was about fifty and, naturally, he was smartly dressed but he walked so fast it was quite difficult to keep up with him. From the square, he made his way purposefully up Buchanan Street to Sauchiehall Street, along to North Street, down to Argyle Street, up West Nile Street and along Bath Street and so on. His whole stroll about town took around three hours. Eventually, he went back to his car and headed home to Giffnock. We hadn't a clue what he was up to.

But we were back on station the following morning and, sure enough, almost to the minute, at 10 a.m., he pitched up again in that black Mini. Once again I took up my position in behind him but this time, as we turned into Argyle Street, I lost him. I was standing there, looking around and wondering what to do next, when I felt a tap on my shoulder. It was McKay and he just smiled broadly and asked if I had enjoyed my walk the previous day. He had us baffled and that was the end of that investigation.

However, he and I now knew each other and, later on in his career, he would use me to get back at some of his rivals at the top of the crime tree in Glasgow.

During their long careers, cops often meet the same criminals over and over again – sometimes in different situations and sometimes these encounters are years apart. This was the case with David Cussins. He played a major role in the famous Albany drugs trial. His life ended when he was murdered and I must accept some of the blame for his death. Our early contacts, however, were less dramatic. A week after the odd business of McKay's city walks, the squad was called on to assist the CID at the Marine Division who were investigating a break-in at a garage where 300 car radios had been stolen. This was a major haul that would be worth a lot of cash as, in those days, cars did not have radios fitted as standard and car owners were always on the lookout for a bargain set to fit into their beloved motors. Cussins was suspected of some involvement in this break-in and I was detailed to find out where he was staying. Luck and being in the right place at the right time are as important in policing as they are in any business and I was lucky to be driving around Kelvingrove Park when I spotted Cussins driving a hired car. It looked as if he was heading for the Gibson Street area but I could see him watching me in his rear view mirror. I pretended to lose him at traffic lights and doubled back to Gibson Street just in time to see him leave the car and enter a main-door flat nearby.

For some reason, Glasgow folk often seem to have the name-plate on the door at almost ground level – letterboxes too are found in this position, something that must give many a postie a bad back. I looked down and squinted at the nameplate which was down near the bottom of the door to the flat I had just seen Cussins go into and, as I did so, the door opened. I looked up from a pair of boots to see Tom Smith, a man with a record and someone 'known to the police', as they say. I told him I was looking for a pal's house and that his name was McDonald.

Smith said someone of that name lived up the next close. Lucky! I went back out to the street and, later, Smith reappeared, carrying a bulky parcel, and walked off. I went back to the house and, this time, I managed to read the nameplate – Cussins. On coming out on to the street again, I saw Smith jump on a bus bound for the city centre and I leapt on after him. He went upstairs and I stood on the platform. From there, I could see Jack Beattie and John Watson in the squad car and, waving wildly, I signalled to them to follow. A flash of the headlights showed they understood. When Smith got off the bus, he was promptly arrested. The bulky parcel contained four radios. He later appeared in court charged with stealing the 300 radios. Cussins was also charged but was found not guilty.

The Flying Squad days brought a few jaunts away from Glasgow. City folk like to make the most of a September weekend jaunt, often heading 'doon the watter' to the resorts like Dunoon and Rothesay. Even the gangs weren't immune from the desire to seek pastures new before the onset of yet another Glasgow winter of freezing wind, rain and sleet.

Intelligence is a big driving force in policing and news of trouble that is about to happen is always more welcome than news of it already happening – at least you stand a chance of stopping it. The word on the street one holiday weekend was that members of the Fleet and the Calton Tongs gangs were heading for Blackpool and such delights as Yates's Wine Lodge, the candy floss world of the big dipper and a shooting gallery or two. There was also the chance to take on each other and do some battling on new territory – an away fixture, you might say.

It was decided that John Watson and I would travel south to assist the local cops in the expected outbreak of violence. Down in Lancashire, with our knowledge of the gangs, it didn't take long for us to spot the Fleet taking a stroll along the streets of the busy holiday resort. I spotted the leader, a guy called Rab, and I suggested we lifted him, then strike a deal. But things happened faster than we expected with the others and, not long after we had seen him, we got a radio call to go to the Blackpool police station where Rab was held after being arrested for shoplifting. We put on our thinking caps and decided to arrange for some of Rab's team to visit him in the cells. We soon agreed with them that, if there was no violence, Rab would be released on the Monday. Rab pled guilty to the shoplifting charge and he was fined a tenner and sent on his way on the Monday.

But, just two hours later, the gangs started fighting as we had feared and one of the Fleet, a gangster called Tom, was stabbed. Years later, Tom would be stabbed again but, this time, his assailant was a woman – the assault took place outside Celtic Park and it resulted in his death. John and I left Blackpool and returned to Glasgow where, within a week, we had arrested four of the Tongs, including their leader who was called Bernie.

However, there was to be a surprising development at their trial in Blackpool when Tom told the jury that he had sustained his injuries after falling through a plate glass window. All four of the accused were found not guilty and released. The gangs' own code of honour had defeated justice. The only bonus in this episode was that I built up a good knowledge of the gangs' membership, hideouts and methods.

In the police, as in most businesses, if you do something right, you are almost sure to get a similar job and so it was with me in the squad. After our success in Blackpool came a trip to Newquay in the summer. Apparently large numbers of Glaswegians were heading to the south-west resort for the Glasgow Fair, the traditional holiday during the last fortnight of July, and it was thought that a couple of street-savvy Glasgow cops would be handy should there be trouble. This was less likely to happen in Newquay than in Blackpool but, along with Detective Constable George Black, I was given a car and we headed for the south coast.

It wasn't the toughest of assignments. Mornings usually

involved a needle game on the putting green and then we went round most of the pubs and hotels, urging the Scottish holiday-makers to behave themselves, which they generally did. At the local picture house, we enquired about complimentary tickets for the current hit musical *Paint Your Wagon*. 'No chance!' we were told since the manager was 'anti-police'. However, we went back to the cinema and told him that we had information that there could be a spot of gang violence at the weekend. We left a telephone number he could ring for assistance.

It seems the thought of a Glasgow rammy in his beloved hall concentrated his mind and he asked if we could sit in the cinema when the film was showing, just in case. We gave this careful consideration and, in the end, thought we might just manage that! That night we saw the first half of the film and the manager even saw fit to bring a pint to me in the circle and one to George in the stalls. We went back the next evening to catch the second half and the manager was now pro-police and thanked us – he had seen groups of troublemakers and warned them that two tough cops were in the audience. I always enjoy *Paint Your Wagon* when it gets a TV showing! Happy days.

I went back to Glasgow and soon got a taste of the real danger on the streets thanks to an example of how a seemingly routine incident can turn nasty. I spotted a criminal, Robert Manson, who was wanted for attempted murder. John Watson was with me at the time but he was not feeling at all well. So I jumped out of the car and approached Manson on my own. As I grappled with him, he attempted to stab me with a carving knife and cut my hand badly. Luckily, a beat cop called Brian Coppins came to my assistance and we arrested Manson. It took us both some effort to overpower him. His name came vividly to my mind in the writing of this book because my co-author, Robert Jeffrey, has a handsome hand-carved replica of a fully rigged galleon in his study. This impressive piece of work bears the nameplate HMS *Injustice* and was made by one Robert Manson who ended up with plenty of time on his hands in Peterhead. The galleon had been given to a fellow inmate of Manson in Peterhead – the famous Glasgow Godfather, Walter Norval – who, in turn, gave it to Robert in appreciation of the best-selling biography of him he had written. For me, it's quite a reminder of the lucky escape I had!

Cops don't get much contact with the secret services on the streets of Glasgow but, shortly before leaving the Flying Squad, I got an interesting insight into how well we train our spies – and how well we test them. The Flying Squad were told that a trainee British spy was coming to Glasgow on a test mission to see what he was made of and the inference was that we had to make life difficult for him. The trainee secret service man had been given a mission to contact a female colleague on the seafront at Ayr and she would give him a package to take back to London. We were aware that our target had booked into the old George Hotel in Buchanan Street and that, of course, he would require a hired car for his trip to Ayr. Without telling the staff of the hotel what was happening, we booked a female detective in for a three-day period that included the night our target was to be there. He arrived in Glasgow and was followed up Buchanan Street to the hotel where he booked in. After about an hour, he headed out to a car hire office and we went into action. We broke into the policewoman's room, damaging the door, and took some of her property, including a purse. We hid this in the cistern of the room next door which was, of course, the one used by our target.

The policewoman then returned, found the break-in and, as instructed, reported it to the police. Two beat cops, who didn't know what was going on, arrived at the hotel and, when our target returned shortly afterwards, he was questioned, as were other guests. Naturally, Mr Big-Spy-in-Training couldn't prove his identity as he was travelling under a false name. This led to the beat cops telling HQ and the Flying Squad were sent along. Our target was then taken to the Central Police Office.

The secret services often tend to recruit from the top universities and the London establishment and this guy was certainly a supercilious bit of work and cheeky with it. He had obviously concluded that it was a set-up to prevent him carrying out his training mission. His attitude changed a bit, however, when an officer, who shall be nameless, took the test a step further and added some reality by belting him. Later, the would-be spy admitted that, up to that point, he thought it was all a bit of a game. Unable to prove his identity, he was locked up and only released after the time of his 'meet' in Ayr had passed.

He then did ask to see the detective inspector and handed him a piece of paper with a London telephone number, said who he was and admitted he had failed in his mission. The call to London was made and the handler at the other end congratulated us on a job well done. What reception our target got on his return I don't know but I doubt if he went to the top of the class. What a pity it hadn't been a Burgess, McLean or Philby we had taught a lesson. But at least the score in this strange game was Flying Squad 1, Secret Service 0.

7

BLACKHILL, CAR BOMBS
AND BIG ARTHUR

Paperwork is a big issue whenever policing is discussed these days, with claim and counter-claim making headlines for politicians trying to wring votes out of the law-and-order card. But no cop catches a bad guy or deters a would-be villain through form filling. The problem is nothing new. After my successful – and happy – two years in the Flying Squad, I returned to the Northern Division. There was no lack of work or reports to be written and filed, even in those far-off days of the seventies. On my return, I was immediately, as they say, 'back on the book' (doing routine enquiries at divisional level). Every crime reported was given a number and assigned in order to a particular officer. You could have half a dozen crimes a day to look into – this was the reality of detective work, not the fantasy of film or TV where the detectives seem to have endless time on their hands and give their brain cells a gentle workout on one case at a time.

In my world, you prayed that there was a good hard-working officer on the previous back or night shift. He could really ease the workload by, for example, going out on calls to the house-breakings which, in areas like Springburn and the schemes in the north of the city, were a daily problem. A system was devised to make life a little more bearable. We would often find the letters NNTC on the flimsy slips of paper recording crimes such as break-ins. The letters stood for 'no need to call' and such a designation acted as an early warning that there were no finger-prints, no witnesses and, sadly, no suspects! But the paperwork was extremely time consuming as various forms had to be filled for Department of Health and Social Security cases and custody cases or the many serious assaults we had to deal with.

However, being 'on the book' brought great experience and gave an insight into the ingenuity of the criminal mind and the living conditions people endured in the huge post-war housing schemes. When I was not long back in the Northern, I got a classic example of what life could be like in a depressed area. One of the toughest of the schemes in the city was Blackhill. Plenty of hard-working honest folk had landed up there thanks to the lottery of housing allocation in the city and they had to put up with gangs and neighbours who would steal from you or attack you at the slightest provocation or even no provocation at all.

A feature of this bleak and unattractive area was the railway line that ran along the outside of the scheme. The trains that used it often carried materials thought to be worth stealing and this was a magnet for daring youngsters. They practised a trick of dropping from a bridge over the track on to the slow-moving trains and, from there, sneaking through any internal doors on the hunt for anything they thought was worth their while nicking. It was a constant problem.

We met with the British Transport Police to discuss it and decided the obvious answer was to get the trains to pass through Blackhill at a higher speed than usual. This was done. However, a week later, a dairy was broken into and a huge quantity of butter stolen. Why? We soon found out – later that night, the butter had been spread on the rails where there was a slight incline, the train wheels lost grip and it slowed down enough for the daring lads to jump on board and carry on thieving. It would have been funny if it was not so serious but that was life in Blackhill, a place where I once found a pony inside a house standing in the bath of a first-floor flat. It was resting before going out on the streets with its owner and a cart to collect scrap! You never knew what was going to happen next in Blackhill.

On one occasion, we climbed the stairs to a top-floor flat in search of a woman we had been told lived 'top, right'. When we knocked on the door, the woman who answered said that it was probably her sister we were looking for. Apparently, she lived through the wall in the flat 'top left' in the next close. We made to leave to climb down the stairs and on to the next close. But the woman then said, 'Hang on a minute!' and drew aside a tapestry hanging on her living room wall revealing a gaping hole in the wall where the bricks and plaster had been hammered out to allow access to the house next door. 'That will save you going up and down the stairs,' said the good Samaritan. The city fathers may have thought they had done well to provide modern new homes for their citizens but the properties didn't stay that way for long.

It was dangerous for vehicles to break down in Blackhill. This misfortune happened to a furniture van and, half an hour after the driver had found it impossible to move, it had been emptied of £30,000 worth of Parker Knoll up-market furniture. Our enquiries took us to a flat where the only piece of furniture was a Parker Knoll armchair. There was absolutely nothing else – bare boards with not even a rug, let alone a carpet, and curtain-less windows. We asked the resident where she had got such a nice reclining chair and were told that it had been sold to her for a fiver by a man on the street. We left her with her only piece of furniture although, technically, we should have seized it, but it really was all she had. What a place.

You had to be tough to live in Blackhill and the surrounding areas – and extra tough if you were to thrive and prosper there. Arthur Thompson Snr prospered financially, if he did nothing else. The man who was to become a Godfather, with his every scam featuring in tabloid headlines, was well known to the detectives in the Northern. A dangerous, malign character, he was behind much of the villainy in the city. He was also an associate of the Krays and other London underworld figures. He and I had only one thing in common – we were both the same age.

I had some intriguing early meetings with this legendary crime figure. My first direct contact with him was when we were tipped off that 'a criminal' from Edinburgh was coming through to Glasgow on a certain train at a certain time. I went to Queen Street Station and, sure enough, a man who fitted the description came off the train. I followed him discreetly, at a distance, till he entered a place in North Hanover Street, just a few hundred yards from the station. This was the Hanover Club, a gambling club, and, as I rang the bell, I was met by Abbie Katz, a well-known fence from Partick.

Inside, Katz offered me a seat and went off to get us some coffee. As we sat sipping our coffees, I looked round the room, watching gamblers playing roulette. I got a shock when I spotted Arthur Thompson operating the wheel. He got a shock, too, when he realised that a detective was on the premises. Thompson was big and strong and gave off a heavy air of menace at the best of times. Surprised in his lair, he shot off his chair and came towards me in a threatening manner. His henchmen in the club upped and grabbed him as he got close to me and tried to calm him down. While they were doing so, I made as casual an exit as I could. Incidentally, the man I followed into the club wasn't who he was supposed to be. Word travels fast in Glasgow and, the next day, Tom Goodall sent for me and asked why I was in the club. He understood the situation but remarked, 'You need to watch Thompson – he's dangerous.' I had already figured that one out.

Just a few months after this scary episode, we were to meet again. Detective Sergeant Arthur Steward and I were going to an enquiry in Ruchazie and, while travelling along Provanmill Road, we saw Thompson carrying what looked like suits from his house to the boot of a car. As I pulled over, my companion asked if I had seen something. I pointed out what was happening and he said, 'We'll take the number of the car and pass it to criminal intelligence.' I said a better idea would be to follow the car and give it 'a pull'.

By the time Thompson waved a cheery goodbye to the car, we had secured the assistance of a car with uniformed officers. We followed the suspect car to the city centre and it was signalled to stop in St Vincent Street. The driver turned out to be the son of Mendel Morris, a character who was well known to the cops. 'Surprisingly', he claimed, at first, he couldn't open the boot as it had jammed just the day before! What a shame. When we said we would take it to the nearest police office, he suddenly found that the key magically worked. Inside the boot were fifty new suits complete with price tags. We took Morris to the Northern and charged him with being an associate of a known thief and being in possession of stolen property. The officer on duty asked who the known thief was and I replied, 'Arthur Thompson.'

We then returned to Thompson's house, only to find his car was gone. We figured he would be in the Hanover Club and, before we went in, I suggested to Arthur Steward that we should get the assistance of the late duty Flying Squad and he agreed. The Flying Squad man was Detective Inspector Willie Stewart and he agreed to keep an eye on the Godfather's house at the time we planned to arrest him.

Inside the club, I cautioned Thompson and charged him with being a known thief and, while acting with an associate, he had been in possession of stolen property in Provanmill Road. I told Thompson to put on his jacket and we escorted him outside. He winked at a pal as we passed through the door and said, 'They'll probably visit my house.' He got that bit right. Thompson asked if he could drive his car back to his house and I agreed. I went with him and Arthur Steward followed behind. Thompson drove round George Square and down towards the Clyde – a route on no one's map of the way back to Provanmill. I asked innocently where he was going and he said, 'This might seem like a longer route but the traffic is lighter.' 'No problem,' I said, 'take as long as you like – the Flying Squad are sitting outside your house.' He went white with anger.

At the house, as we formally arrested him, his wife and son came out of the house pushing a pram loaded with more of the suits. The Thompsons' home was a much altered and enlarged house near Hogganfield Loch which they named The Ponderosa after the ranch in *Bonanza*, a popular TV western of the era. The house was thoroughly searched and one of the items we seized was a price tag from a suit. It was on a table beside a telephone in the hall and had obviously been used when the sale of the suits was discussed. It was one of the highlights of my career when I marched into the CID office with this Mr Big in handcuffs and, pointing to a chair, told him, 'Put your arse there.' He replied, 'Yes, sir.' He was no mug. Morris and Thompson were locked up to appear in court on the following day. We soon tracked down the source of the suits – they had been stolen from a shop in the Argyll Arcade. When I went to see Tom Goodall to report it, it would be more than an understatement to say that he seemed pleased at this turn of events.

When they appeared in court, Morris pleaded guilty in an attempt to get Thompson off the hook. It didn't work. Despite being the major 'player' on the streets, involved in all sorts of violent scams, and being able to pull the strings to make some of the hardest men in the city jump to his bidding, the Godfather did not have much in the way of previous convictions and had served surprisingly little time in jail. There were often several years between his court appearances. Now, however, we had him by what the criminal fraternity might call the short hairs.

There was never much chance of him beating this rap despite having the mighty Joe Beltrami as his lawyer. But Thompson was still confident – so much so that one of his relatives, a person I got on surprisingly well with, told me that Arthur had received a call from London gangland's mightiest fixers, the infamous Kray Twins, asking what kind of trouble he was in and offering to come north to fix it. Gang lords are never short of confidence in their ability to bend the justice system!

Thompson dismissed this offer of help, telling his associates that he had a good defence and that he would undoubtedly 'get off'. It was misplaced confidence. His notoriety ensured that there was great public and police interest in the case. Indeed, Tom Goodall himself and other CID bigwigs were in attendance as the trial got under way. I was one of the last witnesses and Joe Beltrami in his best ram-stam courtroom style implied that the price tag beside the telephone had been planted by me. Not true. Big Joe had had some remarkable courtroom successes and was often the lawyer of choice for folk in big trouble but, this time, he was on to a loser with his long-time client, Thompson.

Thompson's defence was basically that he had returned to The Ponderosa to find Morris there, in possession of the suits. He claimed that he ordered him out of the house. Listening to this exchange, I tore a sheet out of my notebook and wrote on it that the fiscal should ask Thompson two questions: why did he order Morris out of the house with only half the suits?; and having heard DC Brown giving his evidence, was he telling the truth? I passed this note to the court officer and he passed it on to the fiscal who looked at it and smiled at me.

When Beltrami had finished his examination of Thompson, the fiscal then asked the first of my two questions. Thompson couldn't answer and said that, with regard to the second question, Brown was telling the truth. At that moment both he and Beltrami knew he would be convicted. He was given four years. Such was Thompson's reputation that many of my colleagues thought I might be in danger of violent reprisals for my part in the case. I was less worried. Thompson knew he had broken the law and that he had been dealt with. It is surprising at times how rational big-time criminals can be about the effect of their actions on their liberty. According to their way of thinking, they are in a sort of war with the law and, in a war, you win some battles and you lose some.

This first encounter with the infamous Godfather had an odd sequel. While he was safely behind bars, some brave criminals broke into his house and stole, among other items, war medals Arthur had been collecting. I was given the inquiry. I got a call from his sister who was the manageress of the Provanmill Inn not far from The Ponderosa. This was a hard drinking pub with hard hard men as customers but there was not much trouble there – no doubt due to the fact that the customers were well aware of the nature of the manageress's brother's way of life.

She was cynical about the break-in, believing that the cops would do nothing about it because they were not exactly friends of the Thompson clan. I suggested she could make a few enquiries herself and she did. She came up with the names of the two men who were responsible and passed them on to me. They were a bit cocky when I tackled them but that attitude soon evaporated when I told them there would be an identity parade and that Arthur would be brought down from Peterhead to see them face to face. That was enough for them – they pled guilty and were jailed for six months. All the property, including the medals, was recovered. Arthur passed on his thanks. On hearing the details, one colleague asked me what was the reason for the ID parade that so scared the burglars. 'None,' I answered, truthfully. But the idea worked.

Over the years, I was to get to know Thompson well. On his release from his sentence for the stolen suits, he was, of course, still mixed up in crime although, for years, he swanned around the city in his expensive suits and silk ties, claiming to be a retired businessman. His activities meant regular visits from me at the request of other forces on some inquiry or other. I always went in the company of a female detective, something that amused him. When the Serious Crime Squad called on him they always went 'six-handed', showing respect for his reputation. I told him that my female detective was a judo black belt – untrue but it did impress him.

The next time I tangled directly with the emperor of The Ponderosa was in May 1978. This was in the heyday of the annual Scotland v England soccer matches and, that year, Hampden was to be the battleground of the old enemies and demand for tickets was, as usual, colossal. And, all around the city, counterfeit tickets for the big game were changing hands at big prices. I was charged with sorting out the mess. A tip-off named Arthur's son, Arthur Jnr – who was later to be fatally shot down in the street in a gangland war – as one of the sellers of the fakes.

I rang old Arthur, arranged an appointment and pitched up at The Ponderosa with my non-black-belt female detective. Arthur's son emerged from the kitchen and was interviewed. Old Arthur then wanted to know what had transpired and, on hearing details of the interview, he said, 'He got the tickets from me.' I pretended not to hear him and turned the conversation to a huge fake oak beam in the roof and asked how it had been placed there. Old Thompson was proud of the ill-gotten wealth that oozed out, in questionable taste, all over The Ponderosa and began a detailed explanation of how he had done it. When he was in full flow, I interrupted with a sudden question – where had he got the tickets? He said he had got them from Jim Baxter, the famous ex-Rangers star, who had gone into the pub business. Baxter, of course, was unaware that they were forgeries.

We had been offered a cup of tea but I told my colleague not to take it as, if he liked you, the worst you would get in it was spit. As the interview ended, Thompson asked me, 'Are you going to question everyone who is selling these tickets?' I told him we were and he proceeded to take the wind out of my sails by wondering, 'Does that include your boss?' I was furious when I returned to HQ to find that he was right. My boss had got fifty tickets from Baxter and, not realising they were fakes, had sold them.

We tried to recover all the tickets but some stayed in circulation. To be fair to my boss and Baxter, I must point out that these tickets were such good forgeries that even the Scottish Football Association could not tell them from the real ones. I had to go to the printers of the real tickets to confirm that the ones we thought were fakes were indeed counterfeit. However, no matter how real they looked, they all had the same serial number. I have to admit, with some satisfaction, that, when we recovered the tickets, many had been bought by people in high places, as they say. These were folk who should have known better than to get involved in such scams but the thought of a ticket for the big day was too much for them.

In the event, it was a case solved, though I have my suspicions that it didn't win me many friends in the aforesaid high places. The ringleaders, including a crooked printer, were arrested and hundreds of the tickets recovered before the kick-off. The ringleaders were arrested and jailed.

Around this time, I got another reminder of how dangerous it could be to mix it with Thompson. The car in which he had driven me from the Hanover Club during the suits case was blown up – apparently in retaliation for the death of a shadowy character called 'Packie Welsh'. This character had been involved in what was called a road accident with Thompson and died from his injuries. The underworld reprisals involved a bomb being placed under the seat of Thompson's car. It was wired up to a direction indicator but, when it did go off, it didn't complete the game plan. Big Arthur survived, protected from the blast by his seat, but his mother-in-law, a passenger in the car at the time, died. Being around the Thompson clan was always a high-risk occupation.

I have to admit it always made me uneasy to be in his

company. When he looked at me, a detective who was nosing him up from time to time, I could see the hate in his eyes.

8

YOUNG KIDS, HARD LESSONS
AND ROUGH JUSTICE

During my time in Springburn in the late sixties, I ran into my fair share of the sort of crime that makes your stomach turn. Coppers, jailed cons and the man or woman in the street are all equally repulsed and disgusted by sexual attacks on young kids. It is the one crime, more than any other, that spawns revenge – in the police force, in the world at large and even in prisons. Men convicted of such offences know that, when the jail gates close behind them, a nightmare that can go on for years lies ahead. Convicts of all types reserve a special hatred for the people they call 'beasts'. Beatings when the prison officers' backs are turned are routine and boiling water from tea urns is regularly thrown over them. They can't relax for a minute because every opportunity is taken to make such vile people pay painfully for their crimes. Sometimes rough justice comes even before the offender is tried. And sometimes it comes from the police!

I clearly remember one case where this had happened before we were finally able to get our hands on a man suspected of several attacks on kids. There had been much talk about this particular 'beast' and great effort and energy had been expended trying to catch him. But the officer in charge of the investigation was doing it by the book. He knew what could potentially happen to this man and he was determined that no harm would come to this sick individual while in our charge so he made it clear to us that, no matter how strongly we felt about his type of crime, this guy was to get into court unharmed. But you can't cover every eventuality. While in the station, the accused went to the toilet and, when he was there, an off-duty officer came in and asked who the prisoner was. When told, he rushed into the toilet and belted the accused in the face – there was blood was everywhere.

Even more dramatic retribution could take place and one incident aroused my suspicions. When on day-shift duty, we often took turns to provide lunch cover for each other by answering the phone and doing other little bits of office work. One lunchtime, during my covering stint, I took a call from a woman who gave a name and address in Garscube Road. She reported that an elderly man had taken a young girl in her close from the back-court up to his top flat. I told her to go out on to the street, speak to the first man she saw and ask for his assistance as it would take us about ten minutes or so to get there. I phoned HQ and asked for a unit to go to the address pronto.

It took me eight minutes to get to the tenement and I arrived to see a crowd standing around the body of a man who was lying dead on the pavement. The beat cops were also there as my call to HQ had got them to the scene just minutes before me. The woman who had phoned approached me, identified herself and said she had done exactly as I had suggested and approached the first two men she met on the street. The men had rushed upstairs to the flat and battered on the door of the house but got no reply. They heard the sound of the child crying so they forced the door and, according to them, the girl was standing in the kitchen but, before they could get a hold of the householder, he jumped out of the window.

Speaking to the men myself after listening to the woman, I noticed one had a huge scar running down his face. Both repeated the story of the window jump just as the woman had told it. I began to think there was something familiar about 'Scarface' and told him I thought I knew him. But no, he said I was confusing him with his brother. 'Who is that?' I asked. 'He was convicted of the murder of three cops in London.' The surname of my witness was Duddy, a name familiar to readers of the crime pages. On 12 August 1966 John Duddy, along with Harry Roberts and John Whitney, had gunned down three London detectives just before a robbery. All three went to prison for life and John Duddy died behind bars in 1981.

I looked his brother straight in the eye and said, 'You didn't throw the old man out of the window, did you?' He thought carefully and replied, 'It never crossed my mind.' Whatever really happened, the intervention of Duddy had at least saved the young girl. She was reunited with her mother and a doctor confirmed she was unhurt.

Worse was to come. Later that year, 1969, a woman brought her three-year-old daughter into the office and told us she thought she had been indecently assaulted. The casualty surgeon confirmed the mother's fears. There was no description of the attacker but the incident was recorded. The injury to that child was slight but, a few weeks later, a five-year-old girl in the same area was attacked and her injuries were more serious – she had been cut about her private parts. It was too early to make a connection between the two attacks but the possibility had to be considered. This time there was a description of man with dark hair, average height and aged around twenty.

This was the sort of crime that had everyone in the area, especially cops and parents, speculating about what could happen next, so a squad was formed to look into the attacks. It was unpleasant to say the least. As we feared, over the next few weeks, similar attacks were reported and the squad investigating the crime was increased with detectives from other divisions drafted in.

A few days after the most recent attack, I was on lunch duty when, once again, the phone rang and I heard the woman at the other end of the line screaming hysterically. All I could make out at first was 'young girl' and 'lots of blood'. Eventually I got the address and, as it wasn't far from the office, I got there quickly. Running out of the office, I had shouted to the staff at the bar to get an ambulance. I will never forget the sight that met me when I arrived at the address. An eight-year-old girl was standing in a pool of blood, with fresh streams of it pouring down her legs. We placed her on a settee and tried our best, with wet towels, to staunch the flow of blood. I was distressed and when I dialled 999 I shouted down the line, 'I am phoning from (the address I was at) and we have a very seriously injured young girl. I am now going out to the street and there had better be an ambulance when I get there.' And as I came out of the close, an ambulance screamed to a halt in front of us. It had been on its way to the Western Infirmary with a patient and had been swiftly diverted.

The attack had taken place at the rear of the building. Reinforcements quickly arrived and a really thorough search was made of the area. There was a palm print on the outer door of a backcourt so we removed the door from its hinges and took it to the police lab for forensics to have a look – but that led us nowhere.

I became aware that there were such strong feelings about the series of attacks that the younger guys had agreed that, if the attacker was caught in the act, he would be dealt with accordingly, such was the feeling in the camp. It was actually the furore over the case that helped to solve it. Again the breakthrough came in a lunch-hour phone call. A female phoned the office and told Detective Constable Joe Jackson that she suspected her boyfriend was responsible. Her suspicions were fuelled by the fact that he had moved from a flat located in the area of the attacks to another part of the city. He was now staying with close relatives who also had suspicions that he was interfering with their children.

When arrested, the man, James Ferguson, aged twenty-four, admitted that he had assaulted the children. Feelings in the office were running high and this was the guy who had his face flattened, despite our bosses' efforts to protect him from rough justice, by that off-duty officer mentioned at the start of this tale. The attacker got life and I often thought that the incident in the police office would only be a first taste of what lay ahead for him in his years behind bars.

One serial predator was behind bars but reports of indecent assaults were still coming into the busy office. One man called in with his ten-year-old son to tell us that the boy had been interfered with at a Saturday morning children's film show in the Princes Cinema in Gourlay Street. The man had given him sweets and followed him out into Palermo Street. In a backcourt, the man had kissed the boy and given him two shillings. He told him not to tell anyone and to meet him the following Saturday outside the cinema. As it turned out, the boy had had a lucky escape. He had had the good sense to tell his dad what was going on.

With the dad and the boy's help, we decided to catch this attacker so we arranged to be outside the cinema the following week. The boy was a bright kid and he was wearing a duffel coat with a hood. This was of assistance to us and I told the youngster to raise the hood over his head if he saw the man who had interfered with him the week before. We were desperately keen to get hold of this pervert – so much so that I took a leaf out of Jack Beattie's book and slipped into disguise. That Saturday I stood at the entrance to the cinema resplendent in the doorman's ornate uniform with its gold flashings and a cap that would have done a four-star general proud. The boy's dad stood at a nearby bus stop, in a position where he could keep a protective eye on his young son at all times. Two detectives also hid in the area.

Within minutes of us taking up our various positions, the boy raised his hood when a man of around fifty appeared. He spoke to the lad, took his hand and led him towards me. In good doorman style, I held the door open for the youngster then closed it in the man's face. 'What's your game?' he said. 'You're about to find out!' was my reply. The boy who had done so well to help us travelled with his dad in one car to the station and a detective colleague and I took the suspect in another car. He gave us abuse all the way to the office, claiming vehemently and aggressively that he had never seen the boy before. When we entered the CID room, the boy's dad noticed that the prisoner was bleeding from a wound in his mouth. I had to explain to him and the others present that the suspect had unfortunately collided with a swing door!

The man gave his name as Brian Luke, said he was fifty-one and surprisingly revealed that he was a janitor at a nearby primary school. This was long before the days when you had to be vetted before you could be employed near children. He claimed he had never been in trouble before and I checked his name and date of birth with the Scottish Criminal Records Office but turned up nothing. We then phoned London and asked them to check their records, including any that Interpol might hold on this sleazy character. Half an hour later, I got the call I was half expecting. Luke had recently been deported from Australia after serving seven years' hard labour following a conviction for two charges of buggery involving a ten-year-old boy and an eleven-year-old boy.

Although the case against Luke seemed indisputable, there were problems. Firstly, the Australian convictions apparently could not be used against him and here he would be classed as a first offender. And, secondly, we didn't have corroboration of the attack – only the word of a ten-year-old boy. Luke was charged, however, and he said, 'I only kissed him. I should have learned my lesson – I did hard labour in Australia for assaulting two boys. I was deported when I was released.' He later pleaded guilty and was given eighteen months. I have no doubt that, if the Springburn boy hadn't immediately told his dad what had happened to him, he would have suffered the same fate as the two boys in Australia. The fact that his attacker had sought and gained employment at a school did not really surprise me – child molesters are often to be found in an environment where children are.

Years of detective work make clear to you that real life crime is as fascinating as any work of imaginative fiction. And that the 'killer' clue so beloved of the crime writers turns up more often than you might expect. Criminals sometimes find it quite easy to give themselves away. I still have a laugh when I think back to one day when we were investigating a gas meter theft. The lady of the house asked if we had much chance of catching the culprit. I jokingly responded, 'Your husband would have to admit that he was the guilty party.' Whereupon the husband who had been listening to the conversation stood up and said, 'I don't know how you twigged but, yes, it was me!'

There can be other amusing giveaways. We had a laugh in the case of the real live one-armed bandit. He had committed assault and robbery in a pub in the Cowcaddens. The officer in charge was called John McVicar (a name to conjure with for fans of true crime and those who follow the fortunes of the London bad guys!). I was on duty when the suspect was brought in and I was asked to keep an eye on him. I was still on my paperwork when I heard a rustling sound and I looked up to see the suspect using his only arm, his left, to put something into his right-hand trouser pocket. I shouted to McVicar and told him what I had seen and he reached into the suspect's right-hand pocket and pulled out a handkerchief and a bank pay-in slip that had been stolen from the pub along with the cash.

When the case reached court the defence QC asked, 'Why would a man with a left arm conceal something in his right pocket?' 'Maybe,' I replied, 'for the same reason he keeps his handkerchief in his right pocket.' The lawyer walked over to the villain and asked him, 'Do you keep your handkerchief in your right pocket?' and the whole court heard him reply loudly, 'Yes, sir.' The one-armed bandit went down for four years. John McVicar was one of the detectives I worked with who impressed me enormously. When he left the police service for domestic reasons it was a big loss.

All this added a touch of humour to sometimes grim days. Another amusing incident was the occasion when, during my stint in Springburn, technology began to catch up with us. Personal radios were issued to a select few beat cops in an experiment. During a particularly busy spell, the duty sergeant came to the detectives' office to tell us that the system had been installed and was working well. He then asked if we wanted to come downstairs so that he could give us a demo. Busy as we were, we trooped downstairs to see the innovation at work. The newly installed console and equipment were impressive and, after a few minutes, a call came through. The sergeant beamed, picked up the mike and said, 'S Sugar receiving you loud and clear – send your message.' Over it came – 'Sugar one to S Sugar, bad news, sergeant, your horse finished down the park. Do you want the prices for the next race?' We laughed but the new system proved to be a great success when devoted to crime rather than beating the bookies.

As a detective you also learn by experience that holding a piece of evidence up your sleeve can be a valuable ploy. There was a good example of this in yet another case involving a sickening attack on a child. This time I was given an indecent assault on a four-year-old girl to investigate. It seemed an impossible case but, when a policewoman and I spoke to the little girl, we were astonished how bright she was for her age and felt she could be of real help in the inquiry, despite her tender years. The attacker had stolen a sixpence from the girl and I decided that we would keep quiet about this. A detective constable, Hugh Wilson, had extensive knowledge of the area and he was teamed up with us.

A policewoman, Hugh and I took the girl, accompanied by

the girl's father, to an unmarked car and toured the area. The wee girl was asked by the policewoman to look out for boys of the same age as the suspect and she did pick out a boy walking past with his mother as being of the right age. He was around ten and went to St Roch's School nearby. We made our way to the school and asked the headmaster to let the wee girl have a look at two classes for ten-year-olds. He refused to allow us access to the classes.

Not everyone is as helpful to the police as they should be but I was astonished that a headmaster of all people would refuse to let us do what we wanted. I cautioned him and charged him with obstructing the police. He then telephoned the education department headquarters in Bath Street. I was asked to speak to the person on the other end of the line and, when I was told I could not lock up this uncooperative headmaster, I simply said that was what I was going to do. Sticking to my guns worked and, when the head ended the call, he turned to me and said, 'I have been instructed to assist you.'

In her original description of the attacker, the bright little girl had said he was wearing a red jersey. When taken into the classroom, she pointed to a boy in a duffel coat. We opened the coat and found a red jersey underneath. We took the boy to the police station and officers went to find his father who was working on the construction of the Kingston Bridge, which, in the spring of 1969, was almost ready to provide another Clyde crossing for Glasgow's growing traffic. The father came to the station. When he was told what had happened, he refused to believe it. I had told the father about the sixpence and, when he heard his son say, 'I didn't take her sixpence!', even he changed his mind. The boy was found guilty.

There was a curious postscript to this tale, years later, when my wife and I went to a kitchen store to buy new units. At the cash desk I was told I was to get a substantial discount. I asked to see the owner to find out why he was being so generous. It turned out that he was the father of that really bright four-year-old girl who had helped solve a difficult investigation!

Life in those days did not all revolve around squalid indecent assaults and rapes although there were too many of these for my liking. There is a much-used Glasgow phrase when someone displeases you – 'Pick a window!' – and, indeed, earlier in this chapter, there was the tale of one child molester who appeared to have been told just that. Others have gone out a window for different reasons.

Around the time of the attack on that four-year-old, the body of a young man was found inside a huge metal dustbin of the type that collects the rubbish sent down chutes in high-rise buildings. Although the guy in the dustbin was not a native of Glasgow, he had fallen in with some local young men in a city centre pub. When it closed, he was invited back to a party and he foolishly agreed. It was to cost him his life. As is the way of many tenement parties, drink piled on drink and, two storeys up, arguments soon flared. The out-of-towner ended up plummeting to his death down in the backcourt and his body was later dumped in the dustbin. It was another crime where attention to detail would be the vital clue.

As is generally the case in incidents like this, the police surgeon, police photographer and sundry others were all involved in the inquiry. I was made production officer and it was down to me to see that everything pertinent to the case was bagged, labelled and recorded for future court evidence. After the body was removed to the police mortuary, it was pointed out to me that an *Evening Times* newspaper, dated the day before the murder, was found under the body. Suspicion fell on one of the party-goers, a guy called Eddie Cavanagh, who was arrested in a pub. In his pocket was a copy of that day's *Evening Times* with the headline 'Body Found in Dustbin'. This was seized as a production. Six months later at the court case, I was the final police witness. All the other officers were still seated in the court when I gave my evidence. The advocate depute took me quickly through the productions, ending with the newspaper found in the pocket of the accused when he was arrested. 'Do you recognise this newspaper as having been found at the bottom of the bin?' 'No,' I replied, 'that newspaper was in the possession of Cavanagh when he was arrested.' 'Are you sure?' 'Yes.' The advocate depute said, 'Other officers have given evidence that this paper was found in the bin.' I had to point out that a copy of the *Times* had been found in the bin but not this one, pointing out the heading on the discovery of the body. It was an interesting little exchange and, in the end, Cavanagh was convicted. But my attention to detail had not gone down too well with the officer in charge of the case who said, 'Are you trying to make a fool of me?' There was no answer to that!

A few months later, I was involved in another murder case in which the victim went head first out of a window but, this time, the issues of police procedure involved were more serious than the little business of a newspaper with the wrong date. On this occasion, the issue went to the heart of the relationship between witness and suspect. It was a gruesome murder. A young man had plunged to the ground out of a window and as he lay there, his assailants dropped bricks down fifty feet on to his body. The owner of the house where the plunge took place was a character called Brannan. I had had dealings with him previously and, with others, I was detailed to find him. He was in a small pub in Springburn Road and I told him to finish his pint and come to the police office with us. There, I was instructed to take a statement from him. I did so and, halfway through, it became obvious that he had thrown the victim out of the window at a party. When I realised Brannan had killed the man, I stopped the interview. Worried about following the correct procedure in such a situation, I sought advice, saying, 'I'm interviewing one of the killers.' 'Just get on with it,' I was told and later Brannan and others were charged with the murder.

At the trial at the High Court, it quickly became clear that the lawyer defending Brannan was unhappy with the statement I had taken from his client. The officer in charge of the case took me into a side room and asked me what I was going to say but, before I could answer, my name was called as the next witness. The defence team had a good look at me, no doubt assessing how I would stand up to the attack on me they were about to unleash. As soon as I gave details of finding Brannan in the pub and asking him to accompany us to the police office, his QC was on his feet to object that his client had, in fact, been arrested. The jury were dismissed as legal argument took place. I knew what was coming and the judge asked, 'What would you have done if Brannan had refused to go with you to the police office?' I replied that the question didn't arise since he came quite willingly. However, having been instructed to locate him and bring him to the office I would not have gone back to say that, having found him, he would not come with us.

The cross-examination continued and the question I really feared came out – 'When you took a statement from my client, was it as a witness or as a suspect?' I replied that I knew that Brannan had been at the party but, at that stage, I did not know the full picture. My understanding was that, if there were several persons at the party, all of them could be interviewed to pinpoint the attacker or attackers. I made the point that it is similar to an attack on a bus – if none of passengers is obviously the assailant, all of them are detained and interviewed because one has to be the attacker.

In his summing-up, the judge instructed the jury to accept the police evidence. In his view, we had acted in a fair and legal manner when the statement was taken from Brannan who, along with some companions, was found guilty and given life. I learned a lot from this case and considered I was becoming a good prosecution witness. Little did I realise that through a stupid error on my part, at a later date, a man accused of murder would walk free. But all life is full of surprises – especially the life of a detective in Glasgow.

9

A Nutcase, a Bayonet and Fivers under the Carpet

You still meet folk who will tell you that the stories of Glasgow hard men with weapons like swords, bayonets, pickaxes and the like are much exaggerated but these cynics never ran into people like Mick Ryan. In the early seventies, I was in the Central Division. It was a step-up from the days in Springburn and Blackhill but I was back mixing it with some of the toughest of the tough in the Gorbals. One day, reports started to come in of 'a nutcase running amok with a bayonet' on our patch. The most recent in a series of attacks had been on a postman who had been hit on the head with the bayonet and was only saved from serious injury by his solid, well-made postman's cap.

Dectective Superintendent James Binnie sent for me and asked if I knew a guy called Mick Ryan. I told him that, indeed, I did and that I was of the opinion that he had 'got away with murder' in an incident in the Railway Club in Pollokshaws Road. 'He's the guy with the bayonet – I want him stopped,' said Binnie. I gathered all known information on Michael McCafferty Ryan. A former leading member of the Gorbals' most infamous gang, the Cumbie, he still lived in the area. He was a bit of a loner with numerous previous convictions for serious assaults. He had been arrested as a main suspect in the murder of a man outside the Railway Club but the case against him was not well handled and, owing to confusion over the productions for the trial, he

105

was released. He was a very dangerous man.

Witnesses to his recent rampages with his bayonet were few and far between and they were terrified of Ryan – not without reason. One of the victims had told of just having bought an early edition of the *Daily Record* from a newsvendor with a pitch at the corner of Cumberland Street. I got a hold of the paper-selling guy and he told me he had seen some of the attacks and that the 'nutcase' was Ryan but he said that there was no way he would come forward as a witness in court. So we needed to do a little original thinking and I told the newsvendor that we understood his fear but we could take a statement from him 'under duress' and make sure in the High Court that it was obvious we had threatened him with jail if he refused. After that, we got a good statement but we still needed Ryan and some corroboration.

A few nights later, we received information that Ryan was staying in a tenement flat in Cumberland Street. With some night-shift detectives, I went to the flat. Ryan's reputation was such that a quiet knock on the door and a polite inquiry did not seem the right thing to do, so I raised my foot and crashed the door open. Six young men were sleeping on the settee and in sleeping bags. The owner of the flat was in the only bed in the house. There was no sign of Ryan. As we left, the owner asked how we had got into the flat and I told him the door was open. 'I don't think so,' he replied.

Over the next few days, we paid the flat a few more visits, using the same effective form of entry, but there was never any sign of Ryan. I took a night off and a Detective Inspector McKinnon volunteered to visit the flat. Back on duty the next day, I asked how McKinnon had got on and was told that he was in the Victoria Infirmary. He had so admired my method of entry he decided to use it himself. He had raised his boot a little too high and smashed his foot through a glass panel, suffering really severe cuts! The same afternoon, the owner of the flat had called round to the station and handed in a key saying, 'Give that to Mr Brown – my door can't take much more.'

A week later, we had Ryan when he was arrested for breaking into a pub. He was as tough and difficult as we had been told and denied he had been responsible for the bayonet attacks. He was, however, charged with the assault on the postman. He claimed it could not have been him as he was 'inside' at the time. This was checked out and proved to be false.

At the trial for the bayonet assaults, the star witness was the postman who identified Ryan as the attacker. The newspaper seller refused to answer any questions, refused to identify Ryan and told the court that his statement had, as we had arranged to happen, been forced out of him with the threat of jail if he did not assist us with our enquiries. The witness was now in a difficult place as the judge, unamused by his lack of cooperation, threatened him with a real term of imprisonment. It got to the stage that Ryan, a realist if nothing else, shouted to the witness, 'Just tell them or you will go to jail!'

When it was my turn in the box, Ryan screamed abuse and denied he had made statements attributed to him when charged. He kept repeating that he had been in jail when the attack took place. 'Was he?' asked the judge. 'Not on that date,' I replied. He got ten years.

But the story was not quite over. About 5 a.m. on the morning following Ryan's conviction, the Govan police called me to ask if I was the key holder of a shop in Albert Drive, Pollokshields. I told the officer that my wife owned the shop. 'Well,' he said, 'you have enemies – every window has been put in with bricks.' Police wives have a lot to put up with and, every time their men go to work, they don't know if they will come back in one piece. My wife was a great support to me – even when the windows in her shop were put in because of my job.

I was to meet Mr Mick Ryan once again – seven years later, when he had been released. I was on a Corporation bus heading home when who should come on but Ryan. He sat down beside me and I thought here it comes. All he said was, 'Hello, Mr Brown, how are you doing? See that ten stretch I got? I was due that.' As I noted, he was a realist.

All this excitement was a contrast to my first days in Central after Springburn. I had a new office which I shared with Detective Sergeant Ian Smith. I was in early on the first day, eagerly awaiting a deluge of crime reports. Nine o'clock came and went. Nothing. I asked Ian where the work was and could hardly believe my ears at his reply. He said, 'We can't be getting anything – that happens quite a lot but something will come in during the day.' From having to deal with at least ten crime reports a day in Springburn, I was having the rare experience of twiddling my thumbs. The two detective inspectors in the Central at that time were Jim McKinnon, best described as eccentric, and Dennis Joyce. The top man was Jim Wands, a true gentleman who let you get on with your work and kept out of the way until, of course, we had a major crime and he assumed command. It was during my stint in Central Division that I first became aware of 'the list'. It contained a detailed assessment of every officer in the CID, from Tom Goodall down to the most humble detective constable. If someone of senior rank died or retired, the guys with 'the list' could tell you who was next in line for promotion. In those far off days, all promotions normally took place within the CID. Once you were in that branch, you were there for the duration of your service. Nowadays, promotion for a detective can mean transfer back to the uniform branch – not, in my view, a good idea. I prefer the horses-for-courses method.

Casting around in the early days for something to get my teeth into, I referred to my police diary and came across an entry on Maurice Swanson, a man of Polish extraction who was to feature in a miscarriage of justice of much the same proportion as that inflicted on Paddy Meehan. My entry told me that, at that time, Swanson lived in Kent Road, Cranstonhill. He was wanted on a serious High Court warrant and was to be approached 'with extreme caution'. Ian Smith agreed to go with me.

We knocked on the door and were confronted by an elderly man. 'Friends of Maurice,' I said. 'He's in the bedroom – second door right,' said the man. He was and he was in bed with a naked woman. He dressed and we took him back to the office. There, James Binnie asked if we had been carrying firearms when we made the arrest. On hearing we had not, he shook his head and repeated what we had been told – 'Swanson is a very dangerous criminal.' At that moment an extremely attractive blonde woman walked into the office, giving me a chance to get some extra street cred by remarking, 'I didn't recognise you with your clothes on!'

Swanson's place in Scottish criminal history came some time after this incident when a bank in St George's Cross was robbed by a lone gunman. The 'usual suspects' thinking came into play after the description of the bank robber closely matched that of Swanson. He was traced and put into an identity parade and, once again, this particular tool at the disposal of the police was to lead to a faulty verdict. Swanson was picked out as the robber at the parade and ended up sentenced to seven years. Like Meehan who was to follow him into criminal history as a victim of wrong identification, Swanson was convicted basically on the evidence of the parade.

There was also another link with the Meehan case as Swanson was represented by the redoubtable Joe Beltrami. At the time of the robbery, fingerprint experts found, as you would expect, numerous prints on the bank counter. Because he had been picked out at the identification parade, the fact that none of the prints belonged to Swanson was considered not to mean too much. Joe Beltrami, who was later in his career to fight for justice for his client Meehan, shouted from the rooftops that Swanson was not guilty of this particular crime. No one listened. And the fact that many of the detectives in the CID, including me, thought that he was innocent did not seem to matter either. He went down for a long stretch.

Some months later, a criminal who had been arrested for a similar crime admitted other robberies, including the St George's Cross piece of larceny. His prints were checked and matched those found in the bank. Maurice Swanson was released and compensated after a case that, once again, had proved the unreliability of identity parades.

You hear a lot these days about jobs being '24/7'. The phraseology may be modern but it is not news to anyone who had taken to earning his corn as a law-enforcement officer. Once you have become a copper, you are always on the lookout for villains. One little bit of luck in my days at the Central proved you didn't have to clock on before you could have success. I was on my way to work on the night shift one day when the bus stopped at the foot of Butterbiggins Road to change drivers – a ritual that is well known to all southsiders who have spent quite a lot of their journey-time parked there while the drivers have a natter! With nothing else to do, I was staring out of the window when a young guy, known to me as John Simpson, walked past. I knew that Simpson was a wanted man – there was a warrant out for him – so I got off the bus and surreptitiously followed him to nearby Preston Street where he entered a close. I went round the back and had a look-see in the kitchen windows. I saw Simpson through one, talking to a woman who said, 'It's all right, John, you can stay here.' I went out into Cathcart Road where I met two beat cops and the three of us went back to the house and found Simpson hiding under bunk beds. We took him to Craigie Street Police Office, off Victoria Road, confirmed he was wanted on warrant and locked him up.

I then continued my journey to the Central and, when I arrived, the place was buzzing. When policemen get hurt in the course of their duties, the service pulls out all the stops to get whoever caused it. This night, the Central was full of top brass

and a major briefing was about to commence. Although I was
not required, curiosity took me into the room. I looked about
and was impressed. The back-shift and night-shift Flying Squad
guys were there, plus officers from the Scottish Crime Squad –
there was a total of about thirty of the finest in the force at that
time. The briefing concerned an incident the night before when
a criminal, driving a stolen car, crashed through a Scottish Crime
Squad roadblock, injuring several officers.

There was a suspect and he was known to frequent six
addresses. The master plan was that all six addresses would be
hit simultaneously at 3 a.m. An officer walked round the room
distributing enlarged photographs of the target. It was John
Simpson. I pondered how I was going to break the news to the
eminent gathering of lawmen. I raised my arm. One of the senior
officers looked at me and, with a shrug, he said, 'Yes, Les, you're
going to tell us you know where we can find Simpson?' I replied,
'Yes, sir, I have just locked him up – he's in custody in Craigie
Street.' There was, as they say, a stunned silence. Tom Goodall
had a word with me later and said, 'Mr Brown, how do you do
it?' I had to say that, in this case, it was all down to luck. 'It's
more than that, much more than that,' said the big boss. Who
was I to disagree with the famous detective?

Fraud is not the sort of crime that sets the excitement running
in Glasgow where more bloody matters tend to be the norm – at
least in the outlying schemes and city centre slum areas. But, in
the Central, we saw plenty of it and one case in particular was
a classic of its kind.

In August 1970, I was detailed to have a word with the
manager of the branch of the Bank of Scotland in West Nile
Street – as close to the city centre as you could get. The manager
was a nervous wreck and he was desperate to have a scam
sorted out. The tale he told me concerned a young man, well
dressed and pleasantly spoken – the sort of fellow your aunt
would call a 'nice young man'. He had called at the bank five

weeks earlier, asking for the manager. He explained he wanted to open an account, deposit money on a regular basis, withdraw money when he needed and have the facility to pay bills by cheque. No alarm bells rang and the manager gave his approval and handed the new client, who called himself Thomas Ferguson, over to a teller to do the needful. The account was opened with £50 and an address in Lansdowne Crescent given.

Over the next two weeks, 'Ferguson' popped in frequently to deposit a tenner or so but, after this spell of depositing money, he told the bank staff that he was going to Aberdeen and needed a chequebook for buying and paying for this and that, including accommodation while he was up north. He was told he would be sent the book in the post but, three days later, he was back claiming the chequebook had not arrived and he was leaving for Aberdeen that very day. So, there and then, the nice people at the bank kindly gave him a chequebook in the name he had given. Of course, the posted chequebook had arrived and he now had sixty cheques in a false name.

A few days later, the cheques started to turn up back in West Nile Street. In one day, in Liverpool, he had creamed in £900 – big money more than thirty odd years ago. The manager pleaded with me to find a way to stop this cheque spree. Back in the office, it became clear that Ferguson had been working this con for more than three years. Banks, shops, hotels, restaurants had all been hit. He had bought everything from a portable TV to a three-piece suite. All the descriptions we had matched – he was around thirty, slim, about 5 foot 8 and with a receding chin – but we hardly knew where to start with this mystery man who had taken cheque fraud to such a sophisticated level. We studied everything he had bought with the duff cheques. A flash of inspiration turned up an oddity – none of his phoney cheques had involved buying a watch. Now we figured a nice Rolex or Omega would be a must-buy for such a guy but no cheques for that sort of thing were in the paperwork.

DC Norrie Simpson and I decided to slog around the city centre jewellers. One was in Buchanan Street and, when we got back to the office, I was told the manager of this particular shop wanted to speak to me. He said the name and address of Ferguson had rung a bell and, when he checked the repairs register, there was an entry for a top-of-the-range Omega Flightmaster and a note that Ferguson of Lansdowne Crescent would call back later in the week for it.

We told the manager we would need to be in the shop when he came in to collect it. Ferguson was not the type to stand calmly in the shop while someone phoned the cops. We got permission to sit in the back shop. It took five days but our man did turn up. The only real link, I have often thought, between a Hollywood-style detective and the real thing is the time each has to spend waiting. The film actors playing detectives have famously to sit around the set till every last detail of lighting etc. is right. The real-life detective spends hours waiting and watching 'in doorsteps' and generally sitting around waiting.

But five days was a long stake-out and, when, after the long boring hours of waiting, Ferguson eventually arrived in the jeweller's shop, I got between him and the door. Norrie also appeared and I told the suspect, 'I have good news and bad news – the good is that your watch is ready, the bad news is that we are the CID.' 'What an idiot I've been,' he said. 'I was approached outside the shop by a man who asked me to pick up a watch and he gave me the ticket for it.' He was a cool customer – it was just a pity about the distinctive weak chin. Of course, he did not actually live at the Lansdowne Crescent address so I knew that we had to find out his real address to discover where the property he'd bought with the phoney cheques was. It was obvious we were dealing with a clever fellow.

By now, we knew his real name was Thomas Miller but there were some twists still left in this tale. After some heavy grilling, he was now admitting that he had taken the watch in for repair.

We worked our own little scam on this crafty character. It was arranged for a colleague next door to phone me and I was to pretend it was the Scottish Criminal Records Office on the line, the suggestion being that the watch was stolen. I turned to Norrie and said, 'You're not going to believe this – the watch appears to be genuine.' 'Can I go then?' asked Miller. I said he could and apologised for the hassle. I handed him the watch and we shook hands. As he made for the door, I said, 'I take it you won't be complaining about false arrest or any of that crap?' 'Of course not,' he replied. 'In that case, you won't mind signing this form to that effect,' I said. He paused for a moment, signed it and wrote his address as Turret Road, Knightswood but, within seconds, he realised he had been conned.

We now had his real address. Knightswood was a nice douce scheme and, when we got there, we were admitted by a Mrs Miller. We explained why we were there. 'Yes, Thomas is my son but he doesn't stay here,' she said. We looked around the living room in this modest house and it was all there – a huge TV set, an expensive music centre and tapes and discs everywhere. I remarked, 'You certainly like your entertainment.'

The mother burst into tears. 'The stuff you're looking for is upstairs in his room.' She got that bit right. On the list of stolen goods we had was an expensive carpet. It was there all right and Thomas Miller didn't need underfelt – we lifted the carpet and found fivers piled five deep. The stolen goods taken from his home filled three vans!

Miller was now concerned about his mother and when we told her she was in the house but she was OK, he began to talk. He had five bankbooks, had made up rubber stamps and used several different names. He told us that he had parked a red sports car outside the jeweller's and that it, too, had been bought with a dud cheque.

He was sent to jail for eighteen months and I will never forget the expression on his face as we closed his cell door. 'You're a bigger con man than I am,' he commented. I took it as a compliment.

After his release, I met him walking through Central Station. We had a coffee (I paid) and chatted about old times. He told me an amusing tale of his time in Saughton. He had shared a cell with a guy called King, a well-known fraudster, and, as keen chess players, they played for money and kept a slate. Before leaving prison, Miller, in an effort to square up his debt, offered to pay by cheque. The offer was refused. That's the last I saw of Miller – a well-educated man who had turned to crime and almost got away with it.

10

FRAUD, SEX, BLACKMAIL, INFORMERS AND OTHER DIVERSIONS

It is an old cliché that truth is stranger than fiction but, during my many years on the streets of Glasgow dealing with the riff-raff and the criminal elite alike, it often occurred to me that some of the things that were happening just couldn't have been made up. The ploys and ingenious scams of the real-life villains would test even the most fertile imaginations of the best crime novelists.

For example, anyone visiting my home in the early seventies might have overheard regular phone calls that would seem to indicate that I had gone bonkers. I would pick up the old, big, black plastic handset and give my phone number and the voice at the end of the line would ask, 'What colour is your dog?' I would invariably reply, 'Red.' And the caller would say, 'Mine is black.' End of conversation. This was a coded exchange with my old adversary and Glasgow criminal legend, the bank robber Samuel 'Dandy' McKay. It meant that we would meet at the 'usual place' in an hour. The place was the Linn Park and, during a stroll around the leafy paths of this well-kept south-side landmark, Dandy would drop me a nugget of two of information on what the criminal classes were up to – especially those not in favour with Mr McKay.

Almost all the top criminals, especially those who seem to get an easy ride from the police, have it whispered around by their enemies that they are informers who have the police in their pockets. In the sixties and early seventies, Dandy was a great help to me on many occasions. He wasn't, of course, my only informant. A detective always keeps an ear to the ground for what is happening with the bad guys.

Another infamous city gangster was Tam McGraw, a man who still makes headlines to this day. He was also in action around the time Dandy and I were exchanging weird phone calls. McGraw's nickname is The Licensee and it has long been rumoured that he got the soubriquet because he had a licence to break the law as a result of his contacts in the police. This, to my mind, is nonsense and there is no evidence to support the theory. A dangerous man, McGraw actually got the nickname because, whenever he was asked his business by the cops, he usually replied 'licensee' because he and his wife owned a pub – it is as straightforward as that.

There is one particular story about McGraw that confirms my view that the nickname simply refers to his ownership, with his wife, of The Caravel pub in Barlanark – an infamous haunt of gangsters and lowlife generally. Incidentally this pub was suspiciously destroyed in the midst of the investigation into the deaths of Joe 'Bananas' Hanlon and Bobby Glover, around the time of the Arthur Thompson Jnr murder. The bulldozing of this place, according to whispers, was timely since any evidence of interest to the police with regard to the killing, which remains unsolved, disappeared into the pile of rubble left by the demolition. Be that as it may, I saw no evidence of McGraw ever helping the police with info.

In the late sixties, I had an interesting run-in with him when an Asian businessman, Maq Rasul, who went on to make a pile with Global Video, was on the end of a lot of thieving from his shop, a general store in Barlanark. There were break-ins and some serious shoplifting. At that time, a gang known as the Barlanark Team was, to some extent, running the scheme that they had taken their name from. Three of the leaders of this well-known outfit were Tam McGraw, Jonah McKenzie and Snadz Adams and I pointed out a fact of life to them – if Rasul was forced to close his shop, the locals would miss it as they would then face the inconvenience of travelling a considerable distance for their fags, milk and bread and so on. After that, the crime wave decreased overnight.

Of more significance is the fact that I locked up McGraw more than once in the old days. Every detective knows that, when someone's informant is dumped into a cell awaiting trial, the phone will ring with an anxious cop on the other end of the line trying to secure as much leniency as possible for his 'man'. In my dealings with McGraw, no one ever tried to interfere with the due course of the law. That simple fact speaks for itself.

Dandy was, however, well able to cooperate with the cops when it suited him. He was helpful to me over the famous case of the company called Rotary Tools. This trial was a bonanza for the press who had weeks of fun out of it – especially, considering the name of the company, the link with blackmail and sex. It was owned by a guy called Maurice Cochrane who had devised a five-star scam. The company took tools in for so-called repair, gave them nothing more than a clean and a polish, charged a top rate and returned them to their owners. You might think you couldn't get away with that. Well, you could if you operated in the Rotary Tools fashion. Cochrane used to invite a representative of a company seeking to have machine tools serviced to come to Glasgow with the items needing looked at or repaired. Then he arranged for such reps to get the sexual services of a good-looking young whore for free. Overnight accommodation was also provided. All the shenanigans of the rep's visit to town were taped and the guy was blackmailed to keep quiet about the nonexistent repairs.

The premises of Rotary Tools were burgled and the assumption was that this was an effort to recover the tapes and photographs by a victim trying to end the blackmail or a crook trying to turn the tables and blackmail Cochrane. The underworld was well aware of what was going on. This is where Dandy came into it – I suspected he had been hired to do the break-in. I mentioned this to him but he denied it. Well, he would, wouldn't he? But he did spill some of the beans about the scam.

On a couple of occasions, I paid a visit to Cochrane and, during one, the cocky ringmaster of this remarkable fiddle picked up the phone and said, 'Tell Willie to take a case of whisky to Cranstonhill Police Office right now.' I leaned across his desk and asked if Willie was single. Cochrane asked what that had to do with it and I said, 'Because he will be locked up when he arrives at the office and it is always better when someone who is jailed is single.' The instruction was cancelled. On another occasion, he threw the keys of a Merc across the table and said I could use it for a few weeks. I said I already had a Merc which, when you think about it, was not very likely for a cop on smallish wages! But he took the hint. In the end, I compiled a report for the Fraud Squad and, not long after that, the place was raided and the scammers went to trial.

I was later told that everything I had said to Cochrane had been taped and my responses to his crude efforts at bribery gave a few laughs to my superiors. But it did show how easy it would be to get caught out.

This was not the only case where McKay helped me. I remember meeting him after he had been stopped by a police car and he was in possession of a large number of expensive looking pullovers. He told me he had been given the clothing by a friend, Bertie Green, a well-known fence. The knitwear was found to be cheap copies of expensive stuff with a fake label. I got a not-too surprising insight into the criminal mind when we got a hold of the guy who had been making the fakes. 'What's wrong with that?' he said when we questioned him. 'Not much to me,' I said 'but maybe this guy next door might think differently.' The guy next door was from Customs and Excise and another case was closed.

On more serious matters it should be recorded that McKay showed some social conscience in that he helped the cops in the case against mass murderer Peter Manuel. The infamous serial killer tried to blame McKay, an accomplished burglar, for some of his actions but the police knew better. Indeed Samuel 'Dandy' McKay, who was as horrified as anyone about the activities of a mass murderer, helped the police no end in building up a case against the evil man who was to die on the gallows in the Barlinnie hanging shed, after running the last few steps to the scaffold.

All this was happening around the time I was moved to Cranstonhill which was a subdivision of the Central. At first, I wasn't too enamoured of the posting to this office in an empty primary school but it turned out to be a very happy office and the entire crew there got on well. The man in charge was Jim Brown and the two detective sergeants were George Mitchell and me. The detective constables included Ian Forsyth, Bryan McLaughlin and John Bekier. It was a busy place and we all got on with it. Funnily enough, my first case there involved the offer of financial backhanders.

A woman who worked at a nearby car hire office phoned to say she had heard a new team had moved in and wanted us to note that five of their vehicles had been stolen. It didn't take us long to find them for her and the next day I was able to inform her that they had been recovered. She expressed her appreciation and said that, if we popped round, we would get 'our money'. Along with a detective constable, I went to see her. She attempted to hand me a bundle of fivers. Dreading the reply, I asked her what the money was for. She replied, 'We give the police a fiver for every car recovered.' She soon got the message that this was not on and, in the future, her reward to us for our help was to be of great assistance in keeping us informed of who was hiring what cars – very helpful info for a crimefighter.

In Cranstonhill, we got more than our fair share of the humour

Paddy Meehan, a non-violent minor crook, who was stitched up and wrongly convicted of brutally murdering an old woman in an Ayr bungalow in 1969

Nicholas Fairbairn who, along with the late leader of the Labour Party, John Smith, defended Meehan in the Ayr murder trial. Despite having this strong defence team, Meehan was convicted, largely due to the convoluted and tainted case presented by the police

Joe Beltrami, 'The Great Defender', who was part of the campaign to get justice for Meehan. After seven years in jail, mainly in solitary confinement, where he constantly protested his innocence, Meehan was pardoned

Fear and panic rule on Great Western Road as deranged gunman James Griffiths fires indiscriminately from the window of a tenement where he is holed up. The police were keen to question Griffiths, an associate of Paddy Meehan, in connection with the murder in Ayr

As a last resort, after nine people were injured, one fatally, Griffiths was killed by armed police. Detectives, including Tom Goodall (looking at the body) and a young Les Brown (over Goodall's shoulder), watch as his body is removed

Les Brown has some interesting theories on the so-called Bible John murders. Posters like these were put up all over the city to try to catch the man – or men? – who killed Jemima McDonald (above, right), Patricia Docker (below, left) and Helen Puttock

The fondly remembered Plaza Ballroom. Around the time of this photo, in the late seventies, Les Brown was investigating a bombing in a pub near here. Despite requiring hospital treatment after the blast, many of the pub's customers were more interested in getting to the jiggin' than in helping the police with their inquiries

Victor 'Scarface' Russo pictured in the 1950s looking like a mob foot soldier from a Hollywood gangster movie. This villain and Les Brown first crossed paths when Les was a cop on the beat in the Gorbals

The well-dressed gangster Arthur Thompson Senior, known as 'The Last Godfather', presents a rather different appearance. His reputation for violence was legendary and he had some serious run-ins with Les Brown who remembers the look of hatred for lawmen that shone from Thompson's eyes

Tom Goodall, the legendary head of Glasgow's CID, in a caravan that has been set up to act as a temporary police office during the investigation of a 1964 murder

A young Les Brown. Early in Brown's career, Goodall recognised his talent for detective work

All too often, Glasgow lived up to its nickname of 'Tinderbox City'. Here firemen train their hoses on the massive blaze at St Andrew's Halls

A Scottish National Orchestra musician examines some musical scores salvaged by firemen from the ruins of St Andrew's Halls where the orchestra frequently played. Les Brown solved the mysterious cause of the fire through the use of some classic detective work

The boarded-up windows of this street on the notorious Blackhill housing estate were by no means unusual in the deprivation that was widespread in the post-war Glasgow schemes. For the kids seen on these mean streets, poverty, drunkenness and violence would have been commonplace

'Gentle' Johnny Ramensky got his nickname because, unlike many Glasgow criminals of the time, he caused the cops no trouble on the numerous occasions they arrested him. An accomplished safe-breaker, Johnny's skills were used behind enemy lines to steal plans during the Second World War

Samuel 'Dandy' McKay was a bank robber and a real Glasgow character. He supplied Les Brown with important information, using secret phone codes, but, when it suited him, he could lead the police, including Les, up blind alleys

Jack Beattie, head of the city's Drug Squad, is pictured with the Albany Hotel behind him. Beattie and Les Brown, who was with the Serious Crime Squad, found themselves on opposite sides in what came to be known as the Albany drug trial, one of the most controversial episodes in the history of Glasgow policing

Wearing the detective's trademark raincoat and soft hat and with pipe in hand, the legendary Tom Goodall, followed by 'Yorkie' Lloyd and Jim Wands, emerges to brief the press about a double murder case they are working in the 1960s

Sir John Orr was one of the most successful men in tackling crime in Glasgow. As a young cop, Les Brown had many adventures on the streets while working with Orr

that turns up in every cop's life. Adjoining the office was a local Catholic primary school. The head teacher was a real character and got on famously with the cops so we liked to help where we could. One night, there was a break-in and we were told the kids were heartbroken as the thieves had stolen, among other items, a pet rabbit. However, by the time we got to the school, the Sister in charge had solved the crime. The first lesson she had given out on the day after the break-in was for the children to write a short essay on their favourite pet. A six-year-old wrote that her favourite pet was the rabbit her brother had brought home last night!

We were not above the odd joke ourselves. Every CID office has a clerk, usually a cop on light duties for one reason or other – basically an office manager but an invaluable aid to the success of the place. After a happy couple of years in the old school, we moved to a new office at the corner of Argyle Street and Finnieston Street but it still went by the name Cranstonhill. The clerk was a guy I will call Alex to save his blushes and, one winter night, we decided to play a practical joke on him. The Kelvin Hall, home of an annual circus and fun fair that were much loved by the old Glasgow public, was on our patch. So we got a detective who could do foreign accents to phone Alex and report that one of his elephants was missing from the Kelvin Hall. We sat around trying not to snigger as Alex took details, including a description of the elephant. He had almost completed his report when someone let slip that he was being set up. He tore up the report, gave the rest of us a sneering look and continued with his paperwork. He had underestimated the scale of our depravity. In the main office, there was a tannoy system on which we could hear calls going out to mobile units from police HQ. A call came in on it and it was timed to perfection – 'Do we have a unit in the area of the Botanic Gardens? We have reports of an elephant damaging plants.' Alex's face was a picture as he retrieved the torn-up report and tried to put it together.

Out on the streets, laughs were fewer but we did get them occasionally and they certainly enlivened the periods between serious assaults, frauds and the usual run-of-the-mill crimes. One night on our patch, a criminal, armed with a jemmy, was trying to crash his way into the rear of a newsagent's shop. Suddenly, he became aware of a presence behind him and turned to see a Boy Scout in uniform and the lad asked the burglar if he would sponsor him for 'Bob-a-Job Week', an old fundraising idea of the Scouts. The boy got a mouthful of obscenities for his trouble and responded by calling 999. The burglar was soon nabbed and, as he was being bundled into the van, the eager-beaver Scout asked the cops if *they* would sponsor him. This time, he got a more positive response.

I also remember a rammy at a Blackhill wedding. The drink had been flowing and both families had been mixing well . . . until a relative of the bride entered a side room and found the best man and the bride in a passionate embrace. Well, it had actually gone a bit further than that! All hell then broke lose with guests on both sides battering each other and the wedding cake ending down the toilet pan. The 'best of order', as they say, was only restored when a guest jumped up on the platform to announce that everything was now fine – the best man had apologised.

The rabbit that was stolen wasn't the only pet to feature in my time in Cranstonhill. A valuable parrot had been stolen from Edinburgh Zoo and suspicion had fallen on a school party from Castlemilk. The law descended on the school and we told the kids that all we wanted was the parrot to be given back and there would be no arrests and no one would go to court. A couple of nights later, a call came in tipping us off that the parrot would be found at an address in Ardencraig Road. There it was, in a large cardboard box, taped up and with suitable ventilation holes. The zookeeper came through to Craigie Street for a reunion and told us that the parrot would recognise him immediately and respond with a greeting. We opened the box and, before the keeper could speak, the parrot beat him to it, squawking, 'The polis are a shower of bastards!' loud and clear. It took the zoo folk six weeks to erase what the Castlemilk lads had taken two days to teach the parrot.

The Glaswegian seems to have a talent for barefaced fraud – and for milking a good idea. We got a good demonstration of this during my time in Cranstonhill when, for once, the guy who got stung was a second-hand car dealer who, in a change of role, was on the wrong end of the financial jiggery-pokery. The guys on the showroom forecourts are generally pretty street savvy with their mission in life to part each customer from the maximum amount of cash they possibly can. But they know too that the buyers are often pretty street sharp, especially in Glasgow, and that they have to have their wits about them all the time. But maybe the guy who got stung was a little too trusting. He advertised for someone to look after his showroom when he went on a brief holiday. The ad produced a man who called himself Alistair Alexander Hain. Hain certainly had the gift of the gab and he quickly showed that he had a talent to shift 'motors' out of the showroom but his real skill came into play when the boss went on the holiday that he had been looking forward to so much.

Hain hardly waited till the owner was on the plane before rolling out the posters advertising a 'once in a lifetime sale'! He was offering 50 per cent off to cash customers. The holiday maker returned to find no Hain and no cars left on the premises. The police identified Hain but could not find him.

About a year later, I overheard a discussion in the Central between two detective constables that had a familiar ring to it. A salesman, this time of carpets, taken on as a holiday replacement, had proclaimed that 'all stock must go' and offered discounts of up to 90 per cent of the price. It was such an attractive offer that even other carpet dealers got in on the action. Again Hain vanished. After another four weeks, Detective Sergeant George Mitchell, who was hunting the fraudster on another inquiry, was tipped off that he was at an address in Hyndland. Mitchell and a colleague visited the flat but no arrest was made. Back in the Central office George told us that Hain wasn't there but that his flatmate had given him coffee and biscuits. We asked George to tell us what the flatmate looked like and he immediately described Hain, who he had never met! George Mitchell was an angry man that day and became more determined than ever to catch the hoodwinker. The cop got his revenge when he received a tip-off telling him that Hain was working in the restaurant at Prestwick Airport as a chef. We went down to Ayrshire, nabbed Hain and removed him from the premises still in his chef's outfit, including hat. The real-life sale-of-the-century expert went north to Peterhead for a number of years where, no doubt, his expertise in the kitchen was put to good use.

Looking back on it, that cup of coffee that Hain had given George to enjoy had its humorous side but it was not very funny when it happened. It reminds me of an incident involving a cup of tea that could have been equally disastrous. One of the rather boring duties of a detective can be to collect prisoners on warrants and bring them to the city for their court appearance. Transferring criminals north from London was a fairly routine task for the Glasgow force but sometimes it went wrong. I remember going to meet a cop off the train in Central Station and I watched him stride purposely down the platform on his own towards me. 'Where's the prisoner?' I asked. 'He got off at Motherwell,' was the unexpected reply!

An incident that happened when I was on such duty could have ended up with a similar outcome but I was lucky. A colleague and I picked up the prisoner in London and settled down for the long train journey home. The drill was to take turns to keep an eye on the guy. One of us read the paper or took a nap while the other watched over the criminal. On this occasion,

I woke from a little zizz to see my colleague sitting opposite me reading a magazine. There was no sign of the prisoner and the train was standing at a platform somewhere in the wilds of England. 'Where's the body?' I asked. 'Don't panic!' I was told. 'He has gone to get us a cup of tea.' I jumped to the window and, sure enough, there was the prisoner casually coming toward me balancing a tray with cups of tea and sandwiches. 'I got you a hot pie, Mr Brown. Is that OK?' It was.

In that case, our prisoner was delivered safely back to Glasgow and no doubt took his medicine when it came to him. But sometimes prisoners, rather than careless cops, get the wrong end of the stick. Friday nights in police stations in this city can get hectic and things can go a little awry. A good friend of mine, Kenny Ross, was the officer on duty at Tobago Police Office in then east end. One weekend, we brought in a bad bit of work, a guy who was something of a serial wife beater. To charge him yet again and go through the rigmarole of charge and trial would probably just compound the problem. So I asked Kenny to hold the guy till he sobered up and not put him through the books. Kenny agreed. I thought no more about it till a week later when I got a radio call to contact Tobago Street. It was Kenny. 'Can I let that guy out?' he asked.

I got another promotion and, this time, I was to join the Serious Crime Squad as a detective inspector based at Temple Police Office in Anniesland on the north side of the city. But, before I left Cranstonhill, I saw another side of the whole flawed business of identity parades. This time, we were investigating an alleged rape of an Asian woman. We asked the owner of an Indian restaurant in Gibson Street for the use of his premises and six of his staff for a parade and he agreed. I took charge and the accused's solicitor watched over the procedure. The victim was brought in and told to have a good look at the men lined up before her and, if she recognised her attacker, she should point at him and tell me the number on the card laid at his feet. She indicated she understood and set off along the line. On reaching the suspect, she punched him full in the face, without any warning. He was sent crashing backwards and there was blood everywhere as the witness was swiftly led out of the premises. I made an entry in the parade log and the defence solicitor asked what I had written. I showed him the entry. It read, 'Positive identification.' No one could argue with that!

11

WAS SHERGAR UP A CLOSE AND DID BIBLE JOHN SLIP THE CUFFS?

No murder inquiry in the recent history of the Glasgow police has made more headlines, provoked more theories and spawned more articles and books than the still-unsolved case of the man – or men! – nicknamed Bible John. What is not in dispute is that three young women, out for a night at the dancing in Barrowland, one of the city's most famous dance halls, were strangled by a mysterious killer. The victims – Patricia Docker, Jemima McDonald and Helen Puttock – all died in circumstances that were, in some ways, strangely similar. I was by now in the Serious Crime Squad and solving murders was our daily business. In the normal run of events, I got involved in this complex and puzzling case which dragged on for years and is still 'open' to this day.

Viewed from the inside, the mystery of Bible John was as intriguing to the detectives involved in it as it was to the millions who read about it almost daily for years. It was Scotland's biggest murder hunt with more than 100 detectives working on the case and more than 50,000 statements taken. Everyone involved has a theory – even thirty-seven years after the news of Pat Docker's rape and death first grabbed the headlines and sent frissons of fear running through the minds of the thousands of dancing-daft Glaswegian women who flocked to the spangled glamour of the many dance halls to escape life in drab tenements and housing estates. Some observers of the case now believe that, despite the similarity in the killings, the murders were the work of more than one man. Who knows? But at the time it seemed that a serial rapist and killer was hunting down his victims in the Barrowland with the swing music of the era echoing off the walls, and the bright lights sparkling, as he chose his next victim.

The name Bible John was the invention of famous Glasgow crime reporter John Quinn who, in one of his stories, put together some of the evidence against the man he called 'a dapper dancer of death'. John came away from a briefing by Detective Chief Inspector Elphinstone Maitland Dalglish, at that time in charge of the case, with the knowledge that the suspect was probably called John and he was thought to talk to dancing partners of a strict upbringing and a parental attitude critical of drinking. He also tended to talk about the Bible. Given this info by the cop known to the press as 'Elphie', John Quinn gave the killer the inspired nickname of Bible John. It stuck.

The investigation struggled right from the start because of a Glasgow tradition. A night at the Barrowland attracted men and women on the hunt for bit of romance or some serious winching, possibly in a darkened close, when the music finally stopped. And, for a variety of reasons, customers of the Barrowland, in particular, didn't want too much to be known about their Friday and Saturday nights at the jiggin'. For a start, many of the men were married and the ritual of pocketing a wedding ring in a pub and swallowing more beer than necessary before going into the hall in search of a one-night stand was a fact of life. Many of the girls in swirling, spangled dresses were likewise married or engaged and just out for a good time. The names John and Mary were pretty popular, too! Talking to the cops and being a witness in a murder hunt was not, perhaps, quite what they wanted to be doing.

The similarities in the Bible John killings were striking – all the girls had been strangled, all were dumped near their homes, all had been at the Barrowland and all had been seen to leave in the company of a personable young man. My involvement in this remarkable inquiry came early in my days in the Serious Crime Squad. Pat Docker was a twenty-five-year-old nurse from the south side who liked an occasional night out at the dancing. She had left the Langside home she shared with her mother and young son that fateful night. Seemingly, her original intention was to go to another city dance hall, the Majestic or the 'Magic Stick' as its clients often referred to it. She apparently changed her mind and went to the Barrowland instead. It turned out to be a disastrous decision for there she met the 'dapper dancer of death'. She may have asked her killer to leave the east end and accompany her towards her home patch on the south side. Whatever happened, her body was found in a lane near the Victoria Infirmary. She was naked and had been menstruating. A sanitary towel had been placed on her body – something her death had in common with the other two Barrowland killings.

All this detail wasn't immediately apparent to me. After the nurse's body had been found, a command vehicle was parked on the murder scene and, from there, numerous enquiries would be handed out to mobile teams, mostly consisting of detectives from the Serious Crime Squad. The police support unit was also involved and the uniformed branch would make house-to-house enquiries in the area. Joe Jackson and I had just completed a successful investigation of another murder when we pitched up at the police command vehicle. It may come as a surprise – but I doubt it – to the reader that members of the police force are not above the rivalry and sometimes jealousy that can be found most other professions. As we made our way into the caravan, I heard the big man in the hunt, 'Elphie', remark to the collator at the scene, 'Here are Jackson and Brown. Give them the most difficult inquiry you have – it will keep them out of the way for a time.' So, with smiles all round, the collator handed me an action form on a crime at the dancing – but it was eighteen months old, long before Pat Docker died. A girl had been picked up at the dancing, just like Pat, and taken to a flat in Maryhill where she claimed she had been raped eight times.

We swiftly headed to Maryhill Police Office and studied the reports which included a description that referred to the suspect being a 'dead ringer' for the singer Frankie Vaughan but much smaller in stature. The address of the rape scene was also given and that was our next port of call. The victim had said that the flat had been opened with a key the suspect had in his possession. The building was being prepared for demolition and, on the wall next door to the flat we were interested in, the name Lurinski was written. We knew of a guy by this name and also where he was currently staying but his appearance was nothing like the description of the rapist. We called on him at his new home and he admitted that he had given the key of the Maryhill flat to a pal but refused to name him. We threatened to charge him with obstructing the police and he then promptly named the man and gave us his address. We went there and knocked on the door, which was opened by a miniature Frankie Vaughan. We carted him off to Maryhill Police Office and handed the case back to the woman detective who had been given it eighteen months before. We went straight back to the Bible John caravan and asked cheekily, 'Don't you have something a bit more difficult?' However, the Docker case was never solved.

The next victim of the so-called Bible John was Jemima McDonald who was killed in the August of the following year, 1969; not long after that, in October, she was followed by Helen Puttock. The McDonald killing led to the production of one of the first identikit wanted posters. They were created from descriptions of the suspect given by witnesses at the Barrowland. The man mostly responsible for what was thought to be a brilliant artist's impression was Lennox Patterson of the Glasgow School of Art. Few folk in the city at that time can forget the vivid portrait of a good-looking man with short well-cut hair and distinctive eyes.

I had more involvement in this third murder. Helen Puttock

had gone out dancing with her sister and at the Barrowland hall had met various men. One particular man seemed to have taken a bit of a shine to Helen and, during the evening, her sister was able to have a good look at him. At the close of play the man and the two sisters decided to share a taxi. They went to Drumchapel first, to drop Helen's sister off, and then the taxi took Helen and the man to the area of her home in Scotstoun – presumably for some serious winching in the usual darkened close.

The next person to see Helen was a man who was out for an early-morning walk with his mutt. He saw the attractive, lively brunette of the night before lying face down. The police were called and they discovered that part of her torn-off clothing had been used to strangle her. There were abrasions to her jaw and the side of her head. Her nose and mouth had been bleeding and some coins were missing from her purse. In death, she lay tragically mutilated just like Bible John's other victims, Pat Docker and Jemima McDonald.

There were some stronger leads this time. A man had been seen heading back into town on a late night bus and he matched the description of the man who had left the dance hall with the sisters. The legendary Joe Beattie was by now in charge of the case and this led to speculation in the force and in the press that a breakthrough was imminent. It never happened and, indeed, shortly before his death many years later, Joe was one of those who raised the possibility that the killings were not necessarily the work of one man – as they had been thought to be at the time – and that there may have been a copycat element. But, again, who knows?

Joe was of the opinion that Helen Puttock's sister was the key witness since she had spent time in Barrowland in the company of the man who killed her sister. I was not so sure that this was the right way to go. Instead, I thought we should be concentrating on women who may have been picked up by Bible John but not killed by him. However, Helen's sister was taken all over town and asked to be on the lookout for guys who looked like the man she shared a taxi with on the night of the murder. It didn't work.

Because of the poster and the press interest, it seemed, at times, that the whole of Glasgow was on the hunt for the killer. Occasionally, possible suspects were picked up but they were all eliminated. One of them was a man called John McInnes but Helen's sister did not pick him out at an identity parade and other witnesses who had the chance to pick him out also failed to finger him. He committed suicide in 1980 aged forty-one. The rumours about him lingered on till the late nineties and only then, after his body had been exhumed and DNA tests carried out, was it finally confirmed that he was not the infamous Bible John.

This puts some of the other 'findings' of the killer into context – including a couple of odd experiences I had myself. The Bible John case filled the minds of the police for years after the killings but life – or, in the case of the Serious Crime Squad, death – went on as usual.

Two years after the Puttock killing, a colleague and I were driving eastwards along Argyle Street when we spotted a man and a woman in heated discussion. For some reason, we decided to talk to them and we followed them into George Square. We separated them and I spoke to the woman who said she only knew her companion as John and he had just picked her up at the Barrowland. The man gave a name and address – 28 St Andrew's Street in the city centre, opposite the old police office. The woman was allowed to take the bus home. The man went to the Central with us. The address he had given us was false. Back at the office, I handcuffed him to a radiator – something he took badly. This time he gave an address in the Gorbals.

I went there, little thinking that my days at the Weirs plant in Cathcart would be brought back to me vividly. The man we had lifted stayed there with his elderly mother. She asked me right out if I thought her son was Bible John. I replied, 'That's what we're looking at.' The old woman said, 'He could be – he regularly goes to the Barrowland.' She went off to make a cup of tea and, as she did so, I had a look, as you do, at the photographs on the mantelpiece and got a shock – I recognised a man as Bob who had been an attendant in the power house at Weirs in my days there. When the mother returned I asked about Bob, her husband, and she told me he had accidentally gassed himself in the kitchen. I found it hard to believe. He had been in the Royal Navy and during his service he had been torpedoed twice so I just did not think he was the sort of man to do away with himself. Odd.

I headed back to the office and, on the way, one of those amusing incidents that could only happen in Glasgow occurred. When I reached the CID car in the street, I found a man in it. He was smelling strongly of whisky and he was trying to start the engine with a key. I opened the door and asked if there was any chance of a lift. 'Sure, mate,' he replied, saying that it wasn't, however, his car and he couldn't start it. 'Here, I'll try my key,' I said and he popped into the passenger's seat. I drove to the Central Police Office where he got the chance to sleep off his whisky!

I turned my attention back to the suspect and he asked how I had got on with his mother. I told him there had been no problem. I also said I thought he might be interested to know that I had once worked with his father. He had other things on his mind. 'Do you think I'm Bible John?' he asked. 'That's up to you,' I responded. 'No, that's up to you, Mr Brown,' was his reply. It was now 3 a.m. and I contacted Joe Beattie. Joe arrived looked him up and down and said that he 'was the nearest yet' but, according to Joe Beattie, he wasn't the serial killer.

I wonder, however, if another incident was more important. Many years later, in the nineties, I was having a chinwag with Detective Inspector Bryan McLaughlin when the subject came round to Bible John. Brian bowled me over by saying he thought he once had him in cuffs but he had escaped. Intrigued, I got him to tell me the tale.

On duty as a beat cop in the Barrowland area, Brian came upon a man urinating in the open in a nearby lane. Without warning, the man ran away and Brian gave chase. He caught up with the man in a backcourt and the man picked up a brick to strike him but Brian felled the guy with a blow from his baton. He hit him such a crack that he required medical attention and the mystery man was taken to the Royal Infirmary in handcuffs. The doctor insisted that he would not treat the man unless the cuffs were removed. Despite Brian telling him what would happen if the handcuffs were removed, they took them off anyway. And, just as Brian had predicted, the mystery man whacked the doctor and ran out the door. Brian thought that the guy would have made a good Bible John suspect. It gets stranger. I asked if he had got the man's name. He said that he had but it and the address he gave had turned out to be phoney. I asked what address he had given and I was stunned when he replied, '28 St Andrew's Street.' It still makes me wonder what if . . .

Life in the Serious Crime Squad had its own rhythm. There were three shifts each with twelve detectives and an inspector in charge. A detective superintendent was in overall charge, answering to an assistant chief constable. 'Serious' mostly meant murder to us and the rate in Strathclyde at that time was around one a week which kept us busy between the bank robberies and the like. This was the first time I ran into serious training in firearms. We could be authorised to carry them by a chief super. There was an irony in that the training was given by Inspector Andrew Hyslop who was to be shot at in Allison Street on the south side when officers tried to arrest an ex-cop, Howard Wilson, who was hiding in a house and was suspected of a bank robbery. Wilson tried to shoot his way out of trouble and two officers, Angus McKenzie and Edward Barnett, were killed before Detective Constable Ian Campbell overpowered Wilson.

On taking up duty at Temple Police Office, we knew that when on the scene of a murder we would stay there till the crime was solved. On a good shift, there would be eight detectives in the office, two on days off and two on court duty. Dividing our time like this was a bugbear as the system was far from efficient and, to my mind, too many good detectives spent too many hours tangled up in court appearances rather than nailing villains.

The work may have lived up to its description as serious but there were lighter moments. One day, we were enjoying a cuppa when the phone rang. It was a chief inspector from Ireland looking for assistance. 'How can we help?' 'Are you aware of the missing racehorse Shergar?' Who wasn't? The horse had won the Derby and was regarded as being worth ten million pounds. The belief at the time was that the horse had been stolen by the IRA and was being held for ransom. The Irishman continued down the line, 'We have information that the horse is being held in a house in Hogganfield Street, Glasgow, by a man called McDonald.' I told the inspector that we knew McDonald and that he lived two floors up on the right of a tenement – not the ideal place to hide a racehorse. However, we agreed we would visit him and it was arranged with this Irish chief inspector that we would go there at 2.a.m. precisely. We asked if the horse answered to its name and the reply was, 'Yes!'

The Irishman had more and said, 'We also have an address in a place called Stirling. Can you raid that address too?' I told him we could not do the visit as it was out of our area and told him to try Stirling CID. 'Where is Stirling?' he asked. 'Near the castle – you must have heard of that . . .' The conversation was becoming increasingly bizarre.

Having satisfied ourselves that we were not being set up, we knocked on the door at exactly 2 a.m. as planned. A Rab C Nesbitt figure in the string vest answered. 'What do you want?' he asked. 'We're CID,' we told him. 'I know that,' he said. With straight faces we said, 'We have received information that you're holding the stolen racehorse Shergar.' 'Have you a warrant?' he asked. 'You don't need a warrant for a racehorse,' we replied, again taking great effort to keep our faces straight. To add to the confusion a woman's voice was heard asking, 'Willie, who's at the door?' Willie replied, 'It's the polis looking for Shergar.' 'Do they have a warrant?' 'You don't need a warrant for a racehorse,' replied Willie.

Amazingly enough, there was no sign of the missing horse. Back in the office, I phoned Ireland to tell our Irish colleague that it looked as if he had been had. He responded by saying, 'There's no CID in Stirling Castle.' No wonder they never found that horse.

12

BLOOD ON THE CEILING AND TWO KIDS BATTERED TO DEATH – ALL FOR A TV SET

For John McMonigle, what was to be the most tragic day in his life started out with a Saturday morning outing filled with optimism. It was a bitter day in January 1976 and thirty-nine-year-old McMonigle could, at last, see some hope of an escape from the squalid surroundings of a top-floor flat in Golspie Street, Govan. He lived there with his three young children, two girls and a boy, the oldest of whom was aged twelve. It was not a pleasant place to bring up the kids – the tenement was being prepared for demolition. Most of the houses round the McMonigles were already empty and the place was a target for lead thieves and the like.

The Corporation were offering him another flat in Pollok and, on the Saturday morning of the 17th, he went to the newish housing estate by bus to look at what was on offer. In what looks like an odd decision to anyone who has not been in the circumstances in which this family lived, he only took one of the kids on the bus with him to Pollok. Young Irene and John were left in Golspie Street to 'guard' the flat and its meagre contents from the prowlers and petty thieves who saw easy pickings in the half-empty tenement buildings that were waiting for the wrecker's ball to turn them to dust and make way for new, decent accommodation for the hard-working folk of Govan.

John McMonigle did not return home till 5.30 in the evening

that day and, when he did, he found his front door ajar. He pushed it open and stumbled into a scene of bloody savagery. His two children lay dead on the floor with horrific head injuries. A hammer lay near their battered bodies. He ran from the house to a nearby phone box. Miraculously, in an area plagued by vandalism, it was working and he dialled 999. The police were swiftly on the scene and they were just as horrified by what they saw as the kids' father had been.

I was relaxing off-duty at home when the call came telling me to get to Govan Police Office immediately. Other off-duty detective squads got the same call. A briefing meeting was held early on the Sunday morning and everyone involved was detailed to go to see the murder scene for themselves. The hunt was on for a savage killer and the horror of that room in Golspie Street affected deeply every cop, from the lowliest PC to the most senior officer, who saw it. I have seen some horrific sights in my career but none was as bad as this. It was possible to count the hammer blows from the trails of blood across the ceiling of the room as the implement was drawn back for the next blow.

Before the horribly mutilated bodies of the kids were removed to the mortuary, the usual preliminaries of a major murder hunt took place. The photographers caught every angle and every detail of that hellish scene. The fingerprint guys crawled over every last inch of the place and forensic examinations were made in great detail.

A conference was called for the next morning. I spent a restless night, the images of the murder scene imprinted on my brain. At the Govan office, the mood was sombre. Most of the men involved, including myself, had children of their own and it was not possible, even for the most professional of us, to stop imaginations running wild. It all added up to a grim determination to catch the merciless killer of these innocent children. But all emotion and feelings had to be suppressed as we began to search for leads – the starting point for what was obviously a difficult investigation.

It transpired that there had been a burglary at the flat a couple of weeks before the killing. John McMonigle had discovered it when he returned home at 7.45 p.m. The door had been forced open with a kick or a shoulder charge and several items had been stolen, including a transistor radio, a gent's watch, some tools and a number of photographs. The break-in had been reported and a Detective Constable Harry Bell had handled the investigation. Flats like this one, that were waiting to be knocked down, often attracted opportunistic small-time thieves and the break-in that John had discovered was typical of this. No fingerprints were found and a limited door-to-door enquiry turned up little. The only information that might have been useful was the fact that Bell had been tipped off that the man responsible was an Alex Miller, who used to stay in the street, but he had not been traced.

Detective Sergeant Pat Connor and I were tasked to find if such a person existed and to bring him to the office. We started with the obvious things – checking with the Corporation housing office in India Street which confirmed that a family called Miller had lived in the very next close to the McMonigles but had been moved to a new address because of the impending demolition. Surprisingly they didn't have the new address to hand but said they would look it out.

Back at the office, there was another shock. We were amazed to learn that, at the time of the discovery of his children's murder, John McMonigle arrived at the public phone box to dial 999 at the same time as another man and that McMonigle had invited him to go first, which he did! The publicity surrounding the crime had prompted this man to come forward.

We then faced a sad task. The next morning, we picked John McMonigle up at the house of a relative to take him to the mortuary to formally identify the victims. I sat in the car while Pat went into the house to get him. He returned two minutes later with John McMonigle. As he climbed into the car, John bade me a pleasant good morning and, later in the drive, he chatted about what a pleasant day it was for the time of the year. It was now obvious why he had let the other man use the phone first – the horror of what happened had simply not sunk in. As I looked at him in the rear view mirror, I could have wept. The actual identification was done by the father looking at the bodies of his children on a closed circuit TV screen. Identification was required before the post-mortems could begin and they confirmed cause of death as massive damage to the children's brains and that it had been caused by the hammer found at the scene.

Driving back to the relative's house, I asked Mr McMonigle if he knew of a family called Miller who lived up the next close. He said he knew the Millers and that his daughter Irene, one of the victims, told him that she had seen Alex Miller entering and leaving the few remaining closes near their house at number 108. The early lead was developing and Pat and I visited some relatives of Miller. His brother, Leslie, told us that Alex now stayed with a woman in Auchengill Street in the Easterhouse scheme and that, as far as he knew, he was continually searching condemned properties looking for scrap and anything worth stealing.

We went to Easterhouse, found Miller and took him to Govan Police Station. I looked at him closely. Was this a man capable of brutally battering two young children to death? He was a man of low IQ who had attended a school for children with special needs. He had red hair and he fitted a description of a man seen fleeing from the murder scene. But, to begin with, we concentrated on that first housebreaking and he gave us a list of what he had stolen which matched our list. He had sold them in a local bar. So far, so good.

Miller was arrested to appear in the Sheriff Court later. He wasn't going anywhere. Pat Connor and I were sure we had locked up a killer but there was much work to be done before a judge and jury would agree with us. We traced the man who had bought the stolen goods. It was not a big-money crime – he had paid Miller £3 for the lot. Others involved in receiving stolen goods were also charged and locked up. We weren't messing around in this inquiry. This was an intense investigation conducted with a background of huge interest and concern from public and media. Some of the emotion spilled out at one of our regular briefings when the officer in charge said that, OK, Miller had been arrested for the break-in but he was not the killer. I shot to my feet and told the assorted officers, 'He did it and we will prove it.'

While we had been occupied with finding Miller, a massive door-to-door inquiry had been mounted in the Golspie Street area and there had been huge TV and newspaper interest. All this resulted in a number of reliable witnesses coming forward. Some spoke of a man with red hair and wearing a grey suit, running down Golspie Street at 4.15 p.m., the estimated time of the crime. Miller filled that bill. He claimed to have an alibi, saying he had spent the day of the murder in the flat at Easterhouse. His girlfriend claimed that, when she left at lunchtime, he was still in bed and, when she returned at 6 p.m., Miller was watching that night's episode of *Dr Who* on TV. It emerged that Miller was something of a TV addict and that *Dr Who* was one of his favourite programmes.

Miller claimed to have turned on the programme as it was finishing and could offer no explanation why he did not see the start. Our suspicion was, of course, that he only watched the end of it because he had only just got back from Govan. We ran some analysis on the bus routes and times and it was clear that he could have left Govan around 4.30 and been in Easterhouse in time for the closing scenes of *Dr Who*. This led us up the path of trying to find someone on a bus at that time who had seen Miller but there was no joy. It was a weak alibi but, as things stood, we could not tie him to the scene.

Motive is a key to detection, as real-life cops and those who watch crime on TV and read books of the true-crime variety know only too well. Where was the motive here? We went back to the bloodstained flat on several occasions before it dawned on us what the motive was. It was in the corner of the room staring us in the face – a TV set that wasn't big or impressive or new but it worked. Miller, we found out, watched TV morning, noon and night. Dragging himself from his pit, the first thing he did was switch on the telly. We went back to Miller's brother's house and, while we were there, talking to his wife, who should knock the door but a man who had come 'to repair the TV set'. The repair man gave us the intriguing information that the fault had been reported on the morning of the murder. We knew that Alex Miller had stayed with his brother on the Friday night and the Saturday morning of the killing. Alex said that he had switched on his brother's TV that morning but the set didn't work. But Alex knew where he could get one that did work – in John McMonigle's flat where he had clocked it in the break-in two weeks before. We went back to the murder flat and examined the TV set. We tilted it and could see fingerprint impressions on either side of the underneath where someone had attempted to lift it or had lifted it.

We took the set away for further examination but the prints were smudged. That was disappointing but it didn't make us alter our theory that Miller had gone to Golspie Street to steal the set but had been prevented by the two children. We then had to fall back on the old stand-by, an identity parade, but it too was disappointing. The main witness was a woman from a house overlooking the backcourts at Golspie Street. In those tenements, as in many in Glasgow, the kitchen sink was at a window and the chore of doing the dishes was made less boring by the chance to watch the comings and goings in the backcourts. Our witness had been doing just such a thing when she saw the suspect. The usual eight men matching the appearance of the suspect as closely as possible had been assembled. As our kitchen-sink witness walked the line, she stopped opposite Miller and said, 'That's quite like him but I am not sure.' No other witnesses fingered him.

After this, Miller appeared in court on the housebreaking charges and got sixty days in Low Moss Prison. It gave us some time to get on with the inquiry knowing we could get him when we wanted. At that time, I had a good relationship with the governor of Barlinnie and I also had an informant in Low Moss. The Bar-L boss helped to arrange for my man to be given access to Miller. The informant raised the subject of the Golspie Street killing several times but Miller refused to take the bait. Although my man told me, for what it was worth, that he thought Miller was the killer.

During this stage of the inquiry, something happened that restores faith in human nature. The folk in every house near the crime scene were questioned and every known criminal in the area was spoken to. Strangely, for a spell, the crime rate in Govan went down because even the criminal element in the area was so horrified by the killings that they had decided the 'polis' should have a free hand to devote all their resources to getting their man. We interviewed all criminals on weekend leave from prison. Every dry cleaner's was visited and any bloodstained clothing that had been sent for cleaning was checked out. Every school in the area was visited and all the pupils were spoken to.

Then, unexpectedly, we got a seriously good break. In another interview with Alex Miller's brother Leslie, we learned more about the TV breakdown and Alex's addiction to the wee box. Then Leslie blurted out that he and his brother had met in Easterhouse around 5.30 on the murder night and Alex had asked Leslie if he had heard about two kids being murdered in Govan. At that time, John McMonigle had not discovered the tragedy so the only way Alex Miller could have known that the children had been killed was if he had committed the double murder himself. Of course, there was one other possible explanation – that Leslie Miller was lying. Witness statements about the grey suit and the red hair could not apply to both brothers as only one of them had red hair. Nonetheless, the two of them could have been at the crime scene.

There was an unusual way to resolve this if only the Crown Office would allow it. I remembered reading in the crime pages of the papers of a case in England where the wife of a prominent newspaper management executive had been kidnapped. Suspicion fell on two Asian brothers who owned the English equivalent of a croft. This was searched without success. What the English cops did was to put hidden listening devices in a room at a police office and let the two suspects chat. In their overheard discussion, the brothers spoke of being responsible for the kidnapping and murder of their victim and the disposal of the body. The taped conversation was allowed in evidence and both were convicted.

We obtained the case papers and the guidelines that had been given as far as secretly taping the brothers' conversation was concerned. We found it was permissible so long as there was more than one suspect and that neither of the two suspects was aware that the conversation was being recorded. The Crown Office agreed to allow us to carry out a similar operation. On the day Alex Miller was released from Low Moss, Pat and I picked him up and took him to Govan Police Station. Our 'techies' in the wireless department had prepared a room to record the conversation and, in another room, headphones and tapes were at the ready. The tension was high as the brothers entered the bugged room. Firstly they discussed harmless family matters but then the talk turned to the break-in and the murders. Alex Miller was clearly heard to say, 'They know it was me. What will they do to me if I tell them?' Leslie Miller replied, 'They won't touch you – tell the truth.' Alex Miller was charged and detained.

In his last interview, Alex Miller said he had gone to the house to steal the TV. He had been disturbed at the door by Irene who said, 'I know your name and I'll tell my dad.' Young John had lifted the hammer, which had just been lying around, in a weak attempt to strike Miller. Miller wrestled the hammer from him and, in a fury, battered the two youngsters to their bloody deaths. Miller then ran from the house and took the bus to Easterhouse where he briefly met his brother. When he got to his girlfriend's house, he switched on the TV to see the end of *Dr Who*.

The legendary and highly respected defence lawyer Laurence Dowdall was contacted. He spoke with the client and listened to the police case. He listened to the tape of the conversation and when it was over he turned to us and said, 'Gentlemen, this will not be going to trial.' And so, on 13 May 1976, Alex Miller pled guilty to two charges of murder. He was sent to that grim, high-fenced and floodlit place that is the Carstairs State Hospital for the criminally insane, there to be detained without limit of time.

Things soon got back to normal in Govan. The crime rate rose again and the odd cop was even assaulted. Despite it all, there was a general feeling of relief that the place was back to its old ways. The nightmare effect of the horrific killing of two young kids was beginning to weaken now that the savage who caused the heartbreak to family and community was safely behind that high wire fence.

During my career in the police, I was involved in the investigation of 200 murders but none affected me like this case. The image of these two young kids, dead on the floor, in their blood-splattered home will stay with me for the rest of my life. All for a TV set. All so pointless.

13

INDIAN WARS IN CASTLEMILK
AND A UNIT SO SPECIAL
THEY CLOSED IT DOWN

In the early seventies, successful policing had resulted in unprecedented numbers of many of the hardest villains in the country being locked up in various prisons throughout the land. The cells were bulging but the hardest of the hard tended to end up in the bleak fortress that is Peterhead, up on the north-east coast, miles from where most of them had committed their crimes. There they were creating havoc – there were dirty protests with excrement smeared on cell walls, break-outs on to the prison roof, mattresses set ablaze, staff taken hostage and, worst of all, violent dangerous attacks on the prison officers.

In an earlier era, many of the prisoners who were involved in this catalogue of outrages would not have been sent to jail at all – they would have found themselves at the end of a rope. But now they were in prison facing years of captivity ahead of them with no hope of freedom and they were confronted by a regime that treated them like animals. With nothing to lose no matter what they did, it is no wonder that there was a group of Peterhead's inmates who became some of the most difficult men the prison system had to deal with – it is no wonder they thought nothing of trying to strangle, stab or beat up their captors.

The papers were saying, 'Something has to be done' and they were right. But what? How could it be possible to end the prison violence that was making headlines in the tabloids week in and week out? The germ of an idea that grew into one of the most controversial experiments in penal reform came from crime psychologists. They recognised that problems occurred amongst long-term prisoners who had no hope of redemption in a society which was taking its revenge for the evil things they had done.

Their solution was the Barlinnie Special Unit where carefully selected hard men were gathered together in a regime that was to be totally different from that of a mainstream prison. There were televisions in cells that had carpets and wall coverings. Classes in art were on offer and the evil men who found themselves there were given encouragement and instruction to bring out talents for writing, painting or sculpture.

It was an idea that sent many on the outside, reading about this 'luxury' life at the taxpayers' expense, into red-faced rages and had them writing letters to the press by the hundred. Even some religious figures were against the whole concept – the notion that even the worst can reform was too much for them to take. And opposition to the Unit increased as stories of visitors having sex with inmates and lurid tales of drugs and booze orgies leaked out.

Eventually, it was closed down in a welter of controversy. But, for some, it had worked. It reformed men such as Hugh Collins and Jimmy Boyle and speeded up their freedom, proving that even the most evil people behind bars can change and opt for a productive life. When the Unit was closed many of the pioneering ideas it had tested emigrated to mainstream penal institutions – all for the good of the prison service.

Collins and Boyle both wrote books on their experiences and both stayed out of further trouble when they were freed. Collins, in particular, was up front with his regret at taking the life of a fellow human being and his story and his writings can only have helped steer some tearaways from following the example of his early years.

When I was active on the beat in the Gorbals, Boyle was, as

they say, a name on the streets, a man to be feared. Although our paths never crossed in those days, I can say that I did once arrest him – and he was in the Special Unit at the time! It came about like this.

The rulebook had it that, as a Category A prisoner, Boyle required an armed escort if he was ever out of jail for whatever reason. It seemed that he required minor surgery to a knee and a colleague and I were instructed to go to the Unit to accompany him and his prison escort to the Royal Infirmary where he would be on the sharp end of a scalpel – this time it would be to improve his health, unlike some of his own activities with a knife. When we arrived and Boyle realised an armed detail was there, he threw a spectacular tantrum – he was not prepared to be hospitalised unless we were sent away. My response was to say, 'That's OK. We have better things to do but he is not leaving this prison without an armed escort.' And this led to more tantrums.

Of course, we got our way and, a short time later, a car drove through the prison gates followed by us. The prison car stopped at the entrance to the Royal and Boyle jumped out to cross the street to talk to a woman he had recognised. That was as far as he got. We immediately arrested him and marched him into the Infirmary. The officer in charge of the prison escort accused us of overreacting – he and I obviously had different views about convicted murderers wandering around the streets chatting to passers-by.

Boyle was still a difficult customer. He wanted a bed near the door of the ward but we arranged for him to go to the far end instead. It was a bit of a security nightmare, with visitors turning up in a stream, but we took it in turn to sit and guard him. We were armed and he was handcuffed to the bed. After treatment, he was returned to the Special Unit.

The Unit, as you might expect, considering its easy-going ethos, made an official complaint about our handling of the whole business to the Chief Constable. Our first interview, with the assistant chief constable (crime), soon cleared up what had happened. The Unit was always being accused of pandering to its inmates and there were even tales of Boyle going to parties outside the prison in the company of warders. Even a television he had in his cell caused some embarrassment when we discovered it had been stolen from a Dixon's store in the city centre. The Barlinnie governor, Bob Hendry, got us its serial number to check it out but, while this was being done, the set was smashed to pieces in the Unit. So any fears about that story getting out and the furore it would have caused in yet another media storm were allayed as the set no longer existed!

My contacts with Bob Hendry, the Bar-L boss at the time, proved useful on another occasion. A prisoner there called John McDuff was the main suspect for a killing in the Coventry area and a detective chief superintendent from the English Murder Squad wanted to come north to interview him. It resulted in one of those amusing little legal contretemps that happen from time to time in the force. I went with my boss, a detective chief superintendent, to meet the English cop at Glasgow airport. Driving to the prison, I became aware for the first time that the Englishman wanted to talk to McDuff as a 'suspect'. I announced to my boss and our passenger that, under the Prison Scotland Act, he would not be allowed to question him as a suspect. 'What a load of crap,' said my boss. 'Just drive the car.'

We went into the governor's office and Mr Hendry greeted me as an old friend. The detective from the south said, 'I would like to interview a prisoner – John McDuff – who is the main suspect in a murder I'm investigating.' I took a deep breath as I knew what was coming. 'Not in this prison, you're not,' said the governor. 'Under the Prison Scotland Act it is not permissible. You can interview him as a witness or you can parade him as a suspect, and you can also charge him, but that is all.' He then proceeded to offer us a coffee and I have seldom had one that I enjoyed more.

After this, there was a pregnant silence. I broke it with the suggestion that McDuff, who had relatives in England, could be moved to a jail there. It would be easier for his relatives to visit him there and the detective could interview him under English Law. That is what happened and, in the end, McDuff was eliminated from the inquiry.

Around this time, I met a man who was to stamp his name on the history of Strathclyde Police as a popular and successful chief constable. When we first met, he was a detective sergeant. Assistant Chief Constable (Crime) Willie Cant called me into his office to tell me that John Orr would join us on the night shift starting next Monday. The big boss said to keep and eye on him and not to let him get into any trouble. With my reputation for getting into controversial scrapes, I thought of saying, 'Why are you putting him on with me?' but I let the idea go. The Monday came and, at 10.30 p.m., John presented himself at the Temple Police Station. I was impressed from the start and the more I saw of him the more impressed I was.

John and I were to find ourselves in scrapes right from the start on that very first night. We went out in a mini, an ideal vehicle for mingling with traffic and not attracting attention. We were tootling along Great Western Road in the vicinity of Park Road when I suddenly wheeled into a garage forecourt and switched off the lights. John knew I had seen something and I indicated a girl about 400 yards away who was swinging her handbag from side to side. 'She's going to be mugged,' I predicted and, sure enough, when she was within a couple of hundred yards of us, a man jumped out of a close, snatched the bag and ran in our direction. He turned into Lansdowne Crescent (you could in those days) closely followed by the victim. I followed and shouted to the girl, who was in the middle of the road, to get out of the way and hit the villain a glancing blow with the car, knocking him to the ground.

John Orr was out of the car in a flash and jumped on top of

the bag-snatcher who was shouting 'Help!' at the top of his voice. A number of youths walking nearby rushed to the bag-snatcher's aid – much to the consternation of John who told them I was a detective inspector. We were, of course, in plain clothes and they were not impressed but wisely decided not to take part in the struggle. Maybe the bag-snatcher was getting the worst of it. The victim had by now caught up with us and said she would go back to Great Western Road to see if she could find a policeman! We just took our man to Maryhill Police Office where we learned that there had been a number of similar attacks. The guy eventually got eighteen months on six charges of robbery and assault. That was John Orr's introduction to the Serious Crime Squad. It certainly didn't do him any harm as he proceeded to the top job in the force – and a well-deserved knighthood.

If John Orr had a nickname at that time, I didn't know it but a suggestion that he did emerged much later at the famous Albany drugs trial which I deal with in detail later in this book. At the trial, he was said to be known to some by the soubriquet 'Punk Rocker' but where that came from or, indeed, if the suggestion is true beats me. But nicknames were certainly common in the force and sometimes the source of a good laugh.

An example of this was the tale of what you might call the Indian Wars in Castlemilk – well, the place was full of cowboys, that's for sure! Shortly before the start of one night shift, the guys in the CID were told that one of our bosses had discovered that he had acquired the nickname Crazy Horse. He was not amused by this and let it be known that anyone caught using the nickname would swiftly find himself back in the uniformed branch – not a pleasant thought and, in fact, it was the ultimate sanction. But we didn't scare easily and, as most of us did have nicknames, it was really no big deal.

That very night we were involved in a major operation which involved sealing off the giant south-side scheme of Castlemilk and making the whole area impossible to access in a car or lorry.

All roads into the scheme had roadblocks in the form of a CID car and one from the uniform branch. Any vehicle moving around the area between 2 a.m. and 5 a.m. would be stopped and searched. I was in charge of this operation and it was to be controlled by radio from HQ. I got a visit from the assistant chief constable (crime) at around two o'clock and he was accompanied by no less than the detective nicknamed Crazy Horse. I explained that everyone was in position and soon anything that moved would be checked. The senior detective with the assistant chief asked if Detective Inspector R L S McKinstry was involved in the operation and, on being told that he was, he asked to speak to him. The big boss picked up the mike and asked how he could get hold of McKinstry. I told him that we were using a system of code names and all the units were named after Red Indians. On hearing this, the assistant chief left in a hurry, having difficulty keeping his face straight. I consulted my checklist and the subject of our little humorous ploy was advised that McKinstry would answer to Geronimo. 'So, he said, 'I just call Geronimo?' I was asked. 'That's all,' I said, 'except that you have to give our call sign – Crazy Horse.' So out it went over the airways 'Crazy Horse calling Geronimo – are you receiving me?' No response. We suggested he tried again. He did and, this time, he got an answer that was not entirely unexpected – it consisted of two words the second of which was 'off'.

I was never brought to task for the use of the nickname – perhaps it wasn't noticed or perhaps creating too much of a fuss would embarrass Crazy Horse. In any case, the operation was a great success with several arrests, mainly for traffic offences. I was asked later on what legal grounds we had the authority to stop and search vehicles. I was of the opinion that uniformed officers were checking the tyres of the cars. 'How does that allow you to search the boot?' 'Where do you keep the spare tyre?' was the easy answer.

We were not completely finished with nicknames however.

Around the same time, two young men, armed with shotguns, entered a Clydesdale Bank in Clarkston Road in the prosperous south side, threatened the staff and disappeared from the bank with ten grand, a huge sum in those days. A third man was the getaway driver. CCTV cameras in the bank got good pics of the robbers but, after a week, the local CID were no further forward.

We had just completed a murder inquiry and were available to help hunt down the two robbers. As occasionally happens, the big lead came from an anonymous tip-off. A man called to say that one of the youngsters we were looking for was called 'Peachy Doc' – that nickname thing again. The call was traced to Roystonhill many miles away from the scene of the crime. We spoke to everyone in crime or on the fringes that we knew in the area without success. We pounded the streets examining every close mouth for the name 'Peachy Doc' in the graffiti that disfigured almost every building. Again no joy.

We were talking about it over a bite in the canteen one day when someone pointed out that 'Doc' was a common Glasgow abbreviation for Docherty. Many with such a name were Catholics and maybe the youngster we were looking for went to the well-known Catholic school in the area, St Roch's. The headmaster suggested a word with the gym teacher who knew most of the older boys. We showed him the photos from the bank camera. He took one look and exclaimed, 'Christ, it's Peachy Doc.'

Detective Inspector McKinstry (Geronimo!) arrested both robbers in their homes and two shotguns and two thirds of the money was recovered. But the incident was not over yet. The driver of the getaway car was an older guy and we discovered that the car was a rented one and then we found out when it was due to be returned to the car hire company. At the given time, we surrounded the area with men, some armed, and, after a two-hour wait, the suspect drove into the yard. As he got out, he was seen to be carrying a plastic bag with what looked like a shotgun in it. As we approached and jumped on top of him, he drew the gun, pulled the trigger and blew holes in the side of a passing bus. All three got hefty sentences.

As I have remarked before, a good contacts book of informants is important to a cop. And one source of good tips-offs is prostitutes. A drunk criminal with his trousers at his ankles can be remarkably indiscreet. One particular street girl had been of great help to us over the years and we were saddened to hear that she was seriously ill in Stobhill Hospital. To make matters worse, her man was in Peterhead at the time.

So Woman Detective Constable Janet Grant and I took up a wee collection from colleagues and decided it was only right to visit her with a bunch of flowers. We took our place in a big queue at a florist's at Anniesland Cross. When it came our turn to be served, the florist kindly asked, 'What can we get you? Is it for your wife or your mother? Who is it for?' The look on her face was a picture when I told her the blooms were for a prostitute. At Stobhill Hospital, we had to do a little detective work. Like many in her profession, our friend had many aliases and we had to find out which one she was registered under. When we found her, she broke into tears on being given the flowers. The ward sister was a little nosey. She remarked that we were in the CID and asked what the patient's husband did – no doubt having noticed he never visited. We told her he was on an oilrig but her nose was still itchy and she persisted. 'Why are you giving her flowers?' she asked. A bit fed up with the cross-examination by this time, I told the sister that the woman's house had been broken into and we had a new policy of giving flowers to victims of break-ins.

Back at the office, they were not amused and I was told a nurse at the hospital had complained that her house had been broken into but no flowers had been forthcoming for her. And the flower shop owner got her own back as well. A few weeks later, Janet was off sick and, after another whip-round, I was back in the florist's. She took one look at me and announced,

'More flowers for the prostitute?' This time it was my face that was the picture!

14

Smith & Wessons in the Albany Foyer and Drugs in Rooms 805 and 909

All careers have a defining juncture, something that transcends all that has gone before and that can cast a long shadow on what comes after. For me, it was the famous Albany Hotel drug trial in 1977. This complex, tortuous case had more twists and turns than a Hitchcock movie. In it, the Strathclyde CID and two members of the Strathclyde Drug Squad were pitched against each other. Drug dealers, out-of town-couriers, shady characters much known about town and the biggest legal names of the day were all involved with a drugs raid in a luxurious hotel in the city centre. No wonder it dominated the headlines in the papers for weeks. It was, some say, the most controversial episode in the history of the force. I was at the centre of it – and I came out of it vindicated by the judge and jury, by my peers in the force *and* by the events that unfolded after the drama of the trial was long over. It was a period in my service that I will never forget – there were many worrying moments and many sleepless nights. For me, this was quite simply the mother of all trials!

The saga finally ended with a mysterious gangland death in a dusty ravine in Pennsylvania but it had all started back in Glasgow many years before that bloody deed was discovered and it is wise to start this labyrinthine tale at the beginning and to remember that seemingly innocuous happenings, as the drama unfolded, would come to take centre stage at the eventual trial of David McHugh and Terence Frank Goodship.

The reader will recall that, in my Flying Squad days, I was involved in a case of a David Cussins and some 300 stolen car radios. Cussins was arrested for being involved in the theft but was found not guilty. However, I came in contact with him again when, some time later, we were hunting down a sex attacker in the Charing Cross area. Cussins lived locally and helped the Flying Squad by pointing out the house of a suspect – although he was subsequently eliminated from the inquiry.

In the following years, our paths crossed from time to time and I found it easy to talk to this relatively minor figure in the Glasgow underworld. I say relatively minor but he was a man who often knew just what was going on in his patch. To illustrate the sort of relationship we had, I will tell of a day at the races. I was on the course at Ayr, looking for a fugitive we suspected would be there, and Cussins was at the pleasant track down the coast to lose some money on nags that failed to live up to his expectations.

When we met that sunny day, he had the cheek to tell me he had done his cash in and ask for a lift home in a squad car. He had no chance of that but I did give him a fiver for the fare home. He repaid me a couple of days later by offering me tickets he had acquired for a World Cup football match in Germany between Scotland and Brazil. I was always wary of him, though, and careful about my relationship with him. So, when he offered me those tickets, it was not hard to say, 'No thanks.'

Cussins had by this time taken over a shop in Great Western Road. He and his family lived in the top end of Sauchiehall Street and, since his ear was usually attuned to what was happening on the streets of the town, I visited him and his family from time to time – but I never went without another member of the squad with me. When we were on night shift and there wasn't much doing we would pop into his shop, even as late as midnight.

The shop was in student territory and it was the sort of place that became busier as the night went on. It was a standing joke with the squad that, whenever we visited the shop, we would have a good look at the stock. One night, we thought he was overstocked with tins of instant coffee so we took one away and had enquiries made by the day shift to see if a consignment of coffee had been stolen. That was the kind of relationship we had.

It is vital to spell this out because, later, our relationship would be the subject of controversy. Cussins knew clearly that, no matter what, if he broke the law and we got to know about it, we would take action against him. It is also important to spell out that, despite what happened later, Cussins was not what could properly be described as a police informer, in the accepted definition of the term. We thought of him more as a likeable rogue who occasionally let slip something that could be a hint in police matters.

But the plot was beginning to thicken. In September 1976, I was on an inspectors' course in Ayr when Cussins phoned me seeking advice. We agreed he should come to Ayr for a chat and, the next day, he told me he was suspected of stealing a large sum of money from a flat in Roystonhill. The owner of the flat, one Thomas Paramasivan, knew where Cussins stayed and was well able to mount an attack on him or his family – and was likely to do so. He said that the theft of the money was being investigated by the Northern Division CID. I told Cussins I was returning to Glasgow the next day and would make some enquiries and speak to the officer investigating the case with a view to having a word with Paramasivan, who I knew, to let him know we were aware of the threats to Cussins. He seemed pleased and we agreed to meet the following day in a pub near his home.

The following morning I phoned Caroline Farmer, the officer in charge of the case, and received some surprising news. She told me that Cussins had attacked Paramasivan with a shotgun and she was looking for him on several serious charges. I told her of my arrangement to meet Cussins and told her of the agreed time and place. She went along with the suggestion that members of my squad and I should arrest Cussins and bring him in to her office. Joe Jackson, Brian Laird and I went to the pub as arranged but he was nowhere to be seen so we went to his house.

I told the guys I would knock at the door and, if Cussins was in, I would signal for them to join me. However, although Mrs Cussins was there, her husband was not at home. Mrs Cussins said she would contact David on his 'Air Call' bleeper, a system of keeping in touch that was popular before everyone and his dog had a mobile phone. She made the call, gave a three-digit code number and said that he should phone home as someone wanted to speak to him. I didn't know it at the time but Cussins had a recently introduced, more sophisticated type of bleeper that could receive verbal messages. He would get the 'someone wants to speak to you' message verbally with no need to contact anyone at Air Call. No sooner had the message gone out than I heard the noise of a bleeper going off nearby and this was followed, almost immediately, by the sound of a key in the door and in walked David Cussins accompanied by Joe and Brian.

I was furious with Cussins, who had broken our arrangement to meet at the pub, and he was immediately arrested for the attack on Paramasivan. The house was thoroughly searched and Cussins was taken to the Northern. As far as David Cussins was concerned, I thought, 'Hell mend him.' I went back to Ayr to complete my course.

On 5 October, I got a call from Mrs Cussins telling me that David wanted to speak to me in Barlinnie. What was said remains controversial to this day. I checked with Ms Farmer who had no objections to me talking to him. At no time in this meeting in the jail did Cussins ask me to get him out on bail and at no time did I mention bail to Ms Farmer or to the Procurator Fiscal dealing with the case. But, despite there being no favours on offer from the police, this is what Cussins told me that day in the Bar-L.

According to him, the man behind most of the drugs coming into Glasgow was an Asian called Khan who lived in Pollokshields. I was told he had an associate called Ahmed who lived in Mount Florida, also on the south side. Another name was mentioned to me – that of Francis Wray from Govan. I wrote all three names in my notebook although, at the time, they meant nothing to me. Apparently, the drugs were coming into the country in specially adapted cars.

The day after this most significant meeting, I called into the Drug Squad's office after first going to the Scottish Criminal Records Office where I obtained a photograph of a man called Khan. I met with two extremely well-known cops: Jack Beattie, head of the Drug Squad, a former night fighter pilot and, according to his newspaper friends, the greatest master of disguise since Sherlock Holmes; and his right-hand man, Detective Sergeant John Brown.

We had a cup of tea and looked at the photograph. Beattie informed me, 'You have the right name and address but the wrong photograph.' Brown chipped in to say, 'We know about Ali Khan and the drugs but you will have to go some to catch him.' At this point, I told them where the info had come from and the temperature in the room dropped – this was clearly not what they wanted to hear. I was in the dark to the fact that Cussins had complained to the police that officers in the Drug Squad were giving students – many of whom he knew because of his shop – drugs provided the cops were given the names of the recipients. The complaint had been investigated and found to be false. Knowing the Drug Squad better than most, I would agree with that finding. But although Jack Beattie and John Brown had been investigated and cleared, they were aware that the source of the complaint had been Cussins. No wonder they responded the way they did to my info – to them anything coming from Cussins was to be treated with suspicion and, in the circumstances, who could blame them?

However, it is worth pointing out that, in January 1980, at Bristol Crown Court, nine men were convicted of illegally importing drugs into the UK in specially converted vehicles. Three were from Glasgow – Ali Ahmed Khan, Bashir Ahmed and Francis Wray – and they were all jailed.

On 27 October 1976, Cussins was released on bail and during the first week of November Brian Laird and I visited his shop and found him sitting upstairs in a small office, ill at ease and obviously with something worrying him. We asked what was wrong and, after some persuasion, he told us he had become involved with 'a right heavy mob'. This transpired to be an invitation from a Glasgow 'businessman' to go to London and negotiate a deal for drugs. Asked the name of the businessman, he initially refused to say but I said, 'Tell me it all or tell me none of it!' and, after that, he said Eddie Topalion was the person involved.

A man well known in the city, Topalion owned the Ad Lib restaurant in Hope Street. Cussins said he was due to go south the very next day. He had known of the trip for about two weeks but had told no one about it. He asked me to go to London with him but, of course, I refused. I suggested he himself should refuse to go but he was told that, if he didn't go, they would just get someone else to do it. I didn't believe this and suspected he had made similar trips in the past. However, we agreed that he would go to London and contact me on his return.

On Friday, 5 November, Detective Sergeant John Corrie, then in the Criminal Intelligence Unit, received information that three men were coming to Glasgow on the Sunday and that they would be in possession of a 'prize'. They had apparently been in Glasgow before and had stayed at the Albany, one of the top places in town. Despite the classy nature of the hotel, they had complained that, for some reason, the room they had been given did not suit their needs. One of them was called Matt.

Around lunchtime on the same day, I received a call from

Cussins saying he would take the 6 p.m. flight from London and asking if we would pick him up at Glasgow Airport. Brian Laird and I drove out to the airport, arriving just before seven, and we heard a call on the public address asking for me. It was Detective Constable Janet Grant at Temple. Cussins had phoned to say he had missed the flight and would arrive one hour later. Sure enough, when the eighty or so passengers appeared down the stairs from arrivals, Cussins was among them.

Later, when the whole saga came to trial, I was asked in court how I knew he had just come from London. The suggestion was that he could have arrived in Glasgow one hour earlier and got up to anything during that time before meeting us. It was true that we only had his word for it that he had missed the earlier flight but I didn't doubt him.

Once inside the CID car, Cussins handed me an envelope which I opened and found that it contained what appeared to be a small slab of cannabis. It was about half the size of a matchbox and gave off an extremely pungent aroma. Cussins opened up about his London trip and the anxiety he had shown before he left seemed to have been well merited. The 'heavy team' he had talked of met him in a pub. Some were wearing shoulder holsters with the weapons on view. Two extremely well-dressed guys sat in a corner. Cussins remarked that they looked like cops and was reassured not to worry – 'they're on our side.' Not so far fetched considering some of the stories of what went on in the Met at that time.

We dropped Cussins at his home and drove to Police HQ where a police scientist, Campbell Stewart, confirmed that the substance in the envelope was cannabis – probably Moroccan gold, the top-of-the-range stuff. We left the HQ and made our way to the home of Detective Chief Superintendent James Binnie, head of the CID, who was aware what was happening as I had briefed him earlier. We showed him the cannabis and he jokingly said, 'It would just about fill my pipe.' I told him my intention was to give the cannabis back to Cussins as he might be required to show the quality to Topalion or anyone else for that matter. I asked for permission for our squad to be armed – such authorisation was required from someone above the rank of chief inspector – and it was given.

The cannabis was returned to Cussins at his house and he was told we would expect it back. He was unable to confirm exactly when the men from London would bring the drugs to Glasgow but thought it would probably be the Sunday. On Saturday, 6 November, Brian and I made another call at Cussins' house to discuss strategy should the couriers arrive the next day. We were inside the house when the phone rang at 12.40 p.m. and Cussins remarked, 'This could be them.' There was an extension to the main phone and I told Cussins to pick up the phone on the count of three and, simultaneously, I would pick up the extension. An English voice said, 'Hello, Dave, it's Matt. I've been in touch with our friend and it's OK. We'll be coming through on Sunday about 5.30.'

On a piece of paper I wrote, 'Are you going to stay at the Albany?' – a question I wanted Cussins to ask this Matt. I gave the note to Cussins who asked the question and he was told, 'I don't know – I'll let you know when I come through. Have you got the money?' David replied, 'The money is OK.' and Matt ended the conversation, saying, 'See you tomorrow.' On the money front, Cussins told us the London team had wanted £7,000 but he had knocked them down to £6,000 We asked Cussins about the cash and he said he hadn't collected it because he knew the drugs weren't reaching their ultimate destination. He didn't want Topalion involved. This made me worry about what would happen if the London team changed the plans and asked Cussins to meet them somewhere else and bring the money. We decided to stay with Cussins all day on the Sunday and, when the London team arrived – wherever that happened to be – we would pounce before they could change their plans. We were vulnerable and I knew it. Before we left Cussins' house, I reclaimed the cannabis sample and lodged it in a safe at the Temple Police Office.

On the Saturday night I went to the Albany and, with the assistance of the security officer, who I knew, ex-Chief Inspector Donald McCulloch, had a good look at the guest register looking for a Londoner who had been there two weeks ago. I asked if the manager was available, only to be told he had just gone on two weeks' holiday. But, at that point, in walked the manager. He had come back to the hotel to pick up something he had forgotten. He said he remembered the incident when a Londoner had demanded a room change. He could not remember the name but told me the guest had been transferred to room 1003. We soon discovered that a Mathew Peters of 121 Agdon Street, London EC1 had signed in. I phoned the Met who told me there was such a street but the numbers did not go as high as 121. So we knew we had a man called Matt with a phoney address.

After the visit to the Albany, it was back to the office at Temple where I called a meeting to plan the operation next day – particularly what would happen at the hotel – and everyone involved attended. The Drug Squad were invited and John Brown did come along, but his boss Jack Beattie was obviously unwilling to attend and, considering his problems with Cussins in the past, I could understand his position. However, it is worth pointing out that, if there had been a serious murder inquiry that weekend, the whole business would have been handed over to the Drug Squad whether they liked it or not. A knife in some drunk's back on the Friday night could have changed the history of Strathclyde Police!

John Brown, the Drug Squad representative, made no comment on the fact that I, from the CID, would be the one to 'write up the case'. He knew that I did this from time to time depending on the demands faced by the team. If we had arrested anyone during the night, I would prepare the case on tape for the typist next morning. This assisted the day-shift officer and I would leave a note saying the case was on tape and in the typists' room. The day-shift man would then get on with other matters till around 10 a.m. when the typist would hand him the papers. He would read through them and then set off for the Sheriff Court to report the case to the fiscal. Not many of the detectives did this while on night duty but it was well known that I did.

Next morning, we moved to the Albany and I checked that there was no sign of 'Matt' so far. Janet Grant was to take up a position behind the reception desk and Detective Inspector Jim Long would be in charge of the officers inside the foyer – one of whom was John Orr, later to become Sir John and the chief constable. Detective Constable Laurence Wilson, Detective Constable Donald Maule and Detective Constable Kerr Nelson occupied a vacant room on the eighth floor. These officers carried .38 Smith and Wesson revolvers in shoulder holsters. Detective Sergeant Joe Jackson and Detective Constables Brian Laird and Joe Wood were patrolling the city centre in a squad car in constant radio contact and ready to go where required. Detective Constable Graeme Pearson and I were to spend the day with David Cussins so that, if contact was made by Matt, we would be in a position to take the appropriate action. At 3 p.m., the three of us went into Heron House, the Post Office telephone exchange building, opposite the Albany. The other teams also took up position at this time.

Inside Heron House, a few typists doing a bit of Sunday overtime were intrigued with what was going on and fed us tea and biscuits. We said we were expecting trouble at the hotel and, when they left for the day, they asked us to be sure to let them know what had happened. At that point, we didn't know ourselves that the Albany raid would eventually fill television and newspapers for the three weeks while a major drugs trial went on, with various factions in the police giving evidence. At about six o'clock, I phoned across to Janet and suggested everyone got a bite to eat as it could be a long night. She laughed and said this was already in hand for the folk on duty in the hotel. I suggested that great Glasgow standby to Cussins, the ubiquitous fish supper. He declined, saying he had to be careful what he ate because of a dodgy stomach, and asked permission to phone his wife. He did so and then turned and said, 'That's our tea organised.' His wife had been instructed to put on three steaks. I told Janet where we were going – Cussins' house was less than five minutes away from the hotel – and told her to keep me informed of what was happening.

I was just polishing off my steak when the phone rang to say the suspects had arrived. I told Janet to tell Jim Long to do what he had to do and not wait for us. We left Cussins at home and arrived at the Albany three minutes after the call. Janet told us that two men had booked in – one had taken room 805 and one had room 809. Graeme and I went up to the eighth floor and entered room 805 where we were met by Jim Long, some of the other cops in the raid and a stranger. Jim showed me a black case which I examined and found it contained twenty-nine slabs of what was obviously cannabis – the smell was very noticeable. Jim said that the man beside him was Dennis Bryan from London. We moved to room 809 and it was a similar scene – some of the cops, Joe Jackson and a stranger. Joe introduced this stranger as Mathew Peters from London. He then handed me a hotel notepad with five telephone numbers:

041.12487.102
221.8991
334.4532
204.2303
204.3103

I was also handed a parking ticket number Kk417232 dated 7/11/76 which Peters said referred to a Rover (YOY 892) parked at Euston Station, London.

The next step was a call to the Drug Squad and a short time later Detective Constables Riddoch and McKinnon appeared and, after being given the suspect slabs to inspect, they confirmed that it was cannabis. I asked them to take the substance to the HQ for examination by scientists.

Downstairs, Janet had interviewed the receptionists and seized the cards filled in by the suspects who were then taken to Temple Police Station. Interrogated individually, their names and addresses emerged as Mathew Patrick McHugh, aged thirty-four, of 63 Patrick Common House, St Johns Street, London and Terence Frank Goodship, aged thirty-seven, 78 Eastcotes Road, Welling, London. They declined to give any information that would help trace the origin of the drugs. They were then taken to the Central where they were cautioned and charged – with the charge sheet reading, 'That you did, on 7/11/76, at the Albany Hotel, Bothwell Street, Glasgow, have in your possession a large quantity of cannabis, a controlled drug, with intent to unlawfully supply it to another, contrary to Section 5 (3) of the Misuse of Drugs Act 1971.'

The two men were searched by the station bar staff and detained. The following morning, I prepared the case for the Sheriff Court. The front sheet contained the names of the accused, the charge and their personal details. Page two contained a list of productions, including the cannabis, and the total value. Pages three, four and five contained a summary of the events that led up to the arrest. Page six was a list of witnesses and, finally, there was a 'back sheet' which gave details of the accused and my details as officer in charge of the case. At this stage, I did not mention the part played by Cussins. Despite this omission, the facts, as supplied to the fiscal, were accurate in every detail. McHugh and Goodship were remanded in custody for further inquiry and this gave me seven more days to prepare the case fully for the fiscal. This would allow him to decide if bail could be granted. If not, the Crown would have 110 days to complete the case and that included the trial. A lot of work lay ahead but I didn't foresee any problems. That was the biggest mistake of my career!

The telephone numbers found in possession of the accused were checked and we discovered the following:

041.12487.102 – no such number, obviously a real number
     disguised
221. 8991 – Topalion's Ad Lib restaurant in Hope Street
334.5432 – home number of David Cussins
204.2302 – Air Call
204.3103 – number vacant at that time

The Ad Lib and Cussins house had been searched at the time of the arrests but nothing was found. We knew Cussins was in with a heavy mob, as he had told us, and the news that his house had been searched might help take the heat off him in the aftermath of the arrests. After the prisoners had been through the court, I spoke to McHugh. When I asked about the telephone numbers, he told me that the owner of the Ad Lib used to work beside him in the comedian 'Cheerful' Charlie Chester's club in London. He said Cussins' number – 334.5432 – belonged to a casual acquaintance he knew only as Dave or David. He again declined to help trace the origin and said he was instructed to take the drugs to Glasgow where he would be contacted. The Flying Squad in London had checked the address given and told us that McHugh's father, who stayed there, said his son had moved out. The address given by Goodship was also checked out and found to be the home of a woman whose husband was doing time and the police had the feeling that Goodship was staying there unbeknown to the jailed husband.

The next few days were taken up with getting statements and doing further paperwork on the case. For his part, David Cussins was quite happy with the way the case had been handled and, indeed, he was appreciative of the fact that his house had been searched, knowing that it would help his position with the London mobsters. At this time, I told Cussins that I would have a word with the fiscal who was involved in his Paramasivan case. Despite what was alleged at the subsequent trial in the High Court, at no time was Cussins given or offered money. I can count on the fingers of one hand when I have paid an informant for information. This was not one of them.

On 8 November, I attended the Sheriff Court and was interviewed by Procurator Fiscal Depute Kowalski in connection with the Paramasivan case. I told him that Cussins had assisted the police in the Albany drugs case but he made no comment on this. I was then astonished to learn for the first time that the two other men alleged to be involved with Cussins in the assault on Paramasivan were still in custody. They had played a minor role yet they were in and Cussins was out. The fiscal told me that Cussins had been given bail because he had a fixed address and a business to run.

As all this was happening, I was, of course, involved in day-to-day serious crime investigations and the next episode of the Albany case came on 7 December when I was again interviewed, this time by Procurator Fiscal Depute Murray. Again, it was a question-and-answer session. I did not refer to Cussins' role and just repeated what I had said in my first statement. A few days later, I received a citation for the High Court to attend as a witness in the assault case against Cussins. This trial was to be on 11 January 77 and, on the 7th, I met Cussins outside his house in a car. I suggested he should plead not guilty as there were mitigating circumstances. I noticed his hair had been cut very short and didn't guess why. He said, 'Les, there is no way I can do time.'

On the day of the trial, I spoke with the prosecuting advocate depute, Hugh Morton. We knew each other well and he was one of the most capable prosecutors on the circuit and a very genuine person. I told him of Cussins' participation in the Albany affair and that, in my opinion, he had prevented or at least delayed the setting up of a major drug ring in Glasgow. Mr Morton suggested I advise Cussins to plead guilty to the major part of the indictment and my comments would be considered. I was pleased with this response.

I didn't stay pleased too long. Minutes ticked by and there was no sign of David Cussins. The Crown asked me if I knew why he hadn't appeared. I had no idea but I would make enquiries. His wife confirmed my worst fears. No one knew where he was. He had 'flown the coop' and a warrant was issued for his arrest. When I went to see Mrs Cussins, it was obvious she had been weeping. And I soon discovered that the whole business was about to get even more complicated. She confirmed that David Cussins had done a runner but she told me that he had written me a letter which she had posted after he had gone. She did not know the contents. On the following day, it arrived by the lunchtime post and I went home to collect the letter. I returned to Temple and opened it there. The L Murray referred to is the famous Glasgow criminal lawyer Len Murray. This is EXACTLY what the letter said:

Dear Les,

A brief epistle to put you in the picture. I am fully aware that there will be a great cry of 'why on earth did he etc' but I am no use to anyone languishing in prison, particularly when most of the charges are to say the least nonsensical – if only they had dropped the theft charges, or only if it were a lower court, if, if, if. I seem to have been caught between petty jealousies and envy between the S.C squad and the Northern CID and L Murray and Kowalski with the former in both cases being in the right. With L Murray talking in terms of 4, 5, 6 etc I feel that this is the

170

only solution, and it is the hardest decision I have ever made in my life. To have to sacrifice my wife and two beautiful children, not to mention a prosperous business, nice house etc etc, but once again it gets back to what use am I in prison? Another factor which helped me make up my mind was having to call you to the stand. I don't think you would have liked it all that much and without your evidence what chance would I have? Don't misunderstand me Les, I am not suggesting for one moment that you would not have told the absolute truth which could of course only do me a great deal of good, but the mix, as it were, I feel was already in, A Simpson etc-reading between the lines. Also you could imagine the consequences regarding any connection between the two of us after recent events. This would have proved very difficult for me where I was going – and the way to fight fire is with fire – so in theory I could have got off with maybe 2–3 years and then either chibbed or stabbed or alternately doing considerable more porridge, either way not a very easy decision. Anyway it will soon be over, so think kindly of me, we could have been good friends if things had been different. I still think of you as a friend anyway. Now I would like to ask you a great favour, my wife, has obviously sufficient problems to cope with without getting a hard time, i.e. constant badgering by over zealous D.C.s every time they are passing so I would be greatly obliged if you would use your influence in this direction.

Anyway Les keep being a good person and have a drink to absent friends.

Yours aye

David

The postmark was Glasgow, 10 Jan 77.

The letter was deposited in the Temple safe overnight and, on

Friday, 21 January, I took it to Mrs Cussins. I told her the contents were as expected and that I would uplift the letter from her later. This was simply to put her mind at rest and, in any case, she knew as much about her husband's disappearance as I did. The following day, another trivial incident occurred – again it was something that was to have unexpected consequences. I was in Castlemilk with a couple of colleagues and decided to drive to the Cussins' home to pick up the letter because, by that time, she would have had time to read it and digest the contents.

On the way there, driving along Cathcart Road, we saw a well-known south-side criminal standing at the junction with Allison Street. He was holding a black bin bag stuffed full of something or other. I got out of the CID car on my own and approached him. On asking him what was in the bag, he went absolutely berserk – much to the amusement of my colleagues watching from the car. Eventually, they had to come to my aid and we looked in the bag and found that it contained nothing more significant than dirty washing. At this point, the man's wife appeared and a full scale 'rammy' started with a crowd gathering to watch the fun. We did what we thought we had to do – arrested the man on breach of the peace charges and locked him up.

We continued with our journey to pick up the letter and, by then, it was around 6.30 p.m. I went into the house to collect the letter and the others stayed in the car in the street. After a little general chit-chat, Mrs Cussins told me that her husband was concerned that I might commit perjury on his behalf. I said to her, most emphatically, 'If you or a member of the public committed perjury, you would go to prison for five years. If I or any other policeman committed perjury, we would go to prison for ten years.'

She also told me that large sums of cash were available and, if the two Londoners lifted in the Albany got off, each member of their defence team would be given a new car of their choosing. She also mentioned that the lawyer, Ross Harper, stood to gain

£20,000. Knowing Ross Harper, I took all this with the largest pinch of salt available. Back in the car, I told my colleagues what had taken place including the talk of large sums available for a successful defence.

The following morning, I visited the fiscal in Govan to explain the breach of the peace case and suggested to him that I had acted as an agent provocateur. If I hadn't approached the accused in the first place, no crime would have been committed. The fiscal agreed and the charge was dropped. There was a brief lurch into normality after this but a big shock was on its way.

On Friday, 14 February, I was on the back shift and having a leisurely time of it when I picked up the *Daily Record*, the tabloid that was required reading for cops and robbers most days, and I was hit between the eyes by the front page. Arnott McWhinnie, a long-serving and much-respected reporter on the crime scene, had what the scribes call a 'belter' of a story. The intro read, 'Two top Scots detectives have been called in to probe claims that the police used a "fixer" to set up a drugs haul.' According to the story, the investigation began after a meeting between Lord Advocate Ronald King Murray and the leading Scots lawyer Mr Ross Harper. This led to Assistant Chief Constable Arthur Bell and Detective Superintendent Douglas Meldrum being drafted in to help. The story went on that Mr Harper claims that the fixer was used by the Strathclyde Serious Crime Squad. It was alleged that the so-called fixer was a criminal desperate for bail and that the police promised he would be given it but they had a price – they asked him to set up a £10,000 cannabis raid in a Glasgow hotel. Ross Harper was said to have investigated these claims for two months and had a dossier which claimed that that the informer travelled to London to set up a crime for the Scots detectives to 'discover'. A follow-up story along the same lines ran the next day.

After the second story was published, I was called to report to Mr Bell immediately. He told me what the *Record* had said was true – along with Mr Meldrum, he had been asked to investigate the allegations made by Harper with regard to the arrest of McHugh and Goodship. I was given the option of telling them the circumstances of the case or writing it all down. Either way, it had to be done there and then so I wrote it all down. Leaving nothing out, what I wrote ran to sixteen sheets of foolscap. At one stage, Mr Bell left the room and I took the opportunity to rest my hand and ask Mr Meldrum how many allegations had been made. He replied that there were twenty-one but that the main one was that I had planted drugs on them. I felt better on hearing this – the defence must be struggling to even suggest such a thing.

Mr Bell returned and I finished my statement and signed it. I was told to discuss it with no one. I was comfortable that Arthur Bell was on the investigating team rather than some back-room pen-pusher with no street experience. My only fear was that the chief constable would be conned by the defence allegations into suspending me. However, all credit to the chief, Pat Hamill, that he didn't fall for it. Had he done so, it would have suited the defence strategy.

So, once again, it was back to work. This time it was a brutal murder in Barrhead where the victim had been done in by a thug wielding a brick. The accused was given life and it did cross my mind, bearing in mind the investigation and all the complexity of the Albany case, that, whatever else is happening, life and death go on.

A few days later, I was back in Mr Bell's office. 'What were you doing on the 21st of January?' he asked. I referred to my notebook and told him that I had arrested a man on breach of the peace charges and locked him up in Craigie Street Police Office. 'Where were you at 6.30 p.m.?' he asked. I told him about picking up the letter at Mrs Cussins.

Meanwhile, the solicitor for the defence, Ross Harper, had been busy. He had recruited an ex-detective super, Willie Prentice, to dig into my past career. Much later, Willie told me that he had said to them that, if they were looking for evidence to discredit me in the witness box, they were wasting time and money. It seems that one of the reasons for the defence case's suspicions and allegations about the way the raid was handled sprang from the fact that McHugh's brother had told a London police officer that McHugh and Goodship had been set up. The whole saga was further complicated when it emerged that, unbeknown to Ross Harper, someone in his office staff was passing information to a friend who had a police officer friend.

The info that came out was sensational. I never found out who this informant was and the information did not come to me directly. However, I heard through this source that Ross Harper had been at a shooting party in Ayrshire and that one of the other guests had been none other than Jack Beattie, head of the Drug Squad. It was said that Harper questioned Beattie on this occasion about the case and was told that the Drug Squad was not involved and that he could draw his own conclusions. At the suggestion of Jack Beattie, Ross Harper contacted Beattie's right-hand man, John Brown, who confirmed what Harper knew or suspected about the case. Beattie and Brown later went over the case with Harper and gave advice on several aspects of it. It is understating how I felt to say that it seemed strange to me that police officers from the Drug Squad, who had declined to be involved in the interception of two drug couriers, should be assisting the defence of the accused.

Much was made in the press of the so-called secrets of the shooting party but the fact that Beattie had discussed the case with Harper out on the moors did not really bother me. It only confirmed what Harper already knew. What did bother me was the possibility that Beattie or Brown named Cussins as the informer. That would have been below the belt. Certainly Harper was giving the defence everything he had. He also asked Jack Beattie to go with him to speak to the fiscal – apparently, with the intention of convincing him that the defence allegations had substance. And he also took the opportunity in a law lecture at Strathclyde University to refer to the Albany case under the heading of 'Agent Provocateur'. I reported this to Arthur Bell who responded that Harper would appear before the Dean of the Faculty of Advocates and be given 'a slap on the wrist'.

There was to be no slap on the wrist or any condemnation of me when, in advance of the trial of McHugh and Goodship, Arthur Bell completed his report. The reverse was the case. The allegations had been reduced to four:

- that there was missing cannabis
- that I had fixed bail for Cussins
- that I had warned Cussins he was about to be arrested
- that the letter from Cussins to me was alleged to contain details of a cover-up.

Mr Bell reported the following:

- the cannabis resin production for the court was still intact
- the police played no part in Cussins' bail
- it was established that he was not warned
- the letter written to Brown by Cussins had been recovered and was found to contain what Brown had always said it did.

Mr Bell added that Ross Harper had been misled by Drug Squad officers and his report concluded that the prosecution should go ahead. It also contained information that the two accused were members of a criminal organisation that owned farms in Morocco where they grew cannabis and shipped it to Europe in two boats owned by them. He concluded that, if he had been in charge of the Albany drugs case, he would have handled it in exactly the same way it had been handled by the

Serious Crime Squad – quite a compliment.

And now the stage was set for that mother of all trials.

15

EDINBURGH LEGAL LUMINARIES AND A GLASGOW DETECTIVE UNDER HEAVY FIRE IN THE WITNESS BOX

Despite the flamboyance of legal dress – the wigs and the robes – the High Court in Edinburgh doesn't have neon lights over the front door advertising present or coming attractions. Nor does it take adverts in the papers to pull in spectators for the battles of the legal lions that take place behind its huge wooden doors. But, if it did, the events that began in that sombre, impressive arena on 5 September 1977 would have more than merited the phrase 'all-star attraction'. The cast was hugely impressive and it is worth listing some of the major players. Apart from David McHugh, Terence Frank Goodship, a certain Les Brown of the Serious Crime Squad and the late Jack Beattie of the Drug Squad, a copper nicknamed 'The Flea' for his seeming ability to pop up everywhere, the legal line-up looked like this:

Lord Allanbridge: trial Judge

Mr J G Milligan: Prosecuting Advocate Depute
(now Lord Milligan)

Mrs A Paton: assisting the prosecution

Mr J P H Mackay QC: representing the accused Goodship
(now Lord Mackay of Clashfern)

Mr R E G Younger: assisting Mr Mackay

Mr N H Fairbairn QC: representing the accused McHugh
(*later Solicitor General for Scotland*)

Mr Malcolm Rifkind QC: advocate assisting Mr Fairbairn
(*later Minister of State for Scotland and Foreign Secretary*)

Mr J Robertson: Clerk of the Court

Looking at that formidable line-up did beg a question – would two alleged drugs couriers from the east end of Glasgow have been so well represented? I think not. There was no question that all the members of the two legal teams were lawyers of the highest integrity but the fact was the accused could afford the best and that is what they got. When the guys in my squad were told the legal line-up, one remarked, 'Christ, that's a bit heavy!' and another jocularly added, 'It's OK – we won't be too hard on them.'

As we waited for the trial to start, we just got on with the day-to-day job but thoughts of what was to come, within the august precincts of Edinburgh High Court, were never far from the minds of anyone who was to be involved. The day before the start, I convened a meeting in the CID room in the Central Police Office. I knew the defence were already aware that Cussins was the informant and I told everyone present that, if they were asked to name the informant, they could do so by writing his name on a piece of paper. The judge could then read it and decide who else could see it. There was tension and expectancy in the air but, again, routine matters like travel warrants to the capital had to be attended to.

Since Cussins and his involvement with us were at the core of the case, it is worth spelling out, in some detail, the guidelines, which are somewhat tricky, for officers involved with informants.

179

Basically the situation is as follows:

1) The identity of the informant is to be kept secret.
2) The identity of the informant is not to be disclosed in court unless directed by the judge – even then the informant's name is to be written on a piece of paper and handed to the judge.
3) There has to be no guarantee to the informant that he or she is to be immune from giving evidence.
4) Participation by the informant is to be allowed only if it is essential to frustrate criminals.
5) Advice must be sought on this from someone holding the rank of chief superintendent or above.
6) The informant must not act as an agent provocateur.
7) The court must not be misled even to protect the informant.
8) There is to be no immunity for the informant.
9) The Procurator Fiscal need not be made aware of informant's identity.

There was plenty of room for dispute here – as we shall see!

If the all-star legal line-up was not enough evidence of unlimited funds for the defence, an amusing little happening underlined it before the trial had started. McHugh had been granted bail and the reception staff at Barlinnie were astonished when a female turned up at the prison with a holdall containing the six grand in tenners. She was directed to Ross Harper's offices in Glasgow where the niceties of paying bail money in Scotland were explained to her, the money was lodged with the defence and the appropriate cheque was made out to effect McHugh's release.

Despite the tension around the trial, we kept our sense of humour and, when the big day dawned at last, we took the 8.30 a.m. train from Glasgow's Queen Street Station to Edinburgh. There, a posse of press photographers lay in wait. There was a shout of 'Which one is Brown?' and I pointed to Detective Constable

Laurie Wilson who was then followed by the pack of snappers and photographed at every opportunity. It was not, however, so easy for me to escape the limelight when the proceedings got under way. Incidentally, we had been given a hint that a defence lackey would travel through on the same train and perhaps overhear something of interest. No chance – we passed the time playing cards.

When we clocked into the court, the prosecuting advocate, Mr Milligan, warned me I was going to have a rough time in the box and that he would leave me to nearer the end of the prosecution case in order that some loose ends could be tied up. The warning was not unexpected – I knew this would be a tough one – but I told him I would have no problem with my evidence since I was only telling the truth.

He also told me that Eddie Topalion, of Ad Lib, would not be called as he had sent in a doctor's certificate excusing him. I got Mr Milligan's permission to investigate this turn of events and we learned that the certificate had been obtained by telling the doctor it was a 'minor' case where his evidence was not really crucial. That didn't wash and the guys back at Temple picked him up and brought him through to Edinburgh.

The bombshells were quickly being lobbed. McHugh and Goodship had hardly responded to the charges by saying, 'Not guilty', when the clerk of the court read out a special defence, lodged by Fairbairn on behalf of his client McHugh. It read, 'He states that the crime, if any, was committed by Detective Inspector Les Brown and David Cussins, a fugitive from justice, whose present whereabouts are unknown.' What a start! The press bench and, no doubt, the editors back at the offices were meta-phorically licking their lips at the feast of controversy that lay ahead. *This* was going to be good for sales!

Also in court were Chief Super William McMaster of the Police Discipline Branch and a shorthand writer. Their job was to listen to the evidence to ascertain whether any police officer had contravened police regulations or, for that matter, if they were guilty of committing a crime.

Detective Sergeant Joe Jackson was the first of our guys in the box and it was instantly obvious that the pattern of the defence would be to claim that everyone, other than the accused, was lying.

Fairbairn pitched in at Joe, saying, 'My information is that Cussins received a call at the Bombardier Pub that the police were coming to arrest him'

Jackson said, 'I did not know that.'

Fairbairn suggested, 'What happened was that you came into McHugh's room and put a parcel on the top shelf and said, "What have we here?" McHugh said that you put the parcel there and that you responded with, "Oh, no, it is yours and you are going down for that."'

Jackson retorted, 'That's a load of rubbish – no Scottish officer would use an expression like that.' Joe Jackson was one hundred per cent right about that. I have never heard the phrase 'You are going down for that.' used by any Scottish policeman. That sort of B-picture crime language just isn't used up here. Anyway, what was being implied was that Joe had taken one of the slabs of cannabis from the other room and planted it in McHugh's room. Why would we need to do that? We had both accused 'dead to rights'. They had travelled up to the city together and booked into the hotel together. Joe was pretty sparky in the box and when he was asked about me and Graeme Pearson eating a meal in Cussins' house, just before the police pounced, he replied, 'We have to speak to a lot of criminals and you don't get information about criminals at church socials.'

During his turn in the box, Eddie Topalion admitted that he had known McHugh and they had worked together in Charlie Chester's club. He said that someone believed to be a major figure in the London drugs scene, a man not to be trifled with, had ordered him to visit McHugh in Barlinnie, which he did.

While this was going on, I was sitting in the witness room like a man waiting for a dentist with no anaesthetics to call him in for some root canal treatment or worse. It was hard to keep my mind straight as my colleagues came in and out at regular intervals for their grillings. Of course, we did not discuss the case prior to my turn in the box but I was aware that Fairbairn was a skilled interrogator, infamous for interrupting a witness's concentration by throwing in a question or two that had no bearing on the case.

And that is what happened when John Orr was called. He had no trouble giving his evidence but, when Nicholas Fairbairn stood up to cross-examine him, he said, 'Mr Orr, do you have a nickname?' Orr replied, 'Not that I am aware of.' Fairbairn persisted, 'Do you not have the nickname "Punk Rocker"?' Neither John nor anyone else in the squad had heard this nickname but Fairbairn must have got it somewhere. In any case, it was a ploy that didn't work with John.

My turn in the box wasn't to come until three days after the start of the trial. Before it did, there was a curious incident. I stood alone in the corridor, mentally preparing for what lay ahead, when I was approached by a well-known crime reporter. He offered me a sheaf of notes and remarked that they might help me as they told what my colleagues had said in the box. I swiftly said, 'No thanks.' I learned later that this reporter and a member of the defence team were friendly. I am not suggesting for a moment that the offer was orchestrated but I am well aware of what would have happened had I been foolish enough to accept the reporter's offer.

When my name was called and I walked across to the witness box, I was carefully watched by the defence team who were obviously making a visual assessment of how I would react to what was to come. I heard later that Nicky Fairbairn had been telling people that he 'couldn't wait to get Brown into the box'. Mr Milligan took me through my evidence slowly and precisely.

There were no problems and, at the end of the day, I felt I had given a good account of myself.

The next day, I was back in the box at 10.25 a.m. and Nicholas Fairbairn QC, deadly interrogator, was about to get his wish. We had crossed swords before on several occasions at Glasgow High Court in murder trials, so I was well aware of the treatment I could expect. He rose to his feet and asked, Do you know it is a criminal offence to have a drug in your possession with the intention of supplying it to another?' 'Yes.' 'You committed a criminal offence by handing back the sample to David Cussins?' 'By strict application of the law, yes.'

Further questions were thrown at me regarding allowing Cussins to travel south to become involved in a drug deal. He then asked, 'Is it correct that you did not inform the London Drug Squad of what was taking place?' This was tricky. There was no way I was going to reveal that, as we spoke, high-level investigations were going on in the south, by Detective Chief Inspector John Smith, (who was later knighted and who became Deputy Commissioner of the Met in London) involving a race-horse owner and other matters.

To digress from the trial for a moment, I can explain that, in the run-up to the raid at the Albany, the informant in Ross Harper's office had let slip the name of a horse said to be the proverbial 'good thing' running at Epsom. This nag, which incidentally won the race, was said to be owned by a Mr Big who had connections with the London drugs scene and the two accused. I made contact with the London Drug Squad boys who investigated and broke up a drugs cartel. The members were given long prison sentences. Because of this undercover stuff, I had to think carefully about the accusation that I had not got in touch with London.

The line of questioning was, however, cut short when the Advocate Depute shot to his feet to say to the judge, 'My Lord, it might not be in the public interest for Mr Brown to answer that question.' This in itself was an illustration of the complexity of undercover investigations as this intervention was to stop the court hearing that some of the London drugs officers were under investigation themselves. Whatever the rights or wrongs of this, it stopped Nicky Fairbairn going down that road.

He moved on by asking which senior officer had given permission for Cussins to continue to be involved in the case. I replied, 'The assistant chief constable (crime), James Binnie.' 'Are you sure?' he asked and I replied, 'Of course I am sure.' The tide was turning in our favour.

The judge asked if Mr Binnie was a witness and was told he was no longer in the police service but he could be contacted quickly. Fairbairn started another question and answer session. To this day, I am convinced that he began the case thinking we were lying but I am also convinced that it suddenly came to him, as the trial progressed, that we were not. Very experienced in cross-examination, he knew one telltale sign that a witness is telling the truth is that he or she appears relaxed and doesn't delay any answers. He pressed on:

Mr Brown, you are not telling the truth.
– I am.
Mr Brown, you and I know that police officers sometimes, when giving evidence, withhold information that would help the defence.
– Not to my knowledge.
Mr Brown, you and I know of a case where police officers told lies – committed perjury – and, as a result, an innocent man went to prison on a charge of murder which he did not commit, didn't he?
– That is correct.

That shocked the court. The press stopped their note-taking in surprise, my colleagues sat bolt upright and even Lord Allan-

185

bridge seemed intrigued. Everyone had jumped to the conclusion that I was talking of Paddy Meehan and the Ayr bungalow case. Fairbairn, who played a major role in Meehan's trial, moved on:

> Mr Brown for the benefit of this court, the ladies and gentlemen of the jury, the press, the advocate depute and myself, would you name the gentleman who was convicted of murder on perjured evidence and later set free?
> – Yes, sir, it was Oscar Slater.

Fairbairn, as was his habit, had balanced his chin on his hand which was supported by the edge of the jury box. On hearing my answer his head slipped out from his hand. The judge gave a generous smile and nodded. Everyone in the legal profession and the police was aware of the case of Slater who was convicted of a murder in Glasgow in 1909 and subsequently cleared and released from prison. That was it for the day – a good one for the prosecution, I thought.

The next day Fairbairn started off with the fact that I had not originally named the informant and he said, 'If it had not been for good detective work by Ross Harper, the informant's identify might never have been known.' I wasn't going to let him away with that. I announced, 'Cussins' name was given by Detective Chief Inspector Jack Beattie. (This goes back, as the reader will recall, to the shooting party on the Ayrshire moors where the Drug Squad officer socialised with a top man in the defence team and the subject of the trial came up. It seemed to me that, included in the conversation, would be the fact that Beattie was unhappy with the use of the informant but that was a matter for him. I didn't really have a problem with that for, after all, Harper could have got the name through other sources.)

The mention of Beattie annoyed Fairbairn who said I should not talk about that matter prior to that witness giving evidence.

Astonishing as it may seem, Jack Beattie was scheduled to give evidence, for the defence, in a case where two London couriers were accused of bringing cannabis to Glasgow to sell on to another. Fairbairn then went on to speak about Beattie's position for at least three minutes before asking me if I would answer the question yes or no. I asked for the question which was, to say the least, vague to be repeated. The judge smiled but the question wasn't repeated. Little by little, it was going our way and a major turning point was coming up – the first really big mistake by the defence.

Where were you at 6.30 p.m. on 21 January 1977?
– Can you guide me as to what you are referring to?
On that date, at that time, you entered Cussins' flat in Sauchiehall Street to pick up a letter and, unbeknown to you, a man named Pearson was in the kitchen and wrote down, at the time, what you and Mrs Cussins discussed.

He then read out extracts from notes and it was obvious that someone had been there at the time specified because some of our conversation had, indeed, been noted. I asked to see the notes and the judge nodded that it was OK for me to do so. When I got them, I could not believe that what I was looking at was a photocopy. I turned to the judge and said so and asked if I could please see the original notes. I could hardly believe it when Fairbairn said, 'There are no originals – these are the notes I am referring to.' I pointed out to the judge that, if I was in the High Court giving evidence as a detective, I would not be allowed to use photocopies rather than originals. Lord Allanbridge asked me to accept that photocopies would be sufficient in this case but I had the bit between my teeth.

– My Lord, with respect, I must tell the court that Pearson was obviously in a position to overhear what was said but not everything that was said has been noted. Ross Harper's name was mentioned several times but it does not show in the copied notes. One of the reasons could be that Mrs Cussins told me Ross Harper stood to make a lot of money out of the case – each of the defence team would be offered a car of their own choosing if they were successful. (You will remember I told my colleagues of this allegation when I returned to the car that night.) That is why we are looking at copies of the notes – they have been edited to remove the name of Ross Harper.

At this, I felt that, somewhere in the court, I heard muted applause. I saw that my colleagues had smiles on their faces and even the jury looked impressed. The tide had turned. The explanation for the copies given by the defence was that Pearson had read from them and without warning had torn them up. Pretty lame stuff. Surely they could have been taped up and presented in that form?

While all this was going on, I glanced at Mr Mackay representing Goodship and got the impression he would rather have been elsewhere. He rose to his feet and asked me a few questions, more to the point than Fairbairn, got the answers and sat down. Then Mr Milligan asked a few more questions to clarify a point or two and, finally, Lord Allanbridge asked me to stand down and thanked me. It was the end of three days of intense interrogation but I still say, if you are telling the truth, such experiences are not a problem.

Next up was Brian Laird and, if you ever want a witness to follow you, Brian is the man. After him was Graeme Pearson who had shared the meal with me and Cussins on the night of the raid. He raised a laugh mentioning that, after his steak, he had bolted down 'two puddings' before heading for the hotel.

The last witness for the prosecution was Assistant Chief Arthur Bell who told of his investigations into the Serious Crime Squad which had been prompted by the Ross Harper allegations. Late in February of 1977, Bell reported to the fiscal that he had completed his investigation and that, in his opinion, proceedings against Goodship and McHugh should go ahead. He then stunned the court when he said the two accused were part of a huge organisation which owned properties in Morocco from where drugs where shipped to the UK in luxury yachts and that the drugs were then sold to 'the creatures of the street'. It seemed like strong stuff but, as events were to prove, he was spot on.

That closed the case for the prosecution. As his first defence witness, John Mackay called his client Goodship who told the court that, for the past four years, he had worked as a property agent in Spain. He said he had never been to Morocco. And the only reason he has assisted McHugh was because McHugh had asked him to. He said he had no idea what was in the bag they brought with them. Next on the stand was McHugh who, when questioned by his QC, said he thought the bag had contained blue movies.

Before the defence case had begun, Fairbairn had requested that the Serious Crime Squad be asked not to attend as, in his opinion, they presented a threatening influence on the defence witnesses. Despite my protests, most of the squad, including Joe Jackson, were told not to attend. When the business of the drugs found in McHugh's room arose, Fairbairn mentioned Joe and then added, 'I see Mr Jackson is not with us today.' The inference was not lost on me.

The next witness was Jack Beattie, whose high profile in the Drug Squad over the years and his friendship with some of the city's top newspapermen caused intense interest for those who worked in the city's papers as well as for those who avidly followed the crime stories in them. It was difficult not to feel sorry for him because, at this stage, he had been transferred from head of the Drug Squad to a uniformed position, still with the same rank, in Shettleston Police Office. I am in no doubt this was done to humiliate him but, in my opinion, he should have been left in his post until any complaints about his behaviour had been calmly investigated after the trial was over. As it was, the famous 'Flea' found himself somewhat brought low and mortified in the midst of a controversial trial. That said, I could not believe my ears when he began to give evidence. He said I had told him about the drugs raid in October 1976 and went on to state, 'It was not rational for strangers to come to the west of Scotland to distribute drugs – all of the drugs arrests in the west of Scotland tended to come from people with Glasgow connections.'

What we discussed at that meeting, as I explained earlier, was the information about Khan and the other Asian. I wrote a note for the court officer to hand to the advocate depute. It read, 'Ask to see Beattie's notebook – he wrote down some notes about the Khan connection in October '76.' In cross-examination, Mr Milligan did just that and Beattie's answer was as shocking as some of his earlier statements. 'I have already reported that two notebooks and other items disappeared from my desk over the weekend prior to me leaving the Drug Squad,' he said.

However, I felt the next defence witness, Beattie's sidekick John Brown, would at least clarify the position – after all, he had been at the meeting when I passed on the information on Khan. But no one will ever know what Brown would have said because the defence declined to call him to the witness box.

About this time, the defence dropped their special defence of blaming me. It was good, if not unexpected, news and I heard of it in an odd way. I had been in the High Court in Glasgow as a witness and arresting officer in a murder case and had gone to the canteen in Police HQ for lunch. I heard two typists, in the queue in front of me, talking about the Albany case and one simply remarked, 'I see they've dropped the special defence.'

Back in Edinburgh, the defence closed its case and Mr Milligan began his final address, asking for convictions. Mackay followed, on behalf of Goodship, and was characteristically short and to the point. Fairbairn was more flamboyant, as was his nature, and he started off by telling the jury:

> To provide a knock for the valuable services of Brown, a complete bogus crime was set up. It would not matter if it was McHugh, one of you, Mickey Mouse or the Prime Minister – anyone would have done. If this is how convictions are to be obtained, where are your liberties now?

On Tuesday, 20 September, Lord Allanbridge addressed the jury and reminded them, at the end of his summing-up speech, that they had the choice of three verdicts – guilty, not guilty or not proven. And he pointed out that, to bring in a majority verdict of guilty, at least eight members must agree.

The jury retired to consider almost three weeks of claim and counterclaim. They left the courtroom at five minutes to noon and returned just under three hours later, finding the case against Goodship not proven. But, for McHugh, the guilty verdict was unanimous.

Lord Allanbridge said, 'Terence Frank Goodship, in view of the verdict of the jury, I discharge you from the dock.' The advocate depute then moved for sentencing and informed the court that McHugh had some minor previous convictions but, in December 1964, he had been imprisoned for a year for robbery. Malcolm Rifkind then rose with a plea of mitigation (Fairbairn was not in court) and said:

> Cannabis, as compared to other drugs, is reckoned to be a soft drug. This particular drug is not one, according to the medical profession, the use of which is likely to cause major damage to the health of those taking it. McHugh can be considered one of the small fry in the drug scene so far as it operates.

Lord Allanbridge seemed unimpressed – the so-called small fry got six years for his trouble.

The papers had a field day with headings like 'Are Drugs Barons Moving in on Scotland?', the 'Moroccan Connection' and similar lurid pieces of speculation. Some of the newsmen were writing about people they knew well and, of course, they would put individual spin on things. But I was a bit put out when the *Herald*'s Murray Ritchie talked of a rift between the Drug Squad and the Serious Crime Squad and wrote several over-lengthy pieces on Jack Beattie's career, from his RAF service to his police adventures, including his involvement in the Albany affair. But even I laughed at one tale about Jack. In his master of disguise role, he had turned up in a pub, complete with fake beard and scruffy clothes, and the first customer he spoke to said, 'Hello, Jack, how's it going?' Murray Ritchie also quoted some outrageous statements from a former Glasgow cop, Bob Wilson, who, by then, was working in Hong Kong. The rough and tumble of life in the Strathclyde police force was getting rougher by the minute.

And, despite the hubbub of publicity dying down, there was a new bombshell round the corner. I was asked to report to HQ to see Arthur Bell. An anonymous letter had been sent to the chief constable claiming that the writer had been present at a secret meeting in the Central before the trial. At this mythical meeting, I was said to have warned everyone that anyone who strayed from the script would be 'set-up' and would finish up in jail. The writer claimed to be a prosecution witness at the trial but was too afraid to tell the truth. The letter was copied to the Lord Advocate, Ross Harper and the *Glasgow Herald*. Told all this by Mr Bell, I laughed and said it was a load of rubbish. But everything about this trial and the aftermath was sensitive and D R Smith, the Procurator Fiscal in Dundee, was sent south to investigate. To this end, he questioned all the witnesses.

While this was going on, Detective Chief Superintendent

Alistair Macrae of the Strathclyde force was investigating who the writer of the anonymous letter was and scientific examination revealed it to have been a woman. She was then interviewed and, lo and behold, her father was a policeman. This was a man who could most kindly be described as 'eccentric' and who was clearly having difficulty in coping with the strain of his job. There was a feeling among his colleagues he should not be in the force at that time. He had been at a photocopier, briefly, in the room when we had our pre-trial meeting but he had got completely the wrong end of it. The allegations were blown out of the water and so another twist in the saga was over and it was back to normal life.

Or so we thought. The next headline-grabbing news was that Jack Beattie was charged under police discipline regulations. Although we had had our disputes, even I thought, with regard to Jack, that enough was enough – but no. Most of us detectives knew that Jack had left his wife and was living with another woman. Some top men knew, too, and made a move that was quite obviously intended to get at him for assisting the defence in the Albany affair. Jack continued to claim rent allowance shared by him and his wife prior to the break-up. He also claimed some other perks that he was entitled to. Had he simply completed a 'change of circumstances form' he would have been entitled to claim the same allowances. He went on trial at the Sheriff Court on fraud charges. It was all a bit of a nonsense and it was no surprise when he was found not guilty, with the sheriff ruling that there had been no attempt to defraud and also criticising the evidence put forward by senior police officers.

And still it went on. Beattie now complained he had been the victim of 'offensive conduct' at the hands of Arthur Bell and the deputy chief constable, Alex Morrison. This was investigated by the chief constable of Grampian and the complaint found to be not justified.

Three years after the trial, in September 1979, a fishing boat called *Guiding Light* was intercepted by Customs on a beach in south-west England as £100,000 worth of cannabis was being unloaded from it. Among those arrested was Terence Frank Goodship. The vessel had been tracked from Morocco. The news started my phone ringing and, at last, all the hassle and worry of the trial was finally completely justified. Other arrests followed, including that of the racehorse owner Mr Big who offered the officers who nabbed him a huge bribe for 'an hour's start'. When the case came to court, the drug gang got lengthy sentences.

Detective Chief Inspector John Smith of the Met (now Sir John Smith) told me a story that shed some light on the huge sums floating around in the world of drugs. Every Friday, this gang banked £200,000 in cash. On one occasion, the teller told the courier that he was two grand short. No sweat – he just reached into his pocket and pulled out a wad and peeled off the missing cash.

At times like this, the Met had a tradition of producing a celebration tie with some kind of appropriate motif on it. For this one, they chose a lighthouse, a nod in the direction of the fishing boat, and a cannabis leaf. In tribute to my role, I was given one of the ties. The reports on the *Guiding Light* affair made my mind spring back to the exciting days in the High Court in Edinburgh and recall some of the comments. Goodship – 'I have never been in North Africa.' McHugh – 'I thought the bag contained blue movies.' Fairbairn – 'McHugh's actions were not that of a major agent.' Rifkind – 'I would suggest he be considered small fry.' Beattie – 'It wasn't rational for strangers to come to Glasgow to distribute such a large quantity of cannabis.' Ritchie in the *Glasgow Herald* – 'All the police got out of the operation was a small-time courier.' And, finally, Arthur Bell – 'I understand that people in London own places where it is grown and processed in North Africa and their employees are sent out to collect it and bring it back to this country.' Sometimes it can be hard not to say, 'I told you so.'

But the story would be incomplete without detailing the final bloody end of poor David Cussins. Eight years after he did a runner, afraid of going to jail for a long time and even more afraid of what might happen to him inside as a police informer, we discovered he had gone, somewhat ironically, to North Africa. While there, he appears to have received the sort of offer he could not refuse and travelled to Pennsylvania. He was picked up on arrival, shot and dumped in a ravine. The assassination came to light when policemen stopped a motorist and found a bloodstained jacket and a phoney passport later found to be Cussins' property. The motorist admitted the murder. There seemed no motive but I believe the drug barons were extracting revenge for his interference in their crimes. It may have been involvement with me that was partly responsible for the death of David Cussins but the family bore no grudge. I was invited to attend a funeral service and I did so.

Footnote
Police officers, lawyers and others interested in the pursuit of justice might like to consider part of Lord Allanbridge's lengthy and complex direction to the jury when they came to consider the allegations that the police set up a crime. In particular, it casts light on my decision to temporarily return the seized cannabis to Cussins. It reads, in part, as follows:

> *It is for you and you alone to answer the question of whether the police evidence relating to the alleged commission of these charges in the indictment was fairly or unfairly obtained. I think I should make one matter clear. Mr Fairbairn has mentioned the phrase agent provocateur and given a definition of it. As far as the criminal law of Scotland is concerned, there is no such defence known to our law. To be fair to Mr Fairbairn, I don't think he*

suggested there was such a defence open to his client but the
expression was used and I want you to be clear on the matter.
The proper test and the proper approach is the one that I have
indicated. Furthermore, whatever may be the practice in England,
where criminal law is administered under a different system from
ours, it is settled in practice here in Scotland that fairness to the
accused is the true criterion for the admissibility of police
evidence.

That statement I have just read is taken directly from the
judgement of Lord Justice General Clyde in the case of *Marsh*
v Johnston, 1959. Thus, though I will refer to one English case
on the subject of informers, I will do so because, in that case,
Lord Chief Justice Parker's remarks on the use by the police of
informers does appear to be accepted by the Scottish police
according to Assistant Chief Constable Arthur Bell, if you
remember and accept his evidence on this matter, as putting
into words better than he could the rules to be followed by the
police as regards informers.

Now, to assist you in answering the question of fairness, I
do not think I can do better than refer briefly to what our
Scottish judges have said in some of their reported cases. They
have all been referred to by the Advocate Depute and, in fact,
read by him to you but that was last week. I am sorry to inflict
them upon you again but I consider them of some importance.
The first case to which I wish to refer is *Marsh v Johnston*. That
was a case, you may remember, about alleged contraventions
of the Licensing Act and evidence was given at the trial by
two police officers who had gone in plain clothes into the
complainer's hotel and seen two customers being supplied
with what appeared to be excisable liquor after closing time
and then ordered excisable liquor for themselves. The complainer, that is the person accused, had supplied the liquor
and received payment for it. After the police officers had
confirmed that the liquor sold to them was excisable, other
uniformed police officers had entered the premises and cautioned the complainer with the offence and he was convicted and
he, in effect, appealed to the High Court. And the point that he
made and the complaint that he had was that, since the two
plain clothes officers had themselves committed an offence in
ordering a drink outside permitted hours, their evidence was
vitiated. The court refused the appeal and what was said by

Lord Justice General Clyde was this, 'It may be that, in ordering a drink outside permitted hours and in tasting it, the police were guilty of a technical offence under the Act but this was a sheer technicality and was not done to procure the commission of an offence but to detect and confirm that offences were being committed.'

Now, a similar thing happened here. The police gave back an informer, on their own admission, a sample and, by doing so, the police accepted that was an offence. But it is a matter for you to put it into what you consider to be a proper perspective. Do you think, as in this previous case, it was done not to procure the commission of an offence but to detect and confirm that offences were being committed? It is purely and entirely for you. The learned judge went on in that particular case [to say], 'In the circumstances it does not appear to me that there was anything in the conduct of the police which was in the least improper, still less does it make their evidence incompetent.' That is what the judge thought in that case. It is for you to decide the matter in this case.

The jury took the point.

16

HIGH JINKS AT HAMPDEN
AND THE STRANGE CASE
OF THE SEVERED FOOT

The shenanigans of the Edinburgh High Court seemed light years away when, in August 1978, I was holidaying with relatives in Baltimore, Maryland. We travelled up by car to Niagara for a break and, as we approached the immigration control for entry into Canada, my cousin Ernie remarked that it normally took around an hour to get through the formalities and move from the US into maple-leaf land.

I was at the wheel when an official, wearing a tartan tie, came out of a booth and asked with a broad Scottish accent, 'Who owns this motor?' I responded with, 'I've no idea – I knocked it last night in New York.' The officer grinned and said, 'Glasgow?' and I said, 'Yes.' The barrier went up in seconds and we were on our way. Ernie was mighty puzzled and I had to explain that the Glasgow sense of humour and Glaswegians themselves could be found in most places of the world. I was in a fine good humour that day, anyway, as I had just received a phone call from home to say I had been promoted to detective chief inspector in 'F' Division in the Gorbals. It was the completion of a career circle and I was back in that infamous south-side area where I had started my career pounding the beat.

Picking my car up at Glasgow airport when I got home, I found a note on the windscreen wishing me luck from the Serious Crime Squad. I was to need it from time to time in my new job.

I prefer active policing to pen-pushing and, although there was plenty of administrative work in my new role, I had the consolation of knowing that, in the event of a serious crime, I would take control. In the Gorbals, there was often the prospect of interesting work at the serious end of the scale but there was less dramatic yet important work to do as well.

As a young beat cop I regularly attended Hampden Park, that iconic temple of sport that towers over parts of the south side and where Scotland these days sometimes get a football education from nations with less history of the game than we have. And, of course, Hampden, partially rebuilt and now dignified with the title of the National Stadium, still hosts cup finals and show games. In the old days, I regularly attended the old Hampden, a dusty and much less glamorous place in the days before all-seating stadiums, on duty as a beat cop, and I loved every moment of the experience. But I did learn some lessons. Everyone knew that, at all-ticket games, you could get into the ground by handing some cash to the right turnstile operator. There was even a sliding gate known as the 'Weirs' gate, manned by an employee of the Cathcart engineering firm – if he recognised any fellow workers, they got in free.

I also remember once when 600 uniformed officers were addressed before a game by a chief super, nicknamed 'Toffee Legs' – the nickname came about as the officer had suffered a little from that old Glasgow trouble, rickets, leaving him a touch bandy-legged – who told us that the world record for arrests at a football match was created in South America where 166 supporters were arrested. 'We'll beat that today,' said Toffee Legs.

It was a Rangers v Celtic game and crowd trouble, at one point or other, was certain. I was patrolling the track at the north terracing when violence started between rival fans. 'Toffee Legs' appeared from nowhere and said, 'Right, lads, get in among them – but don't arrest anyone with a Rangers scarf.' That, sadly, was the face of prejudice in the old days. But later, towards the end of the seventies, there was another incident that made me decide there was work to be done at Hampden. Scotland were playing England in what, in those days, was by far the most important match of the season. I was asked to get tickets for some cops from England, which I did, and, when we arrived at the ground, they could not get in – the illegal cash-paying guys, who had bribed their way in, had filled all the places! I resolved there and then that, if I ever got the chance, I would stop that practice.

Forged tickets were another problem. In May 1978, an officer in Edinburgh phoned me to say he had a suspected forged ticket. When I saw it, it looked authentic and, indeed, it was so good that people at the Scottish Football Association HQ, up in Park Circus, thought it was genuine. At the official printers, a foreman confirmed that it was a forgery – 'a bloody good one' – and showed me what to look for in suspect tickets. I passed the info to CID headquarters and spoke to a senior detective who asked me what the giveaways were and then said, 'Christ, I have just bought six of the bloody things.'

Later, I asked him to hang on to them but, anxious to get his money back, he had returned them to his source, the late Slim Jim Baxter – the Rangers and Scotland legend who had the pub, Baxter's, in Paisley Road West. Jim and his solicitor Joe Beltrami called in to see me and named a person Jim had bought tickets from. He had done so in good faith, without realising they were forgeries. Other names were mentioned – one was a guy who had made a plate and proceeded to print no less than 2,500 tickets. He was charged and the story made the papers. As a result, the punters who had been fooled got in touch with us. Officers had no bother at the game as all the forged tickets had the same number and all those who had been tricked turned up at the same turnstile. No one with a forgery got in.

Slim Jim had named three people as possible sources and one of them was picked up at his home. As he was being escorted down in the lift by some tough-looking cops, one little lady happened to be in the lift too. With a glance at the cops, the suspect said, for benefit of the woman in the lift, that he hoped he wasn't going to get a hammering. The woman replied, 'Give him a hammering if you want – I don't even stay here.' Glasgow folk are nothing if not realists. In the end the mastermind behind this ticket scam got nine months.

Another Hampden problem was pickpockets and we went after them big-style with some success. One day, we made plenty of arrests but the guilty men were so good at sleight of hand that, as well as acquiring wallets, they were pretty adept at getting rid of the evidence. This resulted in one amusing situation when some of the pickpockets appeared in a magistrate's court and Stipendiary Magistrate Langmuir, on the bench, suggested to the fiscal that the police should get a new set of wallets as the ones before him looked familiar!

But my major gripe at Hampden when I took over was the turnstiles scam which turned out to be massive. At that time, there were 122 turnstiles around the stadium and, of course, there was never enough permanent staff to man them all. Extra men were drafted in from Rangers' and Celtic's stadiums. The fee for the work was a mere £3, small even for those days. The officials naively thought that the chance to watch the second half was compensation for the tiny fee. Not so – the big attraction of the job was the cash on the side that could be trousered.

Each turnstile has what was called a 'numerator', which clicked up one number for each turn of the turnstile. The scam merchants turned the numbers back, like clocking the mileage on a car, and then all they did was match ticket stubs to the number of entries shown. A fiver was usually good enough for anyone without a ticket to get in. Of course, not every turnstile operator was bent but the figures were remarkable. At one game, we figured there were more than 100,000 spectators but the ticket figure was 88,000. On hearing this the SFA top man, Ernie

Walker, somewhat florid of face at the best of times, turned purple with anger. This was Scotland v Argentina in 1979 and, half an hour before the kick-off, we gave two five-pound notes to each of ten pairs of detectives. If refused admission, they were told to try another turnstile. None failed to make it into the ground at the first attempt.

As the turnstile operators locked up their booths, they were brought to the police command vehicle under the main stand. Surprisingly, a high number of them seemed to be called John Smith. The stories they told were hilarious. One said he had paid for his daughter's wedding out of his take from just three games. Although the fee was only £3, one claimed to have broken his holiday in Inverness to travel south for it. Most arrested put their hands up and admitted it but not all of them did. One guy told me, 'You can't talk to me like that – I am a civil servant.' I replied, 'Your grammar is not very good – you *were* a civil servant.' Yet another told us he had left his turnstile in his will to his teenage son. The guilty men were fined in the region of £500 and the SFA began to use folk you could trust, like bank clerks. The ultimate solution was to connect the turnstiles to computers. I have since been told, but cannot vouch for its accuracy, that one well-known football ground in Scotland had two turnstiles that were not connected to the computer. Surely not?

The high jinks at Hampden were all part of the job – worthwhile work with sometimes a laugh or two – but mostly life as a detective chief inspector in the Gorbals was a pretty sombre affair – on occasions, downright macabre. And this was never more so than in the unforgettable case of the severed foot. It would have made a pretty riveting tale for the Baker Street sleuth to mull over as he enjoyed a pipe or two, with Dr Watson observing quietly in the background. Indeed, as Sherlock Holmes might have observed, this was puzzling enough to be a 'two-pipe' mystery. It was also a condemnation of the way some

Glasgow folk behave and a demonstration of how the violence abroad in the city had hardened folk into an appalling 'none-of-my-business' attitude. What happened to Robert Smith in March 1980 is the most upsetting example of people looking away and crossing the road at the first sign of trouble that I have encountered in my life as a detective. There was no good Samaritan – not one, not one.

One day, in that drab, bitter month, Robert Smith, who lived in a flat in Govanhill Street, in the south side, failed to turn up for work. A colleague went to the house to find out why. He knocked loudly but could get no response. Fearful of what might lie behind the heavy wooden door, he phoned the police. When officers arrived, they forced open the door and burst in on a scene that they will surely never forget as long as they live. It is a side of police life that, too often, the layman doesn't take into account – the horror that goes with the job.

Smith's home was a flat with a living room, kitchen and a bedroom. On the floor of the living room the uniformed officers were confronted with the sight of a human foot, standing upright on the sole, in a pool of blood. The foot had been severed just above the ankle. In the adjoining kitchen, again on the floor, lay the rest of Robert Smith. There was blood everywhere, including a trail from the mouth of the close up and into the house itself. The blood would have been obvious to anyone who had been in the close.

The duty Procurator Fiscal, Miss Liz Munro, arrived and, knowing my sense of humour, passed a light-hearted remark on the way up the stair. Her mood was soon to change. I told her that, at this stage, it didn't look like murder. Miss Munro, on seeing the horror of the severed foot, made a remark under her breath and, steeling herself, went into the bloody kitchen. Her role, at this stage, was to take charge of the body for subsequent inquiry into the case. The police, on behalf of the Crown, would investigate and report to her. The police casualty surgeon also came to the death site and examined the body there before carrying out a post-mortem examination in the city mortuary the following day. Everyone present agreed that, even at that early stage, it was obvious that a massive loss of blood was the cause of death.

With the body in the mortuary, we began door-to-door en-quiries and I searched the flat for clues to this strange death. Near the severed foot, I found a small pair of bloodstained scissors and it looked as if, incredible as may seem, Smith had cut off his own foot. It also appeared as though he had also made an attempt to apply a tourniquet, just above the ankle.

When we spoke to the neighbours, several admitted to having seen the trail of blood in the common close – a trail that led right to Smith's door. Not one of them had gone to help or to find out what was wrong or even phone the police to get them to investigate. Remarkably, one of the neighbours was a well-known active criminal. By the time I was finished interviewing him, he was in tears. I put it to him that he, of all people, should have known better. And he should.

The inquiry got the full treatment – we threw staff at it. And the intriguing nature of events up that bloody close meant that the media were fully involved in reporting it in depth and asking for witnesses to come forward. Several did, including a woman with an upper-class accent of the kind not found too often in Govanhill at that time. She said that, along with her husband, she was driving in Inglefield Street when they had seen a man, in obvious distress, crawling along on all fours. I asked why they hadn't offered assistance or gone to get help for an obviously seriously injured man. She had nothing to say – she simply could not explain such shocking behaviour. Angry, I ended the conversation by telling her to get stuffed.

Someone else had seen the crawling man in Butterbiggins Road, in the area. To this person, who also did nothing about it, he appeared to be trying to get to Govanhill Street. It occurred to me that such injuries could be caused by a person kicking in a plate-glass window and I arranged for the area to be searched for evidence of something like that happening – but without any success. However, the enquiries did turn up the fact that Robert Smith had been drinking in Kitty's Bar in Stockwell Street, near the bridges over the Clyde to the south side. Drunk, he had left there to walk home. Having a look at the route to his flat, we realised that, at some stage, he must have staggered down to the busy railway line, passing under Cathcart Road, just north of Butterbiggins Road. Clearly, the damage to his ankle could have been caused by a train.

Other witnesses came forward, including one who had assisted Smith part of the way when, at that point, the full extent of his injuries might not have been so obvious. This guy had eventually to leave Smith and, when he looked back, he saw Smith on the ground and two youths searching his pockets as he lay in agony on the road. He shouted and ran back but the youths were running away, carrying something – probably Smith's wallet. Not only had Robert Smith been struck by a train, he had crawled around 700 yards on all fours, dripping massive quantities of blood, and he had been mugged. Sometimes your belief in your city and its citizens is sorely tried.

On reaching home, Smith had crawled into bed and then, finding the pain unbearable, had struggled through to the living room and desperately applied, as best he could, bandages to his injured leg. Finally, he used the tiny scissors to cut through the rags of flesh that held his ankle to his leg. Then he died. The post-mortem confirmed that all this was the case. The bone showed the signs of the train running over it and there was massive loss of blood.

If any of the witnesses who saw the crawling man had had the humanity to do their duty to assist or, at least, had found someone who could help, then Robert Smith might have survived. It was an ugly side of human nature. I was angry when I told that posh lady to get stuffed. She reported me to the chief constable and I was reprimanded for speaking to her the way I did. Big deal.

17

A Pub Bombing and a 'Grab a Granny' Night at the Plaza

In the late seventies, the Troubles in Northern Ireland were continuing to make headlines. The police and security forces in Scotland, particularly in Glasgow, were aware that there was a fuse just ready to be lit. We were in a permanent state of 'fingers crossed' in case the orange and green started a war on our patch. The west of Scotland was home to many who had come over the Irish Sea, to live and work in areas like the Gorbals and Bridgeton in particular, sometimes bringing their prejudices with them. We also had a heavy crew of home-grown headbangers who were likely to get involved in any IRA–UVF battles. It would not have taken much to tip Scotland into the serial sectarian violence that was rife in Belfast and the surrounding areas.

Looking back, I sometimes think that perhaps the real reason we escaped such violence was the realisation that, if it started here, it could have made what was happening over the water look like small beer. Whatever the cause, Scotland was lucky enough to stay largely out of this conflict. However, in my second spell in the Gorbals, I was to find myself investigating a pub bombing that just could have acted as the fuse to light an outburst of violence – the sort of thing that the Ulster Constabulary dealt with practically on a day-to-day basis. It happened in the Clelland Bar in Hospital Street.

On Saturday, 17 February 1979, we had Detective Constable

Brian Brock on the late shift. He was the sort of officer who was always on the go and he would regularly phone me at home with something or other. He was always on top of the job so, when I heard him on the phone that Saturday night, I knew there was trouble but it was not at all what I expected. He shocked me when he said there had been an explosion in a pub and that he and his fellow officers thought it was a bomb. It was not pleasant news. Were our worst fears about to be realised? Brian said that the pub was believed to be a place frequented by Catholics and that the car was already on the way to pick me up. Incidents like this definitely did not feature on my CV at this stage in my career. Murder inquiries were my forte – this was something new.

When I arrived at the pub, I was met by several uniformed officers and I was surprised by the violence of the explosion. Parts of the roof had been blown off. Bizarrely, ten pence pieces were embedded into the walls and what remained of the ceiling. They must have been sprayed round the bar like machine gun bullets when the force of the explosion burst open the fruit machine. Scary. As one wag on the scene put it, 'Imagine being killed by a two-bob bit.' Hard on my heels was the Bomb Disposal Squad who arrived to search the premises. They eventually declared it safe but I still feared there might be a second device that they might have missed – one aimed at the police – so we placed a guard on the pub and postponed further investigation till daylight.

Six casualties were taken to the nearby Victoria Infirmary but luckily none was badly hurt and their lucky escape did not deter even the injured from going to the Plaza dancehall in Eglinton Toll. They had said in the hospital that, after all, it was Saturday and 'grab a granny night' – something not to be missed even after being caught up in a pub bombing. The nursing sister I spoke to did hand me a bit of a clue – a zip from a holdall that had been removed from one of the victim's thighs by the casualty surgeon. I then went to the Plaza in search of the injured. I let them enjoy their night at the jiggin' and arranged for fuller interviews the next day.

How to handle this inquiry was a bit of a puzzle but I just decided to proceed as if I was involved in one of my 'normal' murders. Back at the pub on the Sunday morning at eight o'clock, we were able to get a much better idea of what had happened in the daylight. The Clelland was a single-storey pub that was situated on the corner of Ballater Street and Hospital Street. It had three areas – the public bar, the lounge and the working area. The public bar had been extensively damaged. In this part, there were numerous tables with an average of four chairs to a table. On each table, there was an assortment of glasses – some for beer, some for spirits. In the centre of the room was a pool table and a stone fireplace. A few feet from the entrance was a large hole in the floor between a one-armed bandit and a juke box. The two machines appeared to have acted as a funnel, directing the blast into the room and up towards the roof. It was time for some routine work. We numbered the tables, labelled the glasses on each table as possible productions in court later and for fingerprint examination. We figured the bomber might have bought a drink and left some dabs on a glass.

While the other officers got on with this, I spoke to the bar manager who had been on duty at the time of the explosion. I asked if any strangers had come in and he told me that one guy had and that this fellow had carried a holdall. 'Did he buy a drink?' I asked. 'Yes, he bought a pint and a glass of sherry.' 'Where did he drink them?' According to the manager, he had downed them at the bar. It was too much to hope that the pint glass and the sherry glass – that unusual combination the stranger had asked for – would still be on the bar but there they stood. Good fingerprint impressions were found but this was in the days before computer recognition and to do a search of all criminals on file would take three weeks, with searchers working three shifts a day, and it would only produce a result if the bomber was already on file.

So sensitive was a pub bombing that the Special Branch were involved from the outset and they came up with a list of their usual suspects – people suspected as being members of the Glasgow branch of the Ulster Volunteer Force. One name on the list was the alleged leader of the UVF – a William Campbell of 16 Heron Street. My visit to him was quite an experience and gave me insight into the depth of sectarian feeling around. For starters, outside his house the number 1690, rather than 16, was painted on the door, clearly a reference to the defeat of James II by William of Orange at the Battle of the Boyne. Before making this house call, I had been warned that Campbell was considered by the Special Branch to be a dangerous fellow. We went in a team of six officers. He was a pretty fearsome looking guy of about six feet three and I identified myself as he answered the door and told him I was in possession of a warrant to search his house. To wind him up a bit, I referred to the fact that the warrant was for number 16 and asked where the 1690 had come from. Stony-faced, he said that the figures referred to the date of the Battle of the Boyne. By this time, we were all in the living room of the house and I said, 'William, I understand you can become very violent. If so, do it now and let's get it over with but I have to tell you I have a slight advantage.' At this point, I opened my jacket and showed him the gun in my shoulder holster.

He and I sat on a couch in the lounge while the others searched the house. A Special Branch man reappeared armed with a Rangers football scarf and placed it on the table in front of us. The knuckles on Campbell's fingers turned white at this and it looked as if he was going to explode. I asked the officer why he had seized the scarf and he replied along the lines that it showed Campbell's 'leanings'. I said, 'Well, if that is the case, when we leave here, we will have to go to my house since my son has a similar scarf. Put it back.' This relaxed Campbell no end.

The mindset of those of the orange persuasion was further illuminated during this house search. I noticed a large painting of William of Orange on a white horse. For a bit of devilment, I asked Campbell who it was astride the horse. 'Oh, that's King Billy,' he replied and I asked him, 'What did he do?' I was told he was 'on our side'. 'You mean when we fought the English?' 'No, over in Ireland.' Enjoying the banter, I asked Campbell if he was Irish and why he had the picture here in Scotland. He answered that King Billy had helped beat the Catholics at the Battle of the Boyne.

Incidentally, we found nothing to connect him to the bombing but we were instructed to take him back to the office in any case as all known or alleged members of the Glasgow UVF had been picked up in dramatic raids and similarly detained at the Central Police Office, under the Prevention of Terrorism Act. One of the search teams had found bags of sodium chlorate in the garage of their particular target. He claimed he used it as weed killer. The details of all those who had been arrested were shown to the Scottish Criminal Records Office and we learned that the finger-prints of a man called Angus McKenna matched those found on the sherry glass on the bar of the Clelland that Sunday morning.

The Special Branch then took over the inquiry, although we were still engaged in preparing the evidence as far as the pub bombing was concerned. In doing this, we found that our original notion that the pub was much used by Catholics was wrong – indeed, most of those injured were Protestants. This had helped to make the pub an easy target as the pubs favoured by Catholics were more aware of the danger and a stranger with a holdall would not have got the easy run given to the Clelland bomber.

A lengthy High Court trial followed and McKenna was given sixteen years. This was a heavy, heavy sentence and it had the desired effect – anyone thinking of similar capers was well warned that the law would hit them hard. Some others involved also received long jail terms. There were no other pub bombings in Glasgow and thankfully that orange-and-green fuse remained unlit.

But it remained a time of tension and there were a few occasions when trouble could have broken out – as illustrated by the time when an orange lodge at Bridgeton Cross was damaged by an explosion. Police enquiries revealed the fact that someone in the hall had kept explosives hidden in a stove but had neglected to tell the cleaner. One cold morning, she lit the stove and nipped across the road for some milk for her tea. The hall did not look quite the same on her return.

So that was my involvement with the Special Branch. I also had a spell away from frontline detective enquiries, working with Criminal Intelligence. It was not my idea and it came after a disastrous mistake I made during the investigation of the murder of a young girl – the infamous Tracy Main case. This is dealt with at length in the following chapter. This investigation was, I freely admit, a controversial episode in a controversial career. No matter, in 1981, I found myself to my chagrin in a nine-to-five job at Police HQ. I resented the move but at least I had the credentials to take over a department where knowledge of criminals is essential. The detective in the field needs good back-up and some of it comes from the criminal records department which keeps a track of convictions and fingerprint records and holds an index of wanted criminals and helpful details of their preferred modi operandi. Criminal Intelligence dealt purely in information mostly on active criminals.

Some of the work is confidential – and I will give away no secrets to help the bad guys – but some of it is routine. Serving officers would pass on background information to us – things like the registration numbers of vehicles in possession of criminals. They would tip us off on criminals spending a lot of time in each other's company and name pubs and betting shops favoured by them. Files were kept on the main known criminals and in them details of their movements, vehicles, hobbies, favourite sports, weaknesses and even where they would go for their holidays were all logged. We liked to think we kept a collective ear to what was going on on the streets. We were tight on making sure such info was only available to serving policemen. It was a small team but they were a dedicated lot and sometimes we got out of the office on special assignments. When a serious crime investigation was on the go, we would review our info and make some suggestions – the 'usual suspects' ploy yet again.

We also published a bulletin once a week, mainly aimed at keeping the beat cops informed. In my time I jazzed it up a bit, adding colour and photographs to make it a bit more interesting for the guys who were pounding the streets and knocking on the doors up the closes. One of the most valuable aspects of this was to inform the force of prison releases and to warn them of people known to be violent or dangerous and who should be approached with real caution. Another task was to lecture at the training college on the services we could provide. Most days we got visits from Serious Crime Squads and I was pretty sure, at first, that most visitors were curious and anxious to find out the reason for what must have been perceived as this blip in my career. But we provided such helpful stuff that the visits continued.

One of the first major crimes we assisted in during my time in Criminal Intelligence had an IRA link. It was the theft of a payroll at Yarrow's, the navy shipbuilding yard, and it was a big-time heist. During the night, masked men overpowered the security staff and stole almost £200,000. Irish accents had been heard and the link was made, wrongly as it turned out, that it was the work of desperate men from over the water looking for funds to aid their armed struggle against the British. The intelligence was that the leader of the gang spoke politely and had an Irish accent, which made me think of someone I had run into before – a guy called Mac. I decided to prepare a file on him as our suspect and had bit of fun with the then chief constable, Pat Hamill. A police photographer, fresh from the crime scene, was

213

having a cuppa with us when he let on that he knew that, years ago, the chief had arrested two men at a robbery in the same shipyard. I asked someone to check it out and was handed a note just as Mr Hamill entered the office. He was in playful mood and looked at me and said, 'I am led to believe you know everything that is going on and that you personally know most of the Glasgow criminals.' I modestly acknowledged that it was true and he then responded by asking if I knew he had arrested two men inside Yarrow's five years ago. I said, 'Sir, you arrested Joe McAdam and Willie Turner, charged them with being known thieves found in suspicious circumstances, they appeared at the Stipendiary Court the following morning and were sent to prison for sixty days.' The chief's face was a picture as he muttered that he was 'impressed' and left to go about his business. The officer who had handed me the info immediately asked how I knew the details of the court hearing as it hadn't been in his note. I had to say I had made it up! The crime was never solved and, many years later, I accidentally ran across Mac. He said hello and remarked he hadn't seen me for a while. I agreed our paths hadn't crossed for some time and then I observed, 'The last time I saw you, it was when you climbed the wall at Yarrow's.' He turned bright red. Could it be that my hunch back in Criminal Intelligence was bang on?

18

A TEENAGER DEAD IN HER LOUNGE AND A CALAMITOUS MISTAKE

A career in the police is a bit like investing in the markets: your stock can go down as well as up, as the oft-quoted warning in the brokers' advertisements has it. And the cause of the movement can, as in the stock market, often be one tiny happening, the effect of which is not immediately apparent. Despite my previous history of success in the force, my standing took a knock after I made a bad mistake in a murder investigation – a mistake much jumped on by the press, the legal profession and anyone around who wanted to take a kick at Detective Les Brown. Writing about it is difficult for me but I am sure the parents of murder victim, Tracy Main, will forgive me for telling a story that I feel must be told. The Tracy Main case also has a legacy of lessons to be learned, even by today's cops, and this also makes detailing exactly what happened in a piece of police history a necessary, if sometimes disturbing, exercise.

As I've said, you never know what's next when you are a cop. Although it started like many other days, 5 February 1980 was a day that would have a dramatic effect on my career. The detective knows the phone can ring at any time day or night so the call I got at home at 6.30 that morning was no special deal. A woman had been found dead on a couch in her lounge in Langside Road. She was fully clothed and there were no signs of a break-in or violence. We quickly ruled out foul play and a post-mortem confirmed it was a natural death. It was an early start to the day but it involved a fairly run-of-the-mill investigation. The day continued along the usual lines – the detectives on duty were allocated assignments, correspondence was attended to, I had a chat with my two detective inspectors and we received a visit from an informant looking for cash.

By mid afternoon, I was chairing a meeting discussing bag-snatching in the King's Park area when HQ came on the line. This was more serious: they had just received a call from a near-hysterical woman saying that there had been 'a rape and murder' at Norfolk Court in the Gorbals. Detectives from the nearby Gorbals Police Office were on their way and it only took ten minutes or so before I was climbing the stairs to flat 2/3 at house number 17. The cop on the door took my name, rank, police number and time of arrival – routine was working even in a fraught situation.

I walked along the hallway into the living room. The early arrivals, detectives and uniformed men, were grouped round a settee positioned on the right of the doorway. Lying partly on the settee and partly on the floor was the body of a young girl, thirteen-year-old Tracy Main. She looked to have been there for some time. She was wearing a parka, which had a partially opened zip, and her trousers had been pulled down to her knees.

The police surgeon arrived soon afterwards and went through the formality of confirming that the victim was dead. The police photographer had arrived as well and I told him to photograph the body from four different angles. When this was complete, we could look more closely at the body. I was horrified to see dried blood on the garments under her parka jacket and various stab wounds in the area of her heart. The only sign of disorder was a metal stand type of ashtray which had toppled over, spilling the foul-smelling contents on the floor.

The forensic squad were next up and I told them I wanted everything examined even if it took them a week. (The parents had agreed to leave the house till the forensic work was finished.) I took a good look round myself. There was no sign of forced entry. The door had two locks, a Yale and a mortise. Both were in the unlocked position which meant that, as in most houses, the door could be secured by simply pulling it shut and the Yale would come into play. A set of house keys was lying behind the front door. The hall light was on, as were the living-room standard lamp and the kitchen ceiling light. There was no bulb in the main light in the living room but, nonetheless, we checked that the socket was live. It was.

On the coffee table in the living room there was a curious mixture of objects – three carrots, a book lying open, two ashtrays, two table lighters, a can of hair spray and a folder that contained school books, a plastic bag and a handwritten note saying, 'Please excuse Tracy for being absent from school, she was sick.' (The parents later told me they had not written this note.)

A murder inquiry unit was set up at the Police Training College, near to the scene of the crime. Two detective sergeants, Archie Crichton and Bob McElvenney, were appointed as collators. The police command vehicle was positioned at the rear entrance to the Norfolk Court flats and it was manned twenty-four hours a day.

Door-to-door enquiries were made in the two high-rise blocks, 5 Norfolk Court and 17 Norfolk Court. We threw teams of detectives at this work and they were told to concentrate on movements at the material times – 7.15 a.m. and 4.15 p.m. on 5 February. Each interviewee was asked if they had seen or heard anything suspicious on that day. If any members of a family were missing when the officers called, the cops would go back till they got to speak to the person they had been unable to talk to. Each householder was asked to name everyone in the other houses on the same floor. This was to prevent any member of a family covering up for another. Action forms for each house had to be filled in and returned to the collators, no matter the difficulty.

But, during this initial stage, we held back from interviewing the houses on the same floor as the Mains. While all of this was going on, I spoke to Tracy's parents, Thomas and Dorothy, who had left the house at their usual time of 7.15 a.m. Thomas Main drove his wife to her job in a working men's hostel where she worked as a cleaner. He then went on to the rear of the city mortuary and another hostel where he was employed as a superintendent. They had a routine in which Mrs Main phoned Tracy from a coin box at 8 a.m. and, when the youngster picked up the phone, her mum would know she was awake and getting ready for school. Sometimes they spoke but often the call was just to make sure Tracy was awake and, of course, there was the matter of the few pence that would be saved by not chatting to be considered. Tracy went to John Boscoe Secondary School, across the river in Bridgeton, and, each morning, she would walk there accompanied by a pal.

On 5 February, the girl called as usual to pick up Tracy. She knocked on the door at 8.30 a.m. but got no reply. She thought she had heard a bump which could have been the solid ashtray falling over – a possible clue to the time of death. As the girl had knocked on the door, we tried doing so too. If it hadn't been locked, it would have opened slightly when someone knocked – it didn't. Tracy's parents and everyone who knew her insisted she would not open the door to a stranger but our door test suggested she must have opened it to the killer. The routine when the Mains left the house each morning was that they locked the door from the outside and pushed the keys through the letter box. When Tracy left she did the same, or she took the keys with her, depending on her plans for the day.

The parents finished work around four and Mr Main picked up his wife and one of her colleagues, dropping his wife off first and then taking the other female home. The day the body was discovered, Mrs Main noticed the door opened slightly as she put the key in. This made her suspect burglars so she knocked on the door of her neighbour, Miss Lewis, and the pair went into the flat together. The sight of the body sent them screaming away from the horrific scene that met them. Miss Lewis's father then went in and found that the girl was indeed dead. The police were contacted but, at this time, Mr Main was still driving the other cleaner home. Later Mrs Main asked about jewellery hidden in the house but it had not been stolen.

Not too long after the initial discovery, I was asked to prepare a statement for the press and TV pack who were gathering for news of a sensational murder. I have always tried to get the press and TV onside for they can give valuable assistance to an inquiry. But care is needed because the newspaper people can often get info from neighbours and so on that might not be in the official handout prepared for the media by the police – things like the type of weapons used. But it was sensible to have a sound relationship with the media and, on this inquiry, we decided to have a briefing at 10 a.m. each day. The press liked the idea but some of my superiors took the attitude that I was there to catch a murderer not get my name in the papers.

Back at the start of the investigation, I had the sombre task of being present at the post-mortem and, as usual, the findings were important. Tracy had been stabbed seven times around her heart. She also had crescent shaped marks on her face that were obviously caused by a hand over her face to stop her screaming. We got samples of blood, nail clippings, hair clippings etc. to help in the hunt for the killer. In her clothing, a second note excusing her from school was also found. Attempts were made to get fingerprints from the marks on the face but without success. I went home that day, a day that had started in routine fashion at 6.30 a.m., at midnight – shattered.

The following morning we had a briefing with all eighty detectives involved. There was a considerable amount of discussion and I was able to tell them that, as a result of what had been found during the post-mortem, the murder weapon would be at least four inches long and one inch wide. The press conference followed at 10 a.m. and we did our best to answer the questions of the scribblers. Detective Inspector Jim Paul read the action forms handed in after the door-to-door enquiries. We checked everyone interviewed for previous convictions and checked who was said to live where against the electoral roll. The fingerprint guys and the Forensics Squad were still busy. All the prints found in the flat were those of family members or known recent visitors, with one exception – the fingerprints on a glass in the bathroom. However, it turned out that a cop had used it to give Mrs Main a drink of water when she was in shock at the discovery of the body.

It is a sad fact of life that, in all inquiries, detectives must check out the people closest to the victim and, in this case, that meant the parents. So I checked the Mains' hands and wrists for recent injuries as a person striking another with a knife will often injure himself or herself. But there was no sign of any such injury on either parent. The check on visitors to the building threw up one guy, an insurance agent, who had been recently tried for murder but found not guilty. He had a perfect alibi so that theory was ruled out.

I took Mr Main to the murder flat and he accounted for everything we had seen on that first day – including the carrots which were for soup. We looked at the knives in the kitchen and one was missing, about ten inches long and an inch wide. We bought a similar one and the medics confirmed that it was what the weapon was likely to look like. The entire area was searched for such a weapon – with drain covers even being lifted. There is not much fun in such inquires but, when we interviewed the staff at Mr Main's hostel and fingerprinted them, one remarked we had fingerprinted everything other than the hostel cat. We then did just that and, on the form that accompanied it, we filled in 'cat burglar' as the owner's occupation.

Tracy was buried on 15 February and about 1,500 people

attended the funeral. The murder had incensed the local community. She had been a keen Celtic supporter and on hearing this the then manager, Billy McNeill, arranged for the club to be represented. Some of the officers working on the inquiry went to the service but not me – I was at Craigie Street Police Office with a man, Thomas Docherty, who was later to be charged with the murder.

You will recall that, when we did the door-to-door stuff, we left the houses on the Mains' floor to later. It had fallen to Detectives Hamish Innes and Gordon Bowers to visit these flats. According to the electoral roll, the flat next to the Mains was occupied by a Mrs Turner but, when Innes and Bowers knocked on this door, it was Thomas Docherty who answered. It looked as if he was staying at the flat and he appeared to them to be of low IQ. Mrs Turner insisted he was just a visitor but it was soon clear that this claim was to safeguard social security benefits coming into the house. On the night before the funeral, Innes and Bowers brought Docherty to the incident room and told me what they had discovered. I agreed that Docherty appeared to be 'not the full shilling' and would have to be treated accordingly.

What follows is verbatim from my notebook:

8 p.m. commenced interview with Thomas Docherty.
Q Do you know who I am?
A Yes.
Q Do you know we are investigating a murder?
A Yes, I saw it on the telly, it was STV.
Q Was it on the six o'clock news?
A The news that comes on at a quarter to six, and the Scottish news comes on at six. It wasn't John Toye. The man said it was a brutal killing and the girl had been stabbed seven times.
(At this point Detective Superintendent Ian Smith who had left the room re-entered.)

Q Thomas, it is my duty to inform you that, in connection with the murder of Tracy Main, on 5.2.80, and, in an effort to establish the identity of the person responsible, I am going to ask you some questions. I must warn you that any answers you give will be noted and may be given in evidence. Do you understand?

A Yes.

Q Will you tell Mr Smith and I what you saw on TV?

A The man who read the news, it wasn't John Toye, said the girl had been brutally murdered – she was stabbed seven times.

Q Tom, are you seriously telling us that a man on the news said that the girl had been stabbed seven times?

A Yes.

Q Did this man say where she had been stabbed?

A Yes, the man went like this. (Demonstrated by clenching his right fist and punching his chest.)

I could not believe what I was hearing. Later, we would check all television news stations to see if information on the number of stab wounds had bee broadcast. It hadn't.

As I have said, the above is a verbatim note of what was said and shows clearly that, in the caution, I had neglected to write down the words 'you are not obliged to answer these questions'.

After this important – in many ways! – interview the Turner house was searched. The officers were looking for the knife or anything that might link Docherty to the Mains' house. No joy. The word was now out that a suspect was being questioned. A discussion followed and it was pointed out that it would not be good idea for Docherty to return to Norfolk Court. It would be in his own best interest to stay in the police office. Outside, his life would be in danger. A meal and bedding was provided and he stayed in an unlocked cell and slept like a baby – which was more than I did. As I mentioned, I conducted another interview with him on the day of the funeral. Back to the notebook:

> 10 a.m. Saw TD in the presence of DS Innes. Cautioned TD
> and told him to tell Innes what he had seen on TV.
>
> TD The man on the news said the girl had been stabbed seven
> times. (As he said this, Docherty struck his chest as he had
> done before.)
>
> Q Would you show us where the TV showed the stab wounds
> [were inflicted]?
>
> A Yes.
>
> Q Can you count?
>
> A Yes.
>
> I showed TD 3/5/8 fingers and he got them right each time.
> (I did not show him seven fingers.) I then drew the outline
> of the upper half of a human form on a piece of paper
> [which] I handed to TD.
>
> Q Will you show us where the man on TV showed where (*sic*)
> the girl had been stabbed.
>
> A Will I draw small dots?
>
> Q No draw small lines.
>
> TD then proceeded to draw seven small lines in the area of the
> heart.

At this point, I was called from the room. I had been due to give evidence in the High Court that day but had asked to be excused. This call was to let me know that the court authorities had agreed. On returning to the interview, Innes told me that Docherty had said something in my absence that was important. I cautioned Docherty, properly this time, and asked him to repeat what he had just said.

> TD He (Innes) asked me if I knew the Mains and I told
> him they went to work at a quarter past seven and they
> were out all day. They got back at four. Tracy stayed off

school because she was frightened and if she had gone to school it wouldn't have happened.

After lunch, there was another session and this time Detective Inspector Joe Jackson cautioned Docherty and then asked him some questions:

Q Tom, are you telling us that you saw on TV that Tracy had been stabbed seven times?
A Yes, I told you the girl was lying against the settee.
Q Where was the settee?
A At the back of the door. (Indicated his right)

The next day there was extensive discussion with all the detectives involved in the case. I was in the chair and opinion was divided. Some thought he was a good suspect or had, at some stage, seen the body – even if he was not actually the killer. If the door of the Mains' flat had been left open, he could have gone in and seen Tracy. Even if he had done so, how did he know she had been stabbed seven times? One officer raised a point that puzzled me – if Docherty had done the stabbing, would he have counted the blows? There was one way to find if he had been in the flat when the body was there. We took him into it and asked him to lie down in the way the body was and he did so, replicating the position of the body even to a crossed leg and tilted head. So he had seen her but had he killed her? We interviewed him again.

Q Tom, did you show these officers the position of the girl's body as shown on TV?
A Yes I showed them.
Q What was the girl wearing on TV?
A A skirt, not trousers, and a shirt and tie.
Q Why mention trousers?

A No reply.

Q Tom, do you want a lawyer?

A No reply.

At this point I phoned Procurator Fiscal Pat Docherty at his home but got no reply. At 5.30 we resumed the interview.

Q Tom we can't understand how anyone could have got into the house – Tracy always kept the door locked.

A The door was open about an inch and a man could have got in without her knowing.

Q Tom, why would the man stab Tracy?

A He would have panicked and if she tried to scream he would have grabbed her.

Q Would you show us how the stabbing would have been done?

A Yes.

I handed Docherty a ballpoint pen and stood immediately in front of him. 'Tom I am going to scream and you show us what the man did.' He grabbed my face with his left hand, his left thumb under my chin with the fingers across my left cheek and mouth, replicating the marks on Tracy's face. As he did this, he made stabbing motions towards my heart.

Q What would the man have done then?

A He would have gone back to his own house and tried to put the knife down the lavvy but it wouldn't go – it was too big.

Q How big?

A Docherty held his hand about a foot apart.

Q What would the man do then?

A The man would get the bus to Bridgeton Cross and get off at the bakery and walk to the canal and drop the knife in the canal.

Q Would it sink?

A Yes, it was heavy.

Q Some of these bridges have a parapet on the outside.

A What is that?

Q It is a ledge.

A No that bridge doesn't have one.

Interview terminated at 6 p.m.

Clearly we had to look for the knife in the Clyde, which Docherty had referred to as the canal. If it was found where Docherty indicated, the case was over. But, despite searching for a week, it wasn't found. Before the search had started, Inspector Bob McTaggart, the man in charge of the unit, said he was confident that, if the knife was there, they would most likely find it. Nevertheless, when that final interview was over, the Procurator Fiscal arrived and, hearing, among other things, that Docherty seemed to know more about the murder scene than some of the detectives did, told us to charge him and submit a report in the morning. I did, charging him as follows:

> You are charged that you did on 5.2.80 in the house
> occupied by Thomas Main, flat 2/3 at 17 Norfolk Court,
> Glasgow, assault Tracy Main, 13 years of age, daughter
> of and residing with said Thomas Main, seize hold of
> her, by the throat, and strike her on the body with a
> knife or similar instrument, and you thus did murder
> her. You are not obliged to say anything in answer to
> that charge, but I have to warn you that anything you
> say will be noted and may be given in evidence.

He said he would plead not guilty. When asked if he wanted a solicitor, he again said no.

All this leads to a bit of hindsight. It is obvious that, had a solicitor been present at these interviews, Docherty would have been advised not to answer the questions. Had he not talked, we would have had nothing whatsoever on him. Another factor was the fact that he had a low IQ but you can see from the answers he knew he was a suspect. Another point is that friends of Docherty, including Mrs Turner, could have got him a solicitor if they had wanted to.

In the end, Joe Beltrami represented him and Joe, in his splendid book *The Defender: Beltrami's Tales of the Suspected*, pointed out that Docherty made no admission of guilt to him.

The case against Docherty continued to be prepared but no murder weapon was found. Mrs Main was re-interviewed and mentioned someone with red hair acting suspiciously and Joe Beltrami gave us permission to get a sample of hair from his client, provided we didn't ask him any questions about the case. In conversation, I asked Docherty how he was getting on in Barlinnie and he replied, 'It's a great place and the food is good.' That was the mental state of our suspect. When she saw him at an identity parade, Mrs Main did identify Docherty as the person acting suspiciously but, by now, the reader of this tome will be only too aware of how little store can be set by a line-up identification.

It was all pretty academic. The prosecution faced some difficulties. We reviewed some previous cases and a striking one was a murder and robbery in Larbert back in the fifties. It went to an appeal and Lord Justice Cooper said:

> When a person is brought to a police office and faced
> with officers of high rank, I cannot think that his need
> for protection is any less than it would have been if he
> had been formally apprehended. The ordinary person is
> not to know that he could have refused to answer any
> questions.

All this would mean that the judge might rule the prosecution evidence inadmissible. We were not to know, at this stage, that Docherty would be freed on the second day of his trial entirely due to a stupid mistake by me in incorrectly cautioning him as confirmed in my notebook.

As the trial neared, I was interviewed by Taylor Wilson, the Procurator Fiscal, and neither of us looked at the caution twice. Normally, I would write the name of the individual in my notebook and note c/c in the margin meaning cautioned and charged. Then I would write out the full details of the charge. Any reply would be noted and that would be that. If, at court, as sometimes happens, the defence asked the nature of the caution, I could give it from memory. This is not what happened in this case. The fiscal took a bit of stick from the media for not spotting my mistake in not telling Docherty that he did not need to answer questions. That was unfair on the fiscal. I made the mistake, I admitted it at the time and I admit it now.

There was another interesting point in the run-up to the trial. The BBC and STV helped prove that, at no time, was the body's seven stab wounds referred to on any of their news bulletins. However, one newsreader had mentioned the fact that the victim had been stabbed several times. Could Docherty have misheard 'several times' as 'seven times'? I suggested this explanation to Joe Beltrami during a break for coffee at a sheriff court trial. It would be something that the Great Defender could make maximum use of!

The trial started on Monday, 2 June 1980 and most of the first day was taken up with medical and forensic evidence. After lunch on the second day, I was called to the witness box. The advocate depute put me through the usual preliminaries and I went on to tell how Docherty had been brought to the office by Bowers and Innes and how Docherty had told of the seven stab wounds. I then explained how I had called Superintendent Ian Smith back into the room, told him what Docherty had just said and cautioned Docherty. Hugh Morton, for the defence, rose to his feet and said that Docherty had not been cautioned properly.

The jury were instructed to leave the courtroom and legal arguments were heard. Lord Cowie asked if I had recorded the caution in my notebook at the time and I said I had. He asked me to read it out and, suddenly, with a sickening feeling, I realised the words 'you are not obliged to answer these questions' had been omitted. My heart sank. I knew where this was going. I tried to resolve the situation by saying that, regardless of what I had written down, the caution had been properly given. It was pointless – the words were not in the book and that's what mattered.

Ian Smith was called to the box and he gave evidence that he had written it down just as I had – both versions were the same. Docherty had not been advised that he need not answer the questions. I mentioned the second 'proper' caution that had been given in the presence of Detective Sergeant Innes but the damage had been done.

Lord Cowie asked for the jury to be recalled and said:

It is with regret that I have to say that Detective Chief Inspector Brown is wrong in saying he administered the full caution to the accused on this occasion. I would be slow to criticise senior officers on matters of this sort, particularly when something is done in the course of a protracted serious police inquiry. But fortunately I have the benefit of Detective Superintendent Smith who was present at the time of the caution and he confirmed that the caution was administered in the terms written in Mr Brown's notebook.

He then said that everything said by Docherty after the initial caution was inadmissible. The advocate depute stood up and withdrew the charge. All hell broke loose and I left the court staggering under a torrent of abuse. Angry relatives directed hate towards me but, sick at heart and in shock, it was hard to take any notice. An exception in this was Mr Main himself. I can imagine how he must have felt but he even called into the police office to express his support. Ian Smith offered to resign and I objected strongly to that. He was in a difficult position. The vital words were missing from his notebook, like they were from mine, and Lord Cowie could have asked to look at his notebook. I do not attach any blame to Ian Smith.

Since I got on well with Joe Beltrami, some other officers wondered why he hadn't warned me what was coming. That was rubbish – Joe would not do that. In any case, I could not have altered my notebook unless I had wanted to spend several long years in the nick, sharing porridge with many of the villains I had locked up. No, I made a mistake and that was it.

Joe Beltrami, however, did help solve one problem. Docherty's life was now in danger and the resourceful lawyer arranged with the Social Work Department that he be taken to the secure Carstairs State Hospital, under Part 4 of the Mental Health (Scotland) Act 1960, and there he remained, in a high security establishment that is normally used for the dangerously disturbed, till it was judged safe for him to leave and head south.

The press now had a field day. Many of them were asking, if I had made a mistake, how come so many others in the legal arena had failed to spot it? But I had to take my medicine. The next day I was in HQ in front of the chief constable when, slightly to my surprise, he said, 'You've made a mistake, which you've admitted – it could have happened to anyone.'

What do I think of it all now, these many years later? A young girl had been brutally murdered, her parents had suffered in anguish, a trial had been stopped and thousands of man-hours had been wasted because of my horrendous mistake. But, aside from my mistake, it is a most puzzling case and you still get theories about it. The most bizarre came from a well-known criminal who told me it was his opinion that I knew Docherty was innocent and made the error with the caution deliberately to get him cleared. Another, this time an underworld contact, told me that he knew a lot about the case and that Docherty was certainly innocent. Well, there is no doubt in my mind that Docherty saw Tracy's body at some stage. But did he murder her? There was no forensic evidence to link him to her. No murder weapon was ever found. The mystery of who killed Tracy Main goes on but, who knows, some day the truth may yet come out.

For me, however, an unwanted career move was on the way. Sometime after the case, a letter was written to the chief that included the claim that 'I had lost my credibility'. I sought a meeting with Patrick Hamill. We talked for hours on the difficulties of being a working detective. He was sympathetic but responded in the end by saying, 'Mr Brown, we are the servants of the fiscal's department.' I replied, 'No, Mr Hamill, we are the tools of the fiscal's department.'

Within the week, I was transferred to Criminal Intelligence at Police HQ but my days as a crimefighter, in and out of the police, were certainly not over – make no mistake about that.

19

An £18-Million Sting and a New Search for Justice

I loved the life of a cop on the troubled streets of Scotland's greatest city. I loved the challenge of detection, the patient collection of facts, the probing interviews, the occasional flash of inspiration, the satisfaction of nailing villains and making the place safer for those who abide by the law – and I loved the humour. Sure, a cop sees much blood and violence, much twisted thinking from evil men, but also, day to day, there is humour. Some of it comes from your colleagues, some of it from the enemy – the men and women who live outside the law. On any day, there is always time for a laugh or a joke – although sometimes the humour can be a little black.

The Glasgow sense of humour is no myth – it pervades the life of almost every citizen. Such matters were my musings as I stared out of my window as leader of the Criminal Intelligence Department, resentful that my mistake in the Tracy Main case had taken me out of the frontline for a time. But the job I was doing was still important and it turned up one of the most intriguing cases I have ever been involved in. Although I was moping about being off the streets, I ran into a story that made some of the Glasgow robbers I had run into look like small beer – mere gas-meter bandits, as they say on the streets – in the scale of international theft. A few hundred grand was top whack for the city's gun-toting bank and payroll merchants but, before I left the police, I got mixed up in an £18-million sting.

It began in curious fashion. Many years before, I had a contact we shall simply call Bert. One day, in Criminal Intelligence, I got a call from this guy. At this time, he lived in the plush suburb of Newton Mearns, out on the road to Ayr. He asked if I would visit him. I said of course I would. I sat comfortably in his well-furnished home and took notes as a bizarre story emerged. Here is the gist of what the informer told me.

According to him, there was a mine in South Africa at a place called Rustenburg. He explained that it was a kind of company town – a massive complex where the workers were born, educated and died, often never having left the site. The miners were almost all black and the bosses were white – it was South Africa in the eighties, after all. One of the whites with some connection to the mine travelled to London once a fortnight as a courier. In his possession, he had a biscuit tin in which there was £100,000 worth of platinum powder which he sold to a jeweller in the Covent Garden area.

As the boss of Criminal Intelligence, I would have been expected to pass this information on to colleagues in the Met. Bert, for reasons known only to him, would have none of this. What he told me was not to be shared with the London cops. I suspected he knew something that he wasn't telling me. I also immediately asked the obvious – how was this stuff getting through customs? According to Bert, the first time the courier came through customs, he declared it as 'low grade'. It was tested and found to be so and he was given a certificate for future presentation at customs in Heathrow. Bert also said that valuable tins had been coming into the UK illegally for months. Bert had to be given assurances that he would not be involved in any further inquiry.

I thought about it and there seemed to be only one course open to me. The next morning, I pitched up at the South African Consulate building in Nelson Mandela Square in the city centre and asked to speak to the consul. When I was asked what I wanted, I identified myself and said the matter was confidential. The fact that I was a detective chief inspector in charge of Criminal Intelligence opened the door and, minutes later, I was in the consul's office. I told him the tale recounted above and he almost convulsed himself in a bout of genuine laughter. He knew that the security at the country's gold, diamond and platinum mines was so tight that such a scam as I was talking about was simply impossible.

The consul, Mr G J Volshenk, really did know what he was talking about – he had worked at that very mine and he believed that it really was physically impossible to steal from the complex. He explained that anyone in contact with precious minerals was strip-searched and X-rayed at the end of each shift. We shook hands and I left the office wondering if Bert had got the wrong end of the stick.

I told Bert what had transpired and he agreed to try to further investigate the courier whose name was said to be Peter. Over the next eighteen months, I regularly visited Mr Volshenk to tell him that the thefts from Rustenburg were continuing. I didn't lose much sleep over all this. If the South African authorities were not interested, so what? And maybe Bert had got it all wrong. But, one day, the phone rang and it was Volshenk, asking if I could come around right away. He sounded excited. Half an hour later I was ushered into his office and he showed me a fax from the top diplomatic brass in South Africa. An American company had acquired part ownership of the mine and, as part of that process, the stock had been surveyed – £18 million in platinum powder could not be accounted for. I kept my face straight as I pointed out that, if you multiplied the number of fortnights Peter had been travelling to London by £100,000, the figures matched up. Now we had to find the courier.

Bert was delighted his info had been found to be right. Two weeks later he phoned with some detail on Peter. Apparently he worked at the mine, had a big house in the plush outskirts of Johannesburg, with a swimming pool, servants and a Rolls in the garage. Volshenk and I knew that this info did not narrow the search much – most whites living in that area fitted the description!

I now began to wonder how serious the efforts to find Peter were. Was he being shielded? After all a simple trip out to Joburg airport would probably turn up the identity of a man who flew to London on a fortnightly basis. The week after this new turn in events, Volshenk asked me to talk to an investigator who had come over from South Africa. This was a high-ranking officer called Brigadier J F Erasmus, head of the South African Diamond, Gold and Narcotic Squads. He was a tough cookie and I immediately thought I would not like to be a prisoner interrogated by him. He told me that they had failed to identify Peter despite extensive enquiries.

I phoned Bert and told him about Brigadier Erasmus being in town and he astonished me by asking if the brigadier would want Peter's phone number. Here was a criminal from Partick blowing the whistle on a multi-million-pound theft from a mine in South Africa, naming the suspect and, if that wasn't enough, offering to give us his phone number. I showed the number to the brigadier but he said it didn't exist – the number was too long. I had to explain to this hotshot that it was common practice for criminals to add numbers to disguise the destination. With his permission, I phoned the number as written and, as I expected, before I could dial all of the numbers, the phone was answered. A female asked who I wanted and I said Peter. 'Mr Kopco is not available at the moment. Can I take a message?' The brigadier's face was a picture.

The investigator returned to Africa. A couple of days later, I received a phone call and learned that, although Kopco did not work at the mine, he did have connections with it and he had been arrested and charged, with others, over the theft of the platinum. The outcome of the case, however, was a mystery, and I suspect that, for whatever reason, the papers had been marked with 'no proceedings' by the authorities. I did, however, discover that, as a result of the case, one high-ranking police officer was suspended. As I suspected, someone somewhere was obstructing efforts to identify 'Peter' whoever he really was. Bert was a winner, however, as the owners of the mine rewarded him with cash for his valuable assistance. Months later, Mr Volshenk hosted a party for 'Friends of South Africa'. My wife and I were invited. Bert wasn't.

By then, I had completed twenty-six years' service in the police and was on the lookout for a second career – something both challenging and interesting. The majority of retired police officers finish up as clerks, interviewing witnesses on behalf of solicitors, but that didn't appeal to me. I learned from a retired detective chief super in London that he had been asked to form an organisation called The Federation Against Copyright Theft (FACT) to represent the interests of film companies and others. I went down to London for an interview and a chat. He told me that two million people had seen the pirate video of *ET*. 'Make that two million and one,' I said. I was offered the job at good money and took it there and then.

The next day I resigned from Strathclyde Police. It was an emotional moment. The word got around that I was going and one of the people who attempted to dissuade me was the chief constable. In my final interview I expressed the facts of life as I saw it.

I spelled out the difficulties of dealing with informants, the difficulties dealing with the procurators fiscal depute, the difficulties in dealing with solicitors and, most of all, the difficulties of dealing with police officers who had galloped up through the ranks, purely on administrative skills. I told the chief, 'They don't know and, worst of all, they don't know they don't know.' I pointed out that one of his most senior staff openly boasted of never having given evidence in a court of law. I don't know what he expected to hear from me but it wasn't what he was getting. I got a hint that promotion might be in the offing – my response was thanks but no thanks. I had three weeks to clear my desk.

Looking back over the years, the greatest pleasure was working with colleagues in various departments. And an interesting fact is that, of all the criminals I dealt with, none ever complained that he or she was innocent of the crime. In fact, astonishing as it sounds, almost all of them admitted the crime in the first interview. I also look back on working with the fiscals' department. The workload they face on a daily basis almost defies belief. Incidentally, it is a pity that juries never get to know some of the slog, such as manual fingerprint searches in the old days, involved in bringing cases to trial. But it is inevitable since, to acknowledge what went on, would reveal previous convictions.

But the main problem facing the justice system is the backlog of cases involving minor offences like housebreaking, car thefts and minor drugs charges. Most of the offenders are repeat criminals who are guilty yet they plead not guilty right up to the day of the trial and then change their plea. The amount of police time wasted sitting around to give evidence that is, in the end, not required is phenomenal. I see one solution but maybe it is too obvious for the authorities or the libertarians who have plenty to say but never suffer the day-to-day hassle of police work.

The procedures for under-sixteens are complex and should be considered separately – I have no easy answers here. But, for those over that age, some simplification is in order. For the first conviction a sentence of a year in prison could be given. Thereafter, each continuing offence doubles the sentence. This would soon become a massive deterrent. I would set remission for good behaviour at a maximum of 25 per cent. To cut the delays involved in last-minute change of plea I would allow an offender, admitting guilt at the first judicial hearing, but only on that day, to be given the same sentence as last time rather than the double sentence. That would certainly give some repeat offenders the incentive to think twice about pleading not guilty right up to the day of trial.

I would also change some of the laws that protect the so-called rights of the accused. I have often said that, if the criminals in this country formed a union and drew up rules and conditions to protect their members, they could not improve on what is on offer today. For example, if a child murderer is in custody awaiting trial, detectives are forbidden, under the Prison (Scotland) Act, from interviewing him in connection with any other child murder as a suspect in that crime – he can be charged or paraded but not interviewed. That rule is one of the bees in my bonnet still buzzing strongly after many years away from the frontline. In this case, the man could only be interviewed in connection with a crime where he is not a suspect. I personally find that almost unbelievable. There are other reforms that are much needed – in fact, you could write a book about it!

One of the questions I am most often asked is, 'Have you come across many dishonest police officers?' I can answer that with four and not one of them survived to complete their pensionable service. Of course, one is too many but I think that four is a creditable figure considering my twenty-six years' service and the fact that I mingled with thousands of officers.

So it was that, on 3 April 1983, I closed the door of my office in Police HQ in Pitt Street. A new challenge in FACT beckoned. But there was still excitement ahead. Only four dishonest police officers? Yes but, down the years, there have been cases throughout Scotland where villains have escaped because of errors in investigations, lack of evidence at the time and other reasons. Conversely, people have been wrongly imprisoned, locked away for crimes they did not commit, and they are forgotten by the public. There are many cases that deserve – indeed, demand – re-investigation so who better to get involved in that than Leslie

Brown, ex-detective? That's why I now devote my time to a voluntary organisation called A Search For Justice. But that's another story. And I plan to tell it.

INDEX